W9-CJB-896

THE
ACCOUNTING
PROFESSION

Melville Series
         on
Management, Accounting, and Information Systems

Consulting Editor   *John W. Buckley*

THE
ACCOUNTING
PROFESSION

John W. Buckley
and
Marlene H. Buckley

MELVILLE PUBLISHING COMPANY
Los Angeles, California

Copyright © 1974, by John Wiley & Sons, Inc.
Published by **Melville Publishing Company,**
a Division of John Wiley & Sons, Inc.

All rights reserved. Published simultaneously in Canada.

No part of this book may be reproduced by any means,
nor transmitted, nor translated into a machine language
without the written permission of the publisher.

Library of Congress Cataloging in Publication Data

Buckley, John W
  The accounting profession.

  (Melville series on management, accounting, and
information systems)
  Includes bibliographical references.
  1. Accounting as a profession. I. Buckley, Marlene
H., 1938- joint author. II. Title.
HF5629.B78   657'.023   74-8880
ISBN 0 471 11609 2 (paper)
ISBN 0 471 11610 6 (cloth)

Printed in the United States of America

10 9 8 7 6 5 4

TO OUR MANY FRIENDS
IN THE ACCOUNTING PROFESSION

PREFACE

In many ways the accounting profession is similar to those foreign countries in which the best qualities of the land and its people are hidden from the casual tourist. Advance preparation often results in travel which is more pleasant and rewarding.

In a similar vein, we seek through this medium to enhance the reader's understanding of the accounting profession, such that he or she understands how it is structured, what functions it performs in society, and where it is headed.

The accounting profession differs from other major professions in the extent of its broad public contact. For unlike the clinical approach of the physician or lawyer, the accountant's work is sequestered from the public view. Much of the effort in accounting is performed within or for large organizations, and even there the contact points tend to be limited to a relatively few people. For example, accountants play a cardinal role in the process which leads to the financial reports which form the basis for investment decisions, yet it is the analyst who deals with investors at first hand.

The accountant (as with architects, engineers, and a number of other professional types) lacks the forum of the public media in which to tell his story in ways which educate and stimulate the viewer toward more positive attitudes with respect to the profession. Accounting lacks its Dr. Kildares, Ironsides, or even Archie Bunkers.

In preparing this work we thought of two groups for whom this book should have particular appeal: (a) those who come into professional contact with accountants and wish to gain a better understanding of the profession, and (b) students who intend to make rational career choices. In too many instances the typical accounting major can complete the entire curriculum and perhaps even work in accounting for several years without knowing as much about the profession as can be obtained from a few hours spent with this book. Other career-oriented individuals may shy away from accounting because of its traditional lack of emphasis on professional matters. Both objectives are facilitated by having access to a work which is factual, comprehensive, and well-illustrated.

In the collegiate market this book offers an alternative to the reader which is often used to supplement basic courses in accounting.

Professionalism in accounting has been an area of keen interest to the authors over many years, but the opportunity to work with Arthur M. Sargent and the California Certified Public Accountants Foundation for Education and Research was pivotal to the completion of this work. Much is owed here to the previous work entitled *In Search of Identity: An Inquiry into Identity Issues in Accounting* (Palo Alto, Ca.: California Certified Public Accountants Foundation for Education and Research, 1972). John B. Farrell, who has chaired the Task Force on Priorities in Accounting at the University of California, Los Angeles, over the past two years has contributed much in the way of ideas and inspiration. The manuscript also benefitted from the constructive comments of Herbert Miller, Douglas R. Carmichael and Lee Seidler. A special debt of gratitude is due A. N. Mosich who assisted in the editing of galleys and pages.

Walker G. Stone and John T. Crain, both with Melville Publishing Company, provided the creative spark for this book and gave us the support and encouragement needed to bring it to completion.

We sincerely hope that this book will prove to be a valuable guide and inspiration to those who are interested in learning more about the accounting profession.

John W. Buckley
Malibu, California *Marlene H. Buckley*

ABOUT THE
AUTHORS

John W. Buckley, Ph.D., is a professor of accounting and information systems at the Graduate School of Management, University of California, Los Angeles. His graduate degrees are from the University of Washington, Seattle. Dr. Buckley has authored a number of books and monographs, including *Contemporary Accounting and Its Environment* (Belmont, Ca.: Dickenson, 1969); *In Search of Identity: An Inquiry into Identity Issues in Accounting* (Palo Alto, Ca.: California Certified Public Accountants Foundation for Education and Research, 1972); *Income Tax Allocation: An Inquiry into Problems of Methodology and Estimation* (New York: Financial Executives Foundation, 1972); with Kevin M. Lightner, *Accounting: An Information Systems Approach* (Belmont, Ca.: Dickenson, 1973); and with Marlene H. Buckley, *A Guide to Accounting: An Information Systems Approach* (Belmont, Ca.: Dickenson, 1973). He is also a regular contributor to the periodical literature in accounting and information systems. In 1967, Dr. Buckley founded the Accounting and Information Systems Research Program at the Graduate School of Management, University of California, Los Angeles, and has been an active participant in many professional conferences and other public affairs.

Marlene H. Buckley, M.S., is a research consultant and author. She completed her masters degree in accounting in 1967 and has had professional public accounting experience with Haskins & Sells. She co-authored *A Guide to Accounting: An Information Systems Approach* (Belmont, Ca.: Dickenson, 1973), and is currently working with John W. Buckley and others on a research project on business decision models. Her professional activities currently are directed primarily at the problems of small businesses and personal finances.

CONTENTS

CHAPTER

3

TO BECOME AN ACCOUNTANT   47

CHAPTER

4

POLICING THE PROFESSION   89

CHAPTER

5

THE LIVING PROFESSION   125

EXHIBITS

THE
ACCOUNTING
PROFESSION

FROM QUIPU
TO COMPUTER

ANCIENT ORIGINS

Long before man learned to write he kept accounts. Such was the case in ancient Peru where the medium employed was the *quipu*, or knotted string [1]. A single knot meant 10, two single knots 20, a double knot 100, a triple knot 1000, and so on to larger numbers. The story was repeated in China and other ancient cultures [2].

When writing emerged in the fertile Mesopotamian valleys it did so in the form of commercial records. The famous Code of Hammurabi (circa 2285–2242 BC) contained several rules pertaining to accounting, for instance [3]:

(104) If the merchant has given to the agent corn, wool, oil, or any sort of goods to traffic with, the agent shall write down the price and hand over to the merchant; the agent shall take a sealed memorandum of the price which he shall give to the merchant.

(105) If an agent has forgotten and has not taken a sealed memorandum of the money he has given to the merchant, money that is not sealed for, he shall not put in his accounts.

A large number of Babylonian accounting records survive to this day. They refer to such activities as selling, leasing, hiring, lending, and joint venturing. Dating from circa 2600 BC, the records are cast in clay which, when moistened, would readily accept the impressions of a stylus. Permanence was then obtained by baking or sun-drying the tablets [4].

Turning to Egypt we find civilizations flourishing in the fertile valley of the Nile as early as 5000 BC. Here, as in other ancient cultures, the necessity for accounts preceded the use of money. The *scribe* (as these early accountants were known) maintained records on papyrus, using a *calamus* (feathered quill) as the writing instrument [5]. Erman observes that "numerous documents have come down to us showing how accounts were kept—these documents show exactly how much was received, from whom and when it came in, and the details of how it was used [6]."

The Bible furnishes a number of references to accounting among the Israelites [7], and, according to Boeckh, the Athenians had a highly developed system of accounting [8]. *Logistae,* as accountants were called in ancient Athens, maintained very detailed records for private individuals as well as public agencies. Important public records were engraved on stone tablets and exposed in public places. A number of these survive to our times, including those contained in the Elgin Marbles collection in the British Museum. Another interesting medium of accounting in Grecian times was the *abax* or sand tray. Appropriate records were maintained by sketching in the sand. Moistening would remove an existing record and pave the way for a new one.

It is understandable that the Romans, with their well-known penchant for administration, should expand further the art of accounting. The Roman genius for rule by law is widely recognized: following his own admonition that "justice is the constant and perpetual will to give each man his right," the Emperor Justinian ordered the codification of Roman law (533 AD). This action greatly influenced the history of the world, for as Lord Bryce observed, "there is not a problem of jurisprudence which it does not touch: there is scarcely a corner of political science on which its light has not fallen [9]." While at its zenith 50 million people lived under the shadow of the Roman Empire, more than a billion people presently live under legal systems which descend directly from Roman law.

But accountants are also indebted to the Romans. The *Italic* tribes which settled upon the site of the Seven Hills of Rome around 750 BC used *pecunia* ("heads of cattle") as currency, from which the term "pecuniary" comes.[10]. The *calculus* developed as a tool of accounting and provided principles of arithmetic logic and numerical manipulation which undergird our present-day computers. *Counters*—those indispensable artifacts of gambling—had their origin in accounting. By moving counters from one box (account) to another, records were maintained. This activity, known as *casting the accounts*, allowed for the first simulations of accounting records [11].

THE RENAISSANCE

As we move to the period of the Renaissance (1300–1600 AD), significant impetus to accounting hailed from the Italian peninsula. Synthesizing the art of accounting to his time and adding his own unique genius, a mathematician named Frater Luca Bartolomes Pacioli published his famous treatise on accounting on November 10, 1494. It bore the awesome title of *Summa de Arithmetica, Geometria, Proportioni et Proportionalita*, which means "Everything About Arithmetic, Geometry and Proportion [12]."

The *double-entry* system of accounting, devised by Pacioli, remains intact to this time, surviving the onslaught of computerized accounting systems. Simply stated, the concept behind double-entry is that every accounting action has a *cause and effect* relationship [13]. If a proprietor invests $1000 in his business, that amount can be traced to some outcome. In the typical instance the payment would be lodged in a checking account in the name of the business, hence:

$$\text{Cash } \$1000 \longleftrightarrow \text{Proprietor } \$1000$$

If $500 is spent to acquire inventory to be sold in the course of business, a reduction in cash would be made in favor of an increase in inventory:

Cash	$500		
Inventory	500		
Total	$1000	$\longleftrightarrow$	Proprietor $1000

By convention, cash, inventory, and other resources are called *assets*, while claims against those assets on the part of owners or creditors are called *equities*. Other familiar terms that are widely used in modern accounting come from this treatise, including debit and credit, inventory, journal, and ledger.

Double-entry made it possible to account for multiple ownership interests, paving the way for the partnership and corporate forms of business. Similarly, *accrual* accounting owes its refinement to double-entry, because Pacioli's method makes it possible to *match* accounting transactions against appropriate events such as sales or time intervals. More importantly, however, the concept of cause and effect in economic transactions undergirds much of the theoretical constructs which deal with such crucial matters as economic welfare, the distribution of wealth, tax burden, cost–benefit analysis, or measurements of efficiency.

During the Renaissance, accounting became firmly established in the curricula of Italian universities. Giorgio Vasari in his *Lives of the Artists* describes the typical education of the Renaissance artist as consisting of reading, writing, and accounts [14]. We also know of the existence of textbooks in accounting and auditing during this period [15].

THE INDUSTRIAL ERA

While accounting flourished in Italy during the Renaissance, its progress in other Western civilizations was less spectacular. For example, accounts were maintained on *tally sticks* in England during this period, a system no more sophisticated than the quipu, abax, or counter. The tally sticks were used until about 1826 [16].

The tally stick was usually of hazelwood, about 8–9 inches long. These sticks were notched to indicate economic transactions. According to Robert, "an incision the width of a man's palm represented a thousand pounds; a hundred pounds a thumb's-width cut; twenty pounds the width of a little finger; a pound the thickness of a grain of ripe barley; a shilling just a notch; a penny a simple cut with no wood removed; and a half-penny a punched hole [17]."

A tally was often split in half under what was known as the *proffer system*, with each party in a transaction retaining one half (called a *stock* and *foil*, respectively). Stenton tells us that tallies were used for recording receipts, notes payable, tax anticipation warrants, and even postdated checks and bills of exchange [18].

As English seafarers and adventurers blazed the trails which led to the colonial and industrial eras (1800–1930 AD), they transformed Great Britain into the world's foremost industrial power. The impetus for accounting thus moved to the "sceptred isle [19]," climaxing in professional status and recognition. It was during this period that the corporate form of business organization emerged with all of its ramifications [20].

The Industrial Revolution spurred the development of cost accounting [21], and the profession of public accounting (auditing) was born and nurtured [22]. A crucial event in the evolution of accounting as a profession was the South Sea Bubble case.

THE SOUTH SEA BUBBLE

The South Sea Company, formed in 1728, would be viewed today as a glamorous conglomerate—a Ling–Temco–Vought (L.T.V.) or Investors Overseas Services (I.O.S.) [23]. While a principal function of the South Sea Company was to develop foreign trade, its activities ranged far and wide, even to assuming the national debt of Great Britain. The South Sea Company provoked unprecedented interest among investors, causing a national hysteria on the scale of the California gold rush of 1849. Smollet, in his History of England, observes that: "The nation was so intoxicated with the spirit of adventure, that people became a prey to the grossest delusion [24]."

Royalty, nobles, poets, and pedestrians alike were trapped by the Sirens of the South Sea and their imitators. Among the investors in South Sea stock were such notables as Queen Anne, Alexander Pope, John Gay, and Mathew Prior.

In addition to driving the price of its stock up through sensational news reports, the South Sea Company engaged in a series of unprofitable as well as illegal practices (including the bribing of members of parliament). Finally the bubble burst, its stock falling in one month from 900 to 190 pounds. An angry public demanded an inquiry into the Company's financial affairs. The task fell to an accountant, Mr. Charles Snell, who studied in the same school as Charles Lamb.

In the course of the investigation, the Company's books were found to have "false and ficitious Entries . . . Entries with Blanks . . . Entries with Rasures and Alterations . . . Leaves torn out . . . Books destroyed, taken away, or secreted [25]." Snell's work led to the Companies Acts which still govern financial reporting in the United Kingdom, and to the audit of public companies by independent accountants. From the debacle of the South Sea Bubble emerged the practice of public accounting.

THE ACCOUNTING IMPERATIVE

This casual walk through history speaks to the imperative of accounting as a social institution. Wherever man meets with man in the economic arena a reference is needed by which to measure and keep score. To anyone who has watched the meticulous care with which Australian aborigines divide their game, the rules which guide investors on the New York Stock Exchange take on added meaning. Which is to say that all known societies have information sets and economic guidelines which serve to moderate behavior.

Accounting is a necessary part of economic man. This was as true in antiquity as it is today. The sophistication of accounting will change in response to the complexity of the social and economic systems it serves, but some level of accounting appears essential to every social order.

Consider some of the decisions which we face as individuals. How much income will I receive in a given period? What expenses will I incur? Are these amounts larger or smaller than in some other period? If income exceeds expenses, what do I do with the surplus? If income is insufficient to meet expenses, how do I make ends meet? What were the sources and amounts of income for the year—and to whom and in what amounts were payments made? Am I wealthier or poorer at the end of the year? What record-keeping or data-processing system is necessary to meet personal and legal requirements for information? What laws are pertinent to these accounting and reporting procedures?

As individuals, we resolve these questions through primitive records and reports. But enlarge the number and scope of this type of question manyfold, multiply the number of decision makers who interact with a single accounting system, and you can begin to understand both the purpose and complexity of accounting in more advanced settings. The processing of information at this level must be systematized and managed by experts.

THE INFORMATION REVOLUTION

We have noted that all known societies have information systems and rules which serve to moderate economic behavior. The complexity of these information systems is geared to the demography and sheer number of persons who interact within a given system.

Complexity is accentuated when systems interact with other systems and nations with other nations. As information systems became larger and more complex, the need for better machinery to process information gave rise to the computer and other modern tools.

The accelerative thrust of knowledge and the information systems it spawns have been discussed widely. Toffler observes that in 1500 Western Europe was producing books at the rate of 1000 per year. In 1960, 1000 titles were published every day [26]! Similar statistics apply to the United States and other countries, leading Siekevitz to note that what has been learned in the last three decades dwarfs the previous cumulative knowledge of mankind [27].

The computer burst on the scene in 1950, bringing about what Burt Nanus refers to as the fourth information revolution [28]:

> The invention of the computer brought on the fourth information revolution by making possible improvements by orders of magnitude in our ability to relate and manipulate numbers, logical concepts and complex activities, thereby accelerating technological and social change.

In terms of this scale the three preceding revolutions were in order: the invention of language, printing, and mass media (periodicals, radio, and television). The fifth revolution will result from on-line mass information systems. Giant data banks will give public, private, and individual users instant access to massive complexes of data, thereby expanding exponentially the flow of information throughout the world.

The rapidly growing body of knowledge in accounting, including computer technology, has been portrayed vividly by Dr. Leo Herbert (Exhibit 1). The computer is not only facilitating such traditional functions as payroll, cost accounting, and general bookkeeping, but increasingly is being used for analytic purposes such as forecasting, cost–benefit analysis, and a wide variety of operations research applications.

EXHIBIT 1

Growth of common body of
knowledge in accounting.
SOURCE: Dr. Leo Herbert, Director,
Office of Personnel Management,
U.S. General Accounting
Office. Dated, August 1971. Repro-
duced with permission.

Human behavior
Manpower values
Intergovernmental relations

SOCIAL ACCOUNTING

Total systems planning
Interdisciplinary applications

TOTAL SYSTEMS REVIEWS
Effectiveness auditing

EFFECTIVENESS EVALUATION
Computers
Cybernetics

INFORMATION SYSTEMS
Organizational models
Organizational planning
Decision theory
Cost—benefit analyses

MANAGEMENT SCIENCES
Management processes
Deficiency findings

MANAGEMENT AUDITING
Management planning

MANAGEMENT SERVICES
Planning and control systems

MANAGEMENT ACCOUNTING

Tax planning
Tax advising

TAX ACCOUNTING
P.P.B.S

Appropriation control

GOVERNMENT ACCOUNTING
Cost standards

Cost—revenue analysis

Cost analyses

Cost and production statistics

COST ACCOUNTING
Principles of financial reporting

Auditing standards

Uniform statements

CPA certification examination

Audits of records and statements

FINANCIAL AUDITING
Computers

Punched cards records

Tax records

Income statement emphasis

Balance sheet emphasis

BOOKKEEPING (SINGLE—DOUBLE ENTRY)

1775   1800   1825   1850   1875   1900   1925   1950   1975

The Dow Jones survey summarized in Exhibit 2 shows that most organizations first saddle computers with tedious and voluminous bookkeeping functions, but steady progression to more advanced applications is typical.

A recent tabulation of the number of computer installations in the United States and the annual cost of operations (including rental, capital investment in computer facilities, salaries of computer personnel, and other operating costs) is shown in Exhibit 3. It is obvious that today even small organizations use computers, and that government and other nonprofit institutions, such as schools and hospitals, are as deeply involved with computerized systems as is the typical business firm.

The computer tide has spawned a variety of new and exotic occupations such as systems analysis, programming, computer operations, computer servicing, keypunch operations, and so forth. A number of these occupations have been projected by the U.S. Department of Labor as being among the most rapidly

EXHIBIT 2
New applications in computing.
(a) Includes next 2 years. (b) Respondents with EDP procurement responsibilities (base = 634). NOTE: Among all respondents, the proportion reporting that their companies now use computers exclusively for accounting/bookkeeping is 13.7%. SOURCE: *Management and the Computer* (New York: Dow Jones, 1969), p. 25.

		Anticipated within			
Computer applications	Use now (%)	Next 2 years (%)	Next 5 years [a] (%)	Do not use or anticipate within next 5 years (%)	Total [b] (%)
Accounting/bookkeeping	**75.6**	**10.2**	**17.7**	**6.8**	**100.0**
Sales analysis	45.1	14.0	18.0	36.9	100.0
Inventory control	43.0	18.8	25.2	31.7	100.0
Production control	33.4	15.0	21.8	44.8	100.0
Engineering, scientific problems	31.7	6.3	13.2	55.1	100.0
Materials management	26.6	13.6	18.0	55.4	100.0
Research and development	24.0	9.0	19.2	56.8	100.0
Market research	19.3	16.4	26.0	54.7	100.0
Decision models	15.8	10.2	23.2	61.1	100.0
Miscellaneous other uses	7.7	3.0	4.1	88.2	100.0

EXHIBIT 3
Government and industry: how their computer inventories compare.
SOURCE: Joseph Cunningham, "Decision Maker," *Computer Decisions,* January 1971, p. 57.

IN NUMBERS

Federal government = 5277   Total (U.S. installed) = 73,077

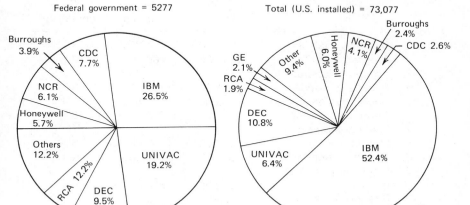

IN DOLLARS (ANNUALLY)

Federal government = $2.8 billion   Total (U.S. installed) = $20.8 billion

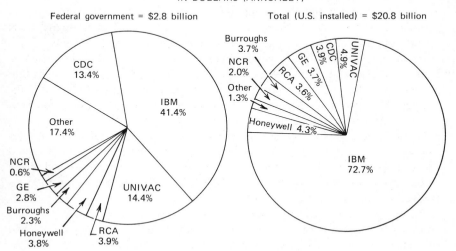

EXHIBIT 4
The ten most rapidly growing occupations,
1968–1980.
SOURCE: U.S. Department of Labor, *The U.S. Economy in 1980*,
Bulletin 1673 (Washington, D.C.: U.S. Government Printing Office, 1970).

		1968 actual	1980 projected	Rate per annum
1.	Systems analysts	150,000	425,000	9.1%
2.	Programmers	175,000	400,000	7.1
3.	Computer operators	175,000	400,000	7.1
4.	Pilots and copilots	52,000	114,000	6.7
5.	Dental hygienists	16,000	33,500	6.4
6.	Computer servicemen	115,000	225,000	5.8
7.	Medical laboratory technicians	100,000	190,000	5.5
8.	Hospital attendants	800,000	1,500,000	5.4
9.	Licensed practical nurses	320,000	600,000	5.4
10.	Oceanographers	5,200	9,700	5.3

growing fields of employment through 1980, as noted in Exhibit 4.

A progressively greater share of the computing dollar is being spent on *software* (systems and programs) as opposed to *hardware* (physical computers and components) (Exhibit 5). Software costs are shared by having many users operate off *canned* programs rather than creating their own systems. Computer-sharing provides such good opportunities to users that Dr. George Feeney, head of General Electric's Information Services Division, predicts that sometime in the next five years a major company president will proudly announce at an American Management Association meeting or similar function that his company no longer has its own computer [29].

Feeney foresees a three-phase development in the evolution of computer-sharing: (*a*) time-sharing, (*b*) networking, and (*c*) computer utilities. General Electric, in common with other major corporations, has already moved to the second phase and transition to the third phase can be expected within the next few years (Exhibit 6).

Accountants are in the mainstream of the information revolution. The accounting system has always been the base to which the other components of an integrated information system are added. The rules which govern the processing and reporting of financial information derive from accounting. Accountants help to define user needs, conduct feasibility studies, design and install

EXHIBIT 5
Hardware/software cost trends.
SOURCE: B. W. Boehm, "Software and Its Impact: A Quantitative Assessment," AIS Working Paper 73-27 (a paper presented at the Computing and Information Systems Colloquium, Graduate School of Management, University of California at Los Angeles, Spring 1973).

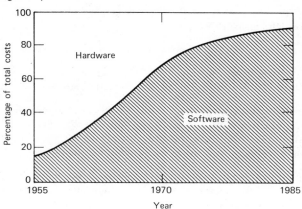

EXHIBIT 6
Three phases of shared computing.
SOURCE: General Electric Information Services, reprint from *Computer Decisions*, November 1971, p. 43.

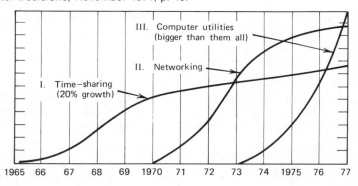

computerized systems, specify controls to minimize fraud, and monitor and audit these systems. They have come a long way from quipu to computer.

WHAT IS ACCOUNTING?

Accounting has been defined in many ways. The Council of the American Institute of Certified Public Accountants (AICPA) adopted the following official statement on October 1, 1966 [30]:

Certified public accountants practice in the broad field of accounting.

Accounting is a discipline which provides financial and other information essential to the efficient conduct and evaluation of the activities of any organization.

The information which accounting provides is essential for (1) effective planning, control and decision–making by management, and (2) discharging the accountability of organizations to investors, creditors, government agencies, taxing authorities, association members, contributors to welfare institutions, and others.

Accounting includes the development and analysis of data, the testing of their validity and relevance, and the interpretation and communication of the resulting information to intended users. The data may be expressed in monetary or other quantitative terms, or in symbolic or verbal forms.

Some of the data with which accounting is concerned are not precisely measurable, but necessarily involve assumptions and estimates as to the present effect of future events and other uncertainties. Accordingly, accounting requires not only technical knowledge and skill, but, even more importantly, disciplined judgment, perception and objectivity.

Within this broad field of accounting, certified public accountants are the identified professional accountants. They provide leadership in accounting research and education. In the practice of public accounting CPAs bring competence of professional quality, independence, and a strong concern for the usefulness of the information and advice they provide, but they do not make management decisions.

The professional quality of their services is based upon the requirements for the CPA certificate—education, experience and examination—and upon the ethical and technical standards established and enforced by their profession.

CPAs have a distinctive role in examining financial statements submitted to investors, creditors and other interested parties, and in expressing independent opinions on the fairness of such statements. This distinctive role has inevitably encouraged a demand for the opinions of CPAs on a wide variety of other representations, such as compliance with rules and regulations of government agencies, sales statistics under lease and royalty agreements, and adherence to covenants in indentures.

The examination of financial statements requires CPAs to review many aspects of an organization's activities and procedures. Consequently, they can advise clients of needed improvements in internal control and make constructive suggestions on financial, tax and other operating matters.

In addition to furnishing advice in conjunction with their independent examinations of financial statements, CPAs are engaged to provide objective advice and consultation on various management problems. Many of these involve information and control systems and techniques, such as budgeting, cost control, profit planning, internal reporting, automatic data processing, and quantitative analysis. CPAs also assist in the development and implementation of programs approved by management.

Among the major management problems depending on the accounting function is compliance with tax requirements. An important part of the practice of CPAs includes tax planning and advice, preparation of tax returns, and representation of clients before government agencies.

CPAs also participate in conferences with government agencies such as the Securities and Exchange Commission, and with other interested parties, such as bankers.

Like other professional men, CPAs are often consulted on business, civic and other problems on which their judgment, experience and professional standards permit them to provide helpful advice and assistance.

The complexities of an industrial society encourage a high degree of specialization in all professions. The accounting profession is no exception. Its scope is so wide and varied that many individual CPAs choose to specialize in particular types of service.

Although their activities may be diverse, all CPAs have demonstrated basic competence of professional quality in the discipline of accounting. It is this which unites them as members of one profession and provides a foundation for extension of their services into new areas.

Even this definition tends to understate the role of accounting in terms of its broad societal mission, for in a very real way accounting policies determine who gets rich and who stays poor.

This fact was recognized by Lord Ardwall as early as 1905 when, in addressing the Institute of Chartered Accountants and Actuaries, convened in Glasgow, he said, "there are really great public and national interests in their hands, because as auditors of public companies, as advisers to great captains of industries, they have an immense power to use for good if they so choose [31]."

Paton and Littleton reiterated this conviction in 1940, saying "the social importance of accounting is therefore clear, especially in relating to the income statement, since dependable information about earning power can be an important aid to the flow of capital into capable hands and away from unneeded industries [32]."

More recently, Toan has posed these provocative questions: "does the accountant by the way he keeps score help to shape and reinforce a particular style of management?" and "will those with different and more radical philosophies someday storm the conventions and conferences of the accounting . . . contending that the bias of accountants supports a pattern of behavior which they would like to see changed [33]?"

Critics of our current economic system are quick to seize upon this point. Quigley, for example, decries those "falsified accounting techniques and mistaken tax methods which encourage the process of environmental decay and conceal what is really happening [34]."

Accountants have long separated the roles of providing information from the actual formulation of decisions. This view, however, is crumbling under the onslaught of information theory which holds that:

1. Information conditions decisions, so that the role of providing information cannot be viewed as being totally (or even significantly) independent of outcomes.

2. Information systems are subject to systematic bias for several reasons, including the fact that by nature they are surrogates for reality and may fail to reflect fully the phenomena they purport to measure and report.

3. Processors of information, however careful, exert influence upon and alter the messages they transmit.

4. Information systems—by virtue of the enormous sunk cost in design, equipment, and training—tend toward entropism and inertia.

For all of these reasons, the accountant does not disclaim responsibility for decisions which are founded upon the information he provides.

Accountants, obviously, are not the sole arbiters of resource allocation, but they share with other groups—such as the Congress, the Securities and Exchange Commission, management associations, and other regulatory agencies—the responsibility for distributing the nation's wealth.

Two imperatives flow from this reasoning: (a) accounting policies should be measured against social goals, and (b) the accountant should adopt a macroeconomic view for policy purposes, one which rises above the client relationship [35].

Those who advocate a broad social perspective for accounting policy have welcomed the position taken by the newly formed Financial Accounting Standards Board (FASB), which, as noted in Chapter 4, is the principal rule-making body for the accounting profession. Its by-laws contain this statement [36]:

In any competitive enterprise system, necessary resources do not exist in unlimited quantities. Therefore there is a need to allocate these resources in the most productive manner within the framework of public policy and social needs. The existence of sound financial and reporting standards facilitates that allocation by providing to the suppliers of resources relevant and useful financial accounting information that is the basis of informed decision making.

Within this broadened context, accounting can be defined as *the science which deals with the design, management, and evaluation of information systems as they relate to decision-making processes incident to societal and enterprise goals.* The objective of accounting is to facilitate effective resource allocation, and accordingly is concerned with all elements which affect this process. These include: (*a*) decision-making, (*b*) policy-making, (*c*) planning, (*d*) control, (*e*) evaluation of results, (*f*) utilization of resources with particular emphasis on human resources, and (*g*) interaction among institutions in relation to each other and their social and physical environments.

Accounting is essentially a measurement and communication science. It is in constant pursuit of better measurement and communication, defined in terms of goal achievement rather than by abstract theoretical standards. "Good" measurement and communication lead to changes in behavior which are beneficial to personal, enterprise, and public welfare.

Given the traditional bias of accounting toward quantitative and economic measurement on the one hand and formal information systems on the other, it must be emphasized that these boundaries no longer exist. Increasingly, accounting is concerned with measurements of all types, especially qualitative and noneconomic factors. Similarly, accountants recognize that informal information, perceptions, and other intangible factors may be as important as the formal system in terms of decision processes and goal achievement.

Defining accounting as a science does not preclude what has commonly been referred to as the "art of accounting." To the degree that science inappropriately carries the connotation of quantitative measurement and formal inquiry, art is needed to add the necessary qualities of perception, intuition, imprecision, and nonquantitative assessment.

THE ACCOUNTING PROFESSION

Accounting is a multidisciplinary profession defined in terms of the problems it addresses. At the broadest level the profession addresses the problem of achieving effective resource allocation. Other problems stem from this focus and include: (*a*) technical assistance in policy formulation, (*b*) the design and management of information systems, (*c*) the evaluation of results, personnel, operations, financial systems, and social goals, (*d*) assessing performance in relation to standards, competing systems, and changing conditions, and (*e*) assisting in the design and evaluating the effectiveness of planning and control activities.

Complex problems of this type require complex solutions including an assembly of skills and specializations. Accordingly, the accounting profession comprises specialists from a wide range of disciplines including accountants, systems analysts, computer programmers and operators, auditors, engineers, operations researchers (including mathematicians and statisticians), behavioral and social scientists, among others. These diverse backgrounds are welded together by learning the *common body of knowledge* in accounting [37], by qualifying for membership in terms of academic standards and by demonstrating proficiency through a professional examination.

It is, however, the set of unique problems and adherence to a common service ideal which bind the diverse members of the profession.

COMING OF AGE

That the profession is coming of age is documented in its literature as well as in its practice. The current career literature of the American Institute of Certified Public Accountants is in marked contrast to its former publications. The publication *We Are Involved* appeals to aspiring accountants in these terms [38]:

> . . . every significant event in modern society—commercial expansion, technical breakthroughs, government programs, social services, the conduct of international relations—requires assessment of resources in manpower, materials and money. Accountants stand squarely in the middle of these activities, recording and budgeting the input and outgo of mankind's work.

Mention is made in this career literature of the "three-pronged professional," referring, of course, to the functions of reporting, attesting, and advising [39]. These statements mirror the realities of accounting practice today.

Far from being limited to the audit function, we find that accountants, and particularly the large accounting firms, are involved in activities which cover the socioeconomic spectrum. In this broader context they are acting not only as verifiers but as designers. Their skill is that of administrative and efficiency experts. Their expertise ranges beyond accounting know-how to include subject matter in engineering, mathematics, computing methods, and behavioral science.

It would come as a surprise to many to discover that accounting firms are developing cost–benefit models for the California public schools, or serving as efficiency experts to the U.S. Postal Service. An accounting firm did the cost engineering for the Feather River Water Project in California; another firm brought programmed budgeting to Pennsylvania schools. Certified Public Accounting firms have assisted in urban renewal projects, the study of transit patterns for the Northeast Traffic Corridor, the restructuring of state welfare programs, and programs for curbing alcoholism and drug abuse. They have been active in developing management information systems for improved health care and engage in many other activities which are far removed from traditional accounting functions.

Looking to the future, the sociologist Montagna observes that the accounting

EXHIBIT 7

A classification of professions in the United States.

NOTE: Dates concern only events in the United States. Among the sources: *Occupational Licensing in the States* (Chicago: The Council of State Government, 1952); *Encyclopaedia of Associations*, 3rd ed. (Detroit: Gale Research Co., 1961); L. E. Blauch, ed., *Education for the Professions* (Washington, D.C.: Government Printing Office, 1955); *Encyclopedia of the Social Sciences* and other encyclopedias; J. W. Kane, *Famous First Facts* (New York: H. W. Wilson Co. 1950); professional association journals, newsletters, and yearbooks; and specialized histories, official or not. In case of disagreement, precedence was given to a competent history, e.g., R. W. Habenstein and W. M. Lamers, *The History of American Funeral Direction* (Milwaukee, Wis.: Bulfin Printers, 1955), or to a date supplied by a professional association cross-checked by one other independent source. I am grateful to Anne Mooney, Ted Cooper, and the headquarters of the dominant professional associations for assistance. (a) Dates in italics in the same row designate the same event. (b) Two dates in the same row designate associated events. (c) Only three or four physicians are known to have resided in the Colonies prior to 1700. From 1607 to 1730 Colonial medical practice was relatively primitive (R. H. Shyrock, *Medicine and Society in America: 1660–1860* [Ithaca, N.Y.: Cornell University Press, 1962], pp. 7, 18). (d) Designates best inference from available information. SOURCE: Harold L. Wilensky, "The Professionalization of Everyone?", *American Journal of Sociology*, September 1964, p. 143.

	Became full-time occupation	First training school	First university school	First local professional association	First National professional association	First state license law	Formal code of ethics
Established							
Accounting (CPA)	19th century	1881^a	1881^a	1882	1887	1896	1917
Architecture	18th century	1865	1868	1815	1857	1897	1909
Civil engineering	18th century	1819	1847	1848	1852	1908	ca. 1910
Dentistry	18th century	1840^b	1867	1844	1840^b	1868	1866
Law	17th century	1784	1817	1802	1878	1732	1908
Medicine	ca.1700^c	1765	1779	1735	1847	Before 1780	1912
Others in process, some marginal							
Librarianship	1732	1887	1897	1885	1876	Before 1917	1938
Nursing	17th century	1861	1909	1885	1896	1903	1950
Optometry		1892	1910	1896	1897	1901	ca. 1935
Pharmacy	1646	1821^b	1868	1821^b	1852	1874	ca. 1850
School teaching	17th century	1823	1879	1794	1857	1781	1929
Social work	1898(?)	1898	1904	1918	1874	1940	1948
Veterinary medicine	1803	1852	1879	1854	1863	1886	1866
New							
City management	1912	1921	1948	After 1914	1914	None	1924
City planning	19th century	1909^a	1909^a	1947	1917	1963	1948
Hospital administration	19th century	1926^a	1926^a		1933	1957	1939
Doubtful							
Advertising	1841	1900(?)^d	1909(?)^d	1894	1917	None	1924
Funeral direction	19th century	ca. 1870	1914	1864	1882	1894	1884

profession is a serious contender for supremacy of the "multi-professional area of administrative science" and "because of [its] unique position as auditors and advisers in financial and related areas to major American and world institutions, [it is] destined to play an increasingly important role in social policy and planning [40]."

Wilensky's well-respected classification of professions (Exhibit 7), notes that accountants attained professional status in the 1880's, but that much has happened in the intervening period. While no milestone marks the spot, the profession has matured most decisively in recent years and stands on the threshold of assuming an even larger role in the conduct of social and economic affairs.

REFERENCES

1. Dating methods have been used to establish that twining existed in Peru as early as 2578 BC according to J. ALDEN MASON, *The Ancient Civilizations of Peru* (Baltimore: Penguin Books, 1957), p. 227. Also, L. LELAND LOCKE, *The Ancient Quipu: A Peruvian Knot Record* (New York: American Museum of Natural History, 1923), p. 325; and LYLE E. JACOBSEN, "The Ancient Inca Empire of Peru and Double–Entry Accounting Concept," *Journal of Accounting Research*, Fall 1964, pp. 221–228.

2. Knot records preceded writing in China according to CARUS, *Tao-Teh-King*, Eng. ed., p. 137, and *Journal of Ethnological Society*, London, 1870, pp. 5, 13.

3. RICHARD BROWN, *History of Accounting and Accountants* (New York: Augustus M. Kelley Publishers, 1968), p. 17. Also, L. W. KING, *The Letters and Inscriptions of Hammurabi*, vol. 1 (Luzac, 1968).

4. References include ORVILLE R. KEISTER, "The Mechanics of Mesopotamian Record-keeping," *NAA Bulletin*, February 1965, pp. 18–24; TOM B. JONES, "Bookeeping in Ancient Sumer," *Archaeology*, March 1956; JAMES H. BREASTED, "The Physical Processes of Writing in the Early Orient and Their Relation to the Origin of the Alphabet," *The American Journal of Semitic Languages and Literatures*, July 1916.

5. ADOLF ERMAN, *Life in Ancient Egypt* (New York: Macmillan, 1894) notes that the scribe was the mainspring of the administrative machinery. His qualifications consisted of demonstrated knowledge of reading, writing, arithmetic, elementary bookkeeping, and proficiency in formulating administrative policy. Scribes often began their careers at the lowest levels of administration but were able to work their way up to such lofty positions as vice-regency of an entire province or nation.

6. Ibid., p. 2. Also see JAMES H. BREASTED, trans., *Ancient Records of Egypt*, 5 vols. (Russell & Russell, 1962).

7. For example, Lev. 25:50, Matt. 18:23–35, Matt. 25:14–30, 2 Kings 22:7, Luke 16:2, Job 33:13.

8. In H. MITCHELL, *The Economies of Ancient Greece* (New York: Barnes & Noble, 1957). Also, J. TOUTAIN, *The Economic Life of the Ancient World* (New York: Barnes & Noble, 1952).

9. See R. H. BARROW, *The Romans* (Penguin, 1949), p. 209.

10. Ibid., p. 31.

11. These and other early accounting tools are discussed by H. P. HAIN, "Casting the Accounts," *Journal of Accounting Research*, Autumn, 1967, pp. 154–163.

12. See WILMER L. GREEN, "Brief Résumé of the Life of Luca Pacioli and His Book Entitled 'Summa de Arithmetica, Geometria, Proportioni et Proportionalita,' " *History and Survey of Accountancy* (Brooklyn, N.Y.: Standard Text Press, 1930), pp. 88–105.

13. The rudiments of double-entry can be found in all beginning bookkeeping and accounting texts.

14. GIORGIO VASARI, *Lives of the Artists: Biographies of the Most Eminent Architects, Painters, and Sculptors of Italy*, BETTY BOROUGHS (New York: Simon & Schuster, 1968), p. 38.

15. A bibliography of early accounting texts to 1800 AD is furnished by RICHARD BROWN, *History of Accounting and Accountants* (New York: Augustus M. Kelley, 1968), pp. 343–360. A bibliography of current research into accounting in the ancient, medieval, and renaissance periods is provided by R. H. PARKER, "Accounting History: A Select Bibliography," *Abacus*, vol. 1, no. 1, September 1965, pp. 62–84.

16. MICHAEL CHATFIELD, "English Medieval Bookkeeping: Exchequer and Manor," in MICHAEL CHATFIELD, ed., *Contemporary Studies in the Evolution of Accounting Thought* (Belmont, Ca.: Dickenson, 1968), pp. 30–38.

17. RUDOLPH ROBERT, "A Short History of Tallies," in A. C. LITTLETON and B. S. YAMEY, eds., *Studies in the History of Accounting* (London: Maxwell & Sweet, 1965), p. 78.

18. D. M. STENTON, ed., *The Great Roll of the Pipe for the Second Year of the Reign of King Richard the First*, vol. 39 (London: Publications of the Pipe Roll Society, 1925), pp. xiii, xiv.

19. From Shakespeare, *Richard II*, act 2:
    This royal throne of kings, this sceptred isle,
    This earth of majesty, this seat of Mars.

20. R. A. IRISH, "The Evolution of Corporate Accounting," *The Australian Accountant*, November 1947, pp. 480–501.

21. SIDNEY POLLARD, "Capital Accounting in the Industrial Revolution," *Yorkshire Bulletin of Economic and Social Research*, November 1963, pp. 75–91. Also,

R. S. EDWARDS, *The Accountant*, "Some Notes on the Early Literature and Development of Cost Accounting in Great Britain," 907 (1937), p. 193; and PAUL GARNER, *Evolution of Cost Accounting to 1925* (University of Alabama Press, 1954).

22. The first association of accountants was formed in Scotland in October, 1854. The *Institute of Chartered Accountants in England and Wales* was incorporated in 1880. In 1882 the *Institute of Accountants and Bookkeepers* was formed in the United States. The *American Association of Public Accountants* emerged in 1886, the *National Society of Certified Public Accountants* in 1897, the *Federation of Societies of Public Accounting in the United States* in 1902, leading in time to the *American Institute of Accountants* in 1917. For these and other early developments, see JAMES DON EDWARDS, "Some Significant Developments of Public Accounting in the United States," *The Business History Review*, June 1956, pp. 211–225.

23. These two groups are discussed briefly by ABRAHAM J. BRILOFF, *Unaccountable Accounting* (New York: Harper & Row, 1972), pp. 68–84 and pp. 183–192, respectively.

24. Quoted in C. J. HASSON, "The South Sea Bubble and Mr. Snell," *Journal of Accountancy*, August 1932, pp. 128–137.

25. Ibid., p. 132.

26. ALVIN TOFFLER, *Future Shock* (New York: Random House, 1970), pp. 30–31.

27. Ibid., p. 31.

28. BURT NANUS, "Managing the Fifth Information Revolution," *Business Horizons*, April 1972, p. 5.

29. In "Decision Maker," *Computer Decisions*, November, 1971, pp. 42–45.

30. The statement appears in the *Journal of Accountancy*, "A Description of the Professional Practice of Certified Public Accountants," December 1966, p. 61.

31. Cited by RICHARD BROWN, *A History of Accounting and Accountants* (New York: Augustus M. Kelley, 1968), p. 442.

32. WILLIAM PATON and A. C. LITTLETON, *An Introduction to Corporate Accounting Standards*, Monograph No. 3 (Sarasota, Fla.: American Accounting Association, 1940), p. 3. A recent comment by William Paton indicates a substantial shift in his viewpoint: "the notion that the goal of the professional accountant is public or social service is nonsense. His function is to provide the best possible service to his specific clients, the people who pay for his efforts" ("Earmarks of a Profession—and the APB," *Journal of Accountancy*, January 1971, p. 41).

33. ARTHUR B. TOAN, JR., "Is Accounting Geared to Today's Needs?", *Management Adviser*, November–December 1971, pp. 17–22.

34. CARROLL QUIGLEY, "Our Ecological Crisis," *Current History*, vol. 59, no. 347, July 1970, p. 11.

35. We may reach the point where accountants will issue broad "state of the economy" messages, or alert the public to emergent practices which should be approached with caution, pending in-depth analysis. Against this standard of social relevance the validity of such issues as "price-level accounting" or "pooling vs. purchase" should hinge on judgments as to whether the resultant shifts in economic welfare are desirable.

36. Financial Accounting Standards Board, *Rules of Procedure* (Stamford, Conn., March 29, 1973), p. 2. Rules of procedure are authorized by article II–A, section 12 of the "By-laws of the Financial Accounting Foundation," as noted in its publication *Certificate of Incorporation/By-Laws* (Stamford, Conn., 1973), pp. 17–18.

37. The authoritative work in this area is ROBERT H. ROY and JAMES H. MACNEILL, *Horizons for a Profession: The Common Body of Knowledge for Certified Public Accountants* (New York: American Institute of Certified Public Accountants, 1967).

38. *We Are Involved* (New York: American Institute of Certified Public Accountants, 1970). *The CPA*, May 1971, p. 7 reports that in the academic year 1970–1971 over 300,000 recruiting brochures were distributed by the AICPA. In addition, their film *Men of Account* was shown 2100 times to an estimated 150,000 students. The audience viewing this film over national television was estimated at 4,000,000 (*The CPA*, July–August 1970, p. 3).

39. A number of these activities are reported by MARSHALL S. ARMSTRONG, "Pressures for Progress," *The California CPA Quarterly*, September 1971, p. 16. However, in recent months, virtually every edition of the house journals of the major CPA firms reports activities of this type.

40. PAUL D. MONTAGNA, "The Public Accounting Profession," *American Behavioral Scientist*, March–April 1971, pp. 488–489.

2

DIMENSIONS OF
THE ACCOUNTING
PROFESSION

A LOOK AT SOME STATISTICS

Accounting is among the most dynamic institutions of our times. Growth statistics alone depict a very unusual rate of development. Ashworth has shown that the CPA trend is considerably more accelerated than the other leading professions and the population as a whole (Exhibit 8). And, of course, CPAs are not the only accountants. In fact, there were an estimated 714,120 accountants in the United States in 1970, of whom 119,000, or 17%, were CPAs, distributed among the occupational groups listed in the table [1].

Occupation	Number	Percent
Public accounting	73,304	61.6
Business and industry	37,247	31.3
Government	4,522	3.8
Education	3,927	3.3
	119,000	100.0

Exhibit 9 provides more detailed statistics on the overall accounting profession. Note that the total number of accountants increased by 189.6% in the period 1950–1970; this represents a compound annual growth rate of 3.3%. The highest growth rates were experienced by minority groups: Spanish-American (19.4%), blacks (13.9%), and women (6.1%).

EXHIBIT 8
Trends in professional and business education and number of CPAs.

The graph compares trends in the numbers of people who graduate each year with first degrees in five professional and/or business fields, the total number of certified public accountants in the United States and population. In the graph, 1951 = 100. (The first year statistics on degrees in accounting became available was 1951. Before 1951, business and commerce includes accounting. In 1951 and after, business and commerce includes all majors in business and commercial subjects except accounting. Between 1951 and 1954, it happens that the index numbers of accounting and of business and commerce are almost identical: therefore the lines for these two fields during these years do not show separately on the graph.)

SOURCE: John Ashworth, "People Who Become Accountants," *Journal of Accountancy,* November 1968, p. 45.

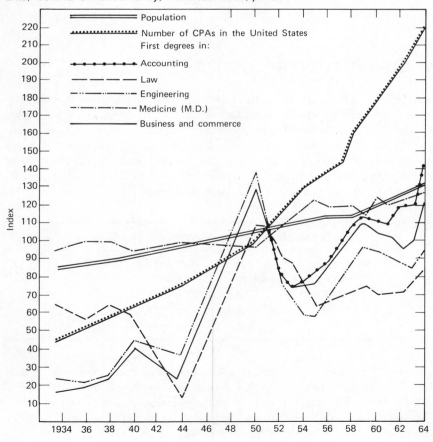

EXHIBIT 9

Statistics on the number of accountants and auditors in the United States, 1950, 1960 and 1970.

SOURCE: Modified from data provided by the U.S. Bureau of the Census, Publication C3.223/10.970/V.2/Pt. 76. October 1970.

Demography	1950			1960			1970			Compound rate of growth per annum		
	Number	%	Trend	Number	%	Trend	Number	%	Trend	1950–1960	1960–1970	1950–1970
Men												
White	319,530	84.8	100.0	386,767	82.3	121.0	514,704	72.1	161.1	1.9	2.9	2.4
Black	870	0.2	100.0	2,397	0.5	275.5	8,995	1.3	1,033.9	10.7	14.1	12.4
Spanish-American and others	330	0.1	100.0	3,093	0.7	937.3	10,343	1.4	3,134.2	25.1	12.8	18.8
Total	320,730	85.1	100.0	392,257	83.5	122.3	534,042	74.8	166.5	2.0	3.1	2.6
Women												
White	55,530	14.8	100.0	75,578	16.1	136.1	169,515	23.7	305.3	3.1	8.4	5.7
Black	330	0.1	100.0	1,217	0.3	368.8	7,291	1.0	2,209.4	13.9	19.6	16.7
Spanish-American and others	60	–	100.0	650	0.1	108.3	3,272	0.5	5,453.3	26.9	17.5	22.1
Total	55,920	14.9	100.0	77,445	16.5	138.5	180,078	25.2	327.4	3.3	9.0	6.1
Total												
White	375,060	99.6	100.0	462,345	98.4	123.3	684,219	95.8	182.4	2.1	4.0	3.1
Black	1,200	0.3	100.0	3,614	0.8	301.2	16,286	2.3	1,357.2	11.7	16.2	13.9
Spanish-American and others	390	0.1	100.0	3,743	0.8	959.7	13,615	1.9	3,491.0	25.4	13.8	19.4
Total	376,650	100.0	100.0	469,702	100.0	124.7	714,120	100.0	189.6	2.2	4.3	3.3

EXHIBIT 10
Distribution of accountants and auditors by
industry classification, 1970.
SOURCE: Modified from data provided by the U.S. Bureau of the
Census, Publication C3.223/10.970/V.2/Pt.76, October 1970.

	Men		*Women*		*Total*	
	Number	%	*Number*	%	*Number*	%
Public accounting and professional services	149,342	28.0	40,323	22.4	189,665	26.6
Manufacturing	136,493	25.6	29,846	16.6	166,339	23.3
Public administration	64,713	12.1	31,960	17.7	96,673	13.5
Finance, insurance and real estate	45,897	8.6	22,893	12.7	68,790	9.6
Wholesale and retail	43,924	8.2	23,069	12.8	66,993	9.4
Communication, transportation and other utilities	30,539	5.7	10,529	5.8	41,068	5.8
Business and repair services	18,933	3.5	9,882	5.5	28,815	4.0
Construction	12,994	2.4	3,806	2.1	16,800	2.4
Mining	8,292	1.6	1,218	0.7	9,510	1.3
Personal services	6,001	1.1	2,932	1.6	8,933	1.3
Entertainment and recreation	2,035	0.4	910	0.5	2,945	0.4
Agriculture, forestry and fishery	1,438	0.3	477	0.3	1,915	0.3
Other	13,441	2.5	2,233	1.3	15,674	2.1
Total	534,042	100.0	180,078	100.0	714,120	100.0

Exhibit 10 shows the distribution of accountants among the major industries. Public accounting, for example, employed 189,665 (26.6%) accountants in 1970, followed closely by manufacturing (166,339, or 23.3%). Some 96,673 (13.5%) accountants worked for governmental agencies in 1970.

ASSOCIATIONS OF ACCOUNTANTS

Accountants are especially active in professional affairs, supporting more than a score of societies and associations. A detailed description of the national accounting associations appears in Appendix A to this book. The top ten associations are listed in the table in the order of membership.

Association	Membership 1972
1. American Institute of Certified Public Accountants	88,200
2. National Association of Accountants	70,000
3. American Accounting Association	15,000
4. National Society of Public Accountants	14,000
5. Hospital Financial Management Association	11,400
6. Institute of Internal Auditors	9,200
7. Financial Executives Institute	8,000
8. Federal Government Accountants Association	7,200
9. Municipal Finance Officers Association	5,200
10. American Society of Women Accountants	4,400

In addition to these national associations there are a variety of state associations (see Appendix D). The largest and most active of these are state societies of certified public accountants. The New York and California societies of certified public accountants had 19,801 and 11,657 members respectively as of December 31, 1972.

THE CERTIFIED PUBLIC ACCOUNTANT

The CPA is the most prestigious member of the accounting profession. He has status and enjoys privileges above those held by other accountants and auditors. Status reflects itself in a superior earning power and the opportunity to occupy high–level positions in industry, government, and public accounting.

The privileges include the right to practice public accounting, i.e., offer professional accounting and auditing services to client organizations and the public. This privilege is vested in law. All states have adopted an accountancy act which regulates the practice of public accountancy. Some pertinent excerpts from the California Accountancy Act illustrate the degree to which accounting services are regulated [2]:

> No person shall engage in the practice of public accountancy in this State unless such person is the holder of a valid permit to practice public accountancy issued by the board . . .

> [A] person shall be deemed to be engaged in the practice of public accountancy within the meaning and intent of this chapter:
> (a) Who holds himself or herself out to the public in any manner as one skilled in the knowledge, science and practice of accounting, and as qualified and ready

to render professional service therein as a public accountant for compensation; or

(b) Who maintains an office for the transaction of business as a public accountant; or

(c) Who offers to prospective clients to perform for compensation, or who does perform on behalf of clients for compensation, professional services that involve or require an audit, examination, verification, investigation, certification, presentation, or review, or financial transactions and accounting records; or

(d) Who prepares or certifies for clients reports on audits or examinations of books or records of account, balance sheets, and other financial, accounting and related schedules, exhibits, statements, or reports which are to be used for publication or for the purpose of obtaining credit or for filing with a court of law or with any governmental agency, or for any other purpose; or

(e) Who, in general or in an incident to such work, renders professional services to clients for compensation in any or all matters relating to accounting procedure and to the recording, presentation, or certification of financial information or data . . .

Any person who has received from the board a certificate of certified public accountant and holds a valid permit to practice under the provisions of this chapter shall be styled and known as a "certified public accountant" and may also use the abbreviation "C.P.A." No other person . . . shall assume or use that title, designation, or abbreviation or any other title, designation, sign, card or device tending to indicate that the person using it is a certified public accountant.

Public accounting practice is categorized by a small number of large firms on the one hand and a large number of small firms on the other. The tendency in accounting, as with other contemporary firms and institutions, is toward larger

EXHIBIT 11
Distribution of CPAs among large and small firms.
SOURCE: American Institute of Certified Public Accountants,
The '70's: A Decade for Decisions (1971), pp. 25, 32.

	1960		1970	
Size	Number of practice units	Percent of membership	Number of practice units	Percent of membership
1. Largest 25 firms	25	24.6	25	38.6
2. 10 or more members	148	6.7	258	7.5
3. 2–9 members	3,455	39.2	5,104	33.6
4. One member	7,787	29.5	9,588	20.3

organizations. As noted in Exhibit 11, approximately 38.6% of public accountants worked for the largest twenty-five firms in 1970.

The propensity toward larger service units in accounting is a concomitant of the surge toward larger organizations in general. As a business extends nationally it requires the services of a national CPA firm which has offices in most major cities. Similarly, as a business grows in complexity it requires a much broader range of specialized services than can be furnished by the typical small CPA firm. We turn now to a closer look at accounting practice as it exists in the large and small service unit.

PROFILE OF A MAJOR CPA FIRM

Arthur Andersen & Co. has provided a rare opportunity to examine the statistics of a major CPA firm (see Exhibit 12). It issued its first annual report in March 1973 (the first for any accounting firm) [3].

Average personnel compensation by Arthur Andersen & Co. for 1973 was: partners—$74,546; managers—$25,234; other professional staff, i.e., juniors and seniors—$13,655; and office support staff—$8614.

Starting salaries ranged between $11,000–$13,000 in 1973 against $6500–$7200 in 1964; the number of clients ranged from about 3000 to 50,000 over the period 1947–1973.

A major CPA firm such as Arthur Andersen & Co. works out of 65 offices throughout the United States and has an additional 100 offices, many in conjunction with affiliates, in as many as 40 foreign countries. These major firms perform 90% of the audit and related services of the 2500 publicly held corporations in the United States. These corporations represent an aggregate market value of stock in excess of $500 billions, with shares distributed among 31 million stockholders. A major CPA firm may have as many as 50,000 client units, and the clientele may extend far beyond business enterprises. One major firm, for example, audits more than 1000 banks, 700 savings and loan associations, 700 insurance companies, and 1200 not-for-profit institutions, including government agencies, schools, universities, and hospitals.

It is reported that in 1965, CPA firms were used in more than 40,000 cases by 26 governmental agencies.

The practice of most large CPA firms is divided into three broad areas: auditing, tax, and management advisory services (MAS). Arthur Andersen & Co. reports income from these categories in the ratio of 69%, 18%, and 13%, respectively.

The growth in management advisory services particularly is impressive. The MAS departments of each of the Big Eight firms is included among the top twenty management consulting groups in the United States. The rate of expan-

EXHIBIT 12

Income statement of Arthur Andersen & Co., March 1973.

(a) The numbers in parentheses represent average employment for 1972–1973 in each category. SOURCE: Annual report of Arthur Andersen & Co. for the period ending March 31, 1973, p. 32.

Item	1972 Amount	%	1973 Amount	%	Increase 1973 over 1972 (%)
1. *Income: professional* fees from 50,000 clients	$244,482,000	100.0	$271,459,000	100.0	11.1
2. *Distribution of income:*					
Personnel compensation [a]					
Partners (732)	49,432,000	20.2	55,835,000	20.5	13.0
Managers (1629)	36,751,000	15.0	41,107,000	15.1	11.9
Professional staff (6421)	82,324,000	33.7	87,680,000	32.3	6.5
Office support (2196)	16,681,000	6.8	18,916,000	7.0	13.4
Total compensation	185,188,000	75.7	203,538,000	74.9	9.9
3. *Operating expenses:*					
Office operating costs	13,068,000	5.3	15,218,000	5.6	16.5
Training and research	7,950,000	3.3	9,639,000	3.6	21.1
Insurance and provision for uninsured risks	6,466,000	2.7	4,463,000	1.6	(44.9)
Interest	1,689,000	0.7	1,850,000	0.7	9.5
Other operating expenses	22,598,000	9.2	26,067,000	9.6	15.4
Total operating	51,771,000	21.2	57,237,000	21.1	10.6
4. *Total current operating* expenses (2+3)	236,959,000	96.9	260,775,000	96.1	10.1
5. *Retained earnings and distribution to former partners or their estates (1–4)*	$ 7,523,000	3.1	$ 10,684,000	3.9	42.0

sion in management services is 15% per annum, which is higher than the growth rate in auditing, and is 5% higher than the growth of non-CPA consulting firms [4]. Projections foresee the maintenance of this growth rate through 1980 [5].

Those who staff the management consulting departments come increasingly from disciplines other than accounting. Many of these specialists do not possess the CPA certificate, yet they play a significant role in the forward thrust of the profession [6]. The Council of the American Institute of Certified Public Accountants passed the following resolution in 1971 in an effort to create a professional home for the non-CPA specialist [7]:

> Resolved, that non-CPA associates on the staffs of public accounting firms who meet educational, technical, and moral standards equivalent to those of present Institute members should be brought into a professional relationship with the Institute.

To date, non-CPA specialists have been unable to become partners of CPA firms, but some firms have created the category of *principal* to cater to the need for top non-CPA executive talent. Further, the ability to incorporate in some states creates positions and titles quite different from those of the conventional partnership.

Dominating the large CPA firms are the Big Eight firms which, in alphabetical order, are: Arthur Andersen & Co.; Arthur Young & Co.; Coopers & Lybrand; Ernst & Ernst; Haskins & Sells; Peat, Marwick, Mitchell & Co.; Price Waterhouse & Co.; and Touche Ross & Co. A summary of their clientele, number of offices, and revenues appears in Exhibit 13.

CPA firms, in common with most professional organizations, are partnerships. Management of the partnership vests in a committee of senior partners, which in certain firms is referred to as the board of directors. The chief executive officer is referred to as chairman or managing partner. The last expression must be viewed in its context, for there are managing partners in charge of local offices, districts, regions and, finally, of the firm as a whole.

The professional staff is divided functionally into the three principal service areas of auditing, taxes, and management advisory services. The audit function is viewed as pivotal, with the responsibility for all services rendered to a client resting finally with an audit partner.

The chain of command ranges downward from partner→ manager→ senior→ junior (or staff) accountant. Typical progression between ranks is: junior to senior, 2–3 years; senior to manager, 2–3 years; and manager to partner, 4–6 years [8]. Heavy emphasis is placed on training, performance evaluation, and career planning at all levels.

An insight into the work of the public accountant is provided in the following description which is extracted from the recruiting brochure of a major CPA firm [9]:

You begin your career with Price Waterhouse as a *staff accountant* in the office of your choice. Typically, you will be assigned to audit engagements with two or more other staff members, including a senior. This provides the individual training and supervision which assures a sound professional relationship with your colleagues from the very start of your career.

As a staff accountant, you will work on a number of different assignments during the course of a year, acquiring a diversity of business experience, and developing the creative ability to handle more complex auditing situations while assuming some supervisory duties. As you work for different people, people who share your challenges, you will find each helping you to develop your talents. This on-the-job training gives you the guidance necessary to stimulate independent thinking and decision making as part of your professional development within the firm and the profession. It also helps you prepare for your CPA examination.

In a relatively short time, you should develop an expanding knowledge of auditing techniques and accounting principles. You would normally be performing as a *senior accountant* in two to three years, in charge of the fieldwork on several audit engagements, and supervising the work of staff accountants. As one of the firm's key supervisors, you will then be responsible for the planning and direction of audits under the general supervision of a manager. You will deal with more and more complex auditing and accounting problems, and will be called upon to discuss these matters with client executives. This position enables you to demonstrate your ability to perform as an independent professional.

The next step in your advancement with the firm—to *manager*—is usually accomplished in four to six years after joining the staff, or two or three years after becoming a senior. As a manager, you will direct several engagements simultaneously, and will be in a position of as much responsibility as a financial officer of a large company. You will spend much of your time in consultation with partners and with client executives.

Each year a number of managers are admitted to partnership in Price Waterhouse. As a *partner* you will have met with distinction all the requirements of the accounting profession in general and of Price Waterhouse in particular. You then carry the ultimate responsibility for the best possible service to clients, and for the administration of the firm. You contribute to the formation of policies and the solution of problems which affect the firm, and often the profession as a whole. As a partner, you share all the satisfactions and rewards of a top executive in today's business world.

It is a distinguishing characteristic of Price Waterhouse that there is only one class of partners and, although they are from varied backgrounds, with few exceptions, all of them have advanced through each of the stages previously described.

The firm has no minimum of either age or length of service for admission to the partnership and, although it usually requires 10 to 12 years of experience, there have been a number of exceptions with fewer years of service. Currently individuals are being added to the partnership when still in their mid-thirties, some even earlier. It has also been the firm's policy that partners retire at age 60, which provides greater opportunities for others, assures upward mobility within the firm, and a continuous renewal of vigorous top management.

THE SMALL CPA FIRM

The nature of a local CPA firm is in sharp contrast to that of a large one [10]. The local partnership has an average professional staff of six persons. Gross annual income is between $150,000 and $200,000 and grows at the rate of 15%. Most of the growth (65%) is from internal expansion, as opposed to mergers. Average net income for a partner is about $30,000. Partners work 57 hours a week during tax season and 42 hours a week at other times. Two-thirds of the income of the local firm is generated from write-up (bookkeeping), unaudited financial statements, and tax services.

The one-man firm, or proprietorship, has a professional staff of 1.5 persons. Gross annual income is between $25,000 and $50,000 and grows at a rate of 10%. Of this growth 60% is from internal expansion. Proprietors work 60 hours a week during tax season and 44 hours a week for the remainder of the year. More than 80% of income comes from write-up (bookkeeping), unaudited financial statements, and tax services.

It is obvious from this analysis that the attest (audit) function is largely absent in local practice; and where it does exist, displacement occurs as clients grow larger, turn public, or are acquired by publicly held corporations.

John L. Carey, in his definitive history of the development of the accounting profession in the United States, notes that displacement of small firms by large ones has occurred "from the earliest days of the organized profession [11]." Ralph Kent, as President of the American Institute of Certified Public Accountants in 1969, identified the displacement of the local firm as one of the three major problems facing the profession; his successor, Louis Kessler, established an ad hoc "committee on displacement" to study and make recommendations concerning the problem [12].

The committee's findings shed some interesting light on the problem of displacement. The sample covered thirty percent of the small member firms of the AICPA, of which 165 firms had participated in a Securities and Exchange Commission (SEC) filing pursuant to the public offering of a client's stock. Of these firms, 103 (62.4%) had been displaced in the process. Displacement in 95.1% of the cases reported was in favor of a "nationally known firm." The rationale in most instances was that "the underwriters informed the client that a nationally known firm was necessary to sell their offering at the highest possible price [13]." Carey notes the influence of bankers in displacement [14], while other reasons range from inexperience in SEC matters on the part of local firms to inability to grow technologically and geographically with the client's development [15].

Apart from displacement, Burton and Roberts have shown that changes of auditors among larger corporations are relatively rare, and are most often caused by a change in management [16]. The SEC now requires written notice of, and justification for, a change in auditors [17]. The public accounting firms which are affected by these actions are, in most cases, invited to respond.

While not seeking to minimize the trauma of displacement, the more pressing challenge facing the small CPA firm arises from the rapidly developing computer technology. Inexpensive computerized accounting services, including time-sharing, have now appeared and will expand rapidly, displacing much of the write-up (bookkeeping) services which now account for a high proportion of the income of the local CPA firm [18].

Interestingly, bookkeeping and tax services can be furnished without certification, and efforts to bring these services within the licensing framework have been unsuccessful [19]. The role of the local firm in a computerized age requires careful planning and analysis. Obviously, more training in systems analysis and computer technology appear to be prerequisites for local practice of the future. Many local CPA firms are modernizing their services.

INCORPORATION OF CPA FIRMS

Until recently, state law as well as AICPA policy has prevented the incorporation of public accounting firms. But this situation is changing. A number of states now permit the incorporation of all types of professional organizations, including medical, legal, and accounting firms. Article 11 ("Accountancy Corporation Rules") was added to the California Accountancy Act on July 1, 1971. It is typical of legislation in this area [20]. Among the more important provisions of the Act are the following:

1. Nothing in the laws or rules relating to accountancy corporations alters the duties and responsibilities of a licensed person to and professional relationships with his clients and others.

2. Each shareholder, director, and officer holds a license issued by the Board.

3. The name of the corporation shall contain and be restricted to the name or last name of one or more of the present, prospective or former shareholders.

4. The words "accountancy corporation," "professional corporation," or "corp.," "incorporated," or "inc.," must be used in conjunction with the name of the firm.

5. Multioffice firms must ensure that each office is under the direction of a licensed person as resident manager.

These rules are similar to those adopted by the Council of the AICPA when its Rule 4.06 was amended on May 6, 1969 to permit the incorporation of member firms [21]. Several local and regional firms have exercised the option, but until all states adopted an incorporation provision (or a federal charter comes into effect), the incorporation of national firms remains in doubt. The incorporation of CPA firms would not limit their liability with respect to professional services, but it might provide for more flexible organization.

THE ACCOUNTANT IN INDUSTRY

Approximately 403,000 accountants occupied positions in industry in 1970, of which 37,247 (9.24%) were CPAs. As noted in Exhibit 10, accountants are distributed among the major industrial groups in these proportions: manufacturing—41.28%; finance, insurance, and real estate—17.07%; wholesale and retail—16.62%; communications, transportation and other utilities—10.19%; business and repair services—7.15%; entertainment and recreation—7.3%; and agriculture, forestry, and fishery—.5%.

The accountant occupies a variety of positions in industry, ranging across such functions as accounting, auditing, cost accounting, financial management, budgeting, controllership, and systems analysis. Within the accounting category, the progression generally is from accountant→chief accountant →controller or financial vice-president. Beginning salaries for accountants with bachelors or masters degrees are comparable with those in government and public accounting. Salary surveys indicate that accountants compare favorably with engineers and lawyers at all levels of employment, and obtain higher compensation than business graduates in other fields [22].

The work of the accountant in industry is varied and highly challenging. He is concerned with future planning and directs and coordinates the preparation of forecasts, budgets, and other financial plans. The processing of financial information falls within his area of competence; in this regard he is responsible for designing and supervising the financial information systems of the firm. The accountant in industry is also charged with protecting and conserving the assets of the firm, and the title of controller is often used to describe the accountant whose principal concern is internal control. The accountant is also responsible for record-keeping and supervises the activities of bookkeepers and clerks.

A number of accountants in industry assume the position of treasurer, which means that they are responsible for the planning and control of the cash resources of the business. Other accountants become internal auditors; as such they review plans and operations and render reports to management which often lead to significant improvements in efficiency.

EXHIBIT 14

Distribution of top level executive positions among major academic disciplines.

SOURCE: Richard C. Bradish, "Accountants in Top Management," *Journal of Accountancy*, June 1970, p. 51.

Title of Corporate Executive	Accounting		Economics		Engineering		Industrial management		Law	
	#	%	#	%	#	%	#	%	#	%
Chairman of the Board	30	13.0	12	5.2	45	19.5	38	16.5	17	7.4
President	37	13.3	14	5.0	63	22.6	35	12.5	29	10.4
Vice Presidents:										
Executive	24	11.7	12	5.8	50	24.3	26	12.7	18	8.7
Financial	127	55.5	31	13.5	4	1.7	14	6.1	16	7.0
Marketing	4	2.1	20	10.3	30	15.6	20	10.3	3	1.6
Other	38	4.4	44	5.3	260	30.1	119	13.8	85	9.8
Controller	199	79.6	14	5.6			10	4.0	1	0.4
Secretary	31	12.1	8	3.1	3	1.2	5	1.9	168	65.3
Treasurer	154	61.3	33	13.1	1	0.4	10	4.0	13	5.2
Total	644	23.3	188	6.8	456	16.5	277	10.1	350	12.7

EXHIBIT 14 (continued)

Title of Corporate Executive	Liberal arts and social sciences		Marketing		Science		Miscellaneous other		Total filled positions	
	#	%	#	%	#	%	#	%	#	%
Chairman of the Board	27	11.6	11	4.8	19	8.2	32	13.8	231	100.0
President	35	12.5	15	5.4	17	6.1	34	12.2	279	100.0
Vice Presidents:										
Executive	28	13.6	10	4.8	8	3.9	30	14.5	206	100.0
Financial	11	4.8					26	11.4	229	100.0
Marketing	58	29.9	23	11.6	11	5.7	25	12.9	194	100.0
Other	106	12.3	29	3.4	72	8.3	110	12.8	863	100.0
Controller	2	0.8	1	0.4			23	9.2	250	100.0
Secretary	20	7.8			1	0.4	21	8.2	257	100.0
Treasurer	12	4.8			1	0.4	27	10.8	251	100.0
Total	299	10.8	89	3.2	129	4.7	328	11.9	2760	100.0

The accountant in industry is responsible for the preparation of financial reports which are distributed widely to stockholders, creditors, government agencies, and other interested parties. He prepares a variety of reports for management—all directed toward the need for providing timely information for decision-making purposes—and is often an integral member of the top management group. There are very few areas in which his expertise is not required.

Accountants have done well in industry. A survey by Richard C. Bradish in 1970 shows that accountants occupy more top-level positions in industry than those from other academic disciplines (Exhibit 14) [23]. The population for the survey included the *Fortune* listing of the 500 largest industrials, the 50 largest merchandising firms, and the 50 largest transportation companies.

Recent developments have served to improve the professional status of the accountant in industry, of the management accountant as he or she is often called. First, the National Association of Accountants (NAA) began its own professional designation program in 1972. The designation is known as the Certificate in Management Accounting (CMA) * and is administered by the NAA's Institute of Management Accounting. In announcing its certification program the NAA noted that [24]:

More and more people—inside the business world and out—realize the significant changes which have been taking place for years in accounting and in the role of the accountant in business. No longer is he simply a recorder of business history. He now plays a dynamic role in making business decisions, in future planning and in almost every aspect of business operations.

This new accountant is called a Management Accountant and he sits with top management because his key responsibility is developing, producing and analyzing information to help management positions. In response to the needs of business and at the request of many in the academic community, the National Association of Accountants has established a program to recognize professional competence and educational attainment in this field—a program leading to the Certificate in Management Accounting.

A second impetus to management accounting has come from the movement to eliminate the experience requirement for the CPA certificate. Until recently two years of experience (in most states) has been required in addition to passing the CPA examinations to qualify for certification. Essentially, the experience must come from completing a prescribed set of duties within public accounting. Those seeking careers in industry have thus been detoured through public accounting in order to be certified or have simply pursued management accounting careers without the benefit of the CPA designation. We note here that a committee of the AICPA has recommended elimination of the experience requirement and that several states have now acted to implement that recom-

---

* The CMA examination is discussed further in Chapter 3.

mendation [25]. This move encourages direct entrance into management accounting without impairing the ability to secure the CPA certificate. The NAA hopes, of course, that the CMA certificate will become the hallmark of excellence in management accounting.

ACCOUNTANTS IN GOVERNMENT

From Exhibit 10 we note that 96,673 accountants worked for government agencies in 1970. All departments and agencies utilize the services of accountants, including the U.S. Department of Defense. The current pay scale for federal employees is given in Exhibit 15 [26].

EXHIBIT 15
GS scale for federal employees, 1973.

Step	Range	Step	Range
1	$ 4,798— 6,238	10	$12,775—16,609
2	5,432— 7,061	11	13,996—18,190
3	6,128— 7,964	12	16,682—21,686
4	6,882— 8,943	13	19,700—25,613
5	7,694—10,007	14	23,088—30,018
6	8,572—11,146	15	26,898—34,971
7	9,520—12,373	16	31,203—39,523
8	10,528—13,687	17	36,103—40,915
9	11,614—15,097	18	41,734

In most federal agencies, accountants are hired initially at step seven and can progress steadily to the position of chief accountant at a scale of GS 15 ($26,898–$39,971). A 10% premium is attached to starting salaries for those who possess the CPA certificate or graduate degree.

The U.S. General Accounting Office (GAO) performs a function analogous to that of public accounting—it audits the operations of the federal government and renders its findings to Congress.

As of June 1972, GAO had a staff of 4826 of which 2628 were accountants, 500 were specialists from other fields, and 1698 consisted of supporting personnel. The ratio of nonaccountants to accountants on the professional staff has increased steadily in recent years, as has the hiring of students with graduate degrees.

A recent publication describes the activities of GAO in the following terms [27]:

Our management audits go beyond the mere verification of financial transactions. In reviewing management performance in Federal agencies, we evaluate management planning, organization, control and decision-making in relation to operating results and program accomplishments. Out reviews and evaluations delve into varied programs and activities involving most substantive fields and technical aspects of our national economy. We take pride in having pioneered in the review of management performance and developing techniques for making these reviews. Our management review work enables us to fulfill our responsibilities to the Congress and, concurrently, to stimulate more effective and efficient management within the Federal Government.

Often referred to as the government's "watchdog," GAO has compiled a significant record of accomplishment. The agency makes an average of 900 audits a year, prepares more than 4000 decisions by the Comptroller General, and submits more than 700 legislative and legal reports to the Congress each year. Its recommendations have led to estimated savings in federal government operations of over $200 million a year for each of the past five years, while the GAO operating budget is only $63 million annually [28].

Many of the activities of GAO have received wide public attention. GAO has inquired into such far-ranging matters as the safety of nuclear generating plants, the effectiveness of drug rehabilitation programs, and the improvement of health care systems. The accountant in government agencies such as GAO is concerned with total organizational efficiency and not simply with the maintenance of financial records and reports. In most instances he is charged with preparing and managing budgets, in designing and operating information systems geared to the needs of his agency, and plays an active role in most of the major activities of the agency. The occupations and titles of accountants in government are as varied as they are in industry.

GAO, however, is the focal point for accounting in government. It is the responsibility of this agency to design and monitor financial information systems for all federal agencies.

GAO operates from 16 regional offices in the United States and 30 suboffices in the major cities. Its international activities are housed in offices in Honolulu, Frankfurt, Manila, New Delhi, and Saigon. Increasingly the Congress looks to GAO for advice on new programs under the broad charge of "giving advice to the Congress."

The U.S. General Accounting Office was created by the Budget and Accounting Act in 1921. In general, the audit authority of GAO extends to all departments and agencies of the federal government, with the exception of the Federal Reserve System, the Comptroller of the Currency, and activities of certain intelligence agencies. Where audit authority exists, GAO has unrestricted access to all facilities and records, and the law provides that such agencies will furnish to the Comptroller General the information he may require concern-

EXHIBIT 16

Organization of United States General Accounting Office.

SOURCE: *Annual Report 1972* (Washington, D.C.: The Comptroller General of the United States; available from the Superintendent of Documents, U.S. Government Printing Office, Stock Number 2000-00102, 1973).

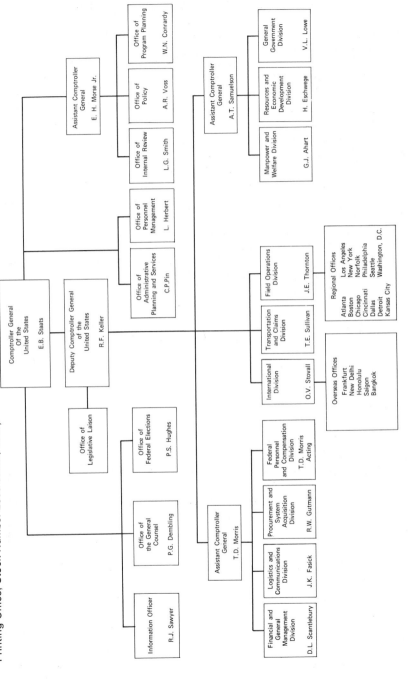

ing their powers, duties, activities, organization, financial transactions, and methods of business.

The present organization of GAO is shown by the chart in Exhibit 16 [29]. The Comptroller General of the United States (currently Elmer B. Staats) is appointed by the President with the advice and consent of the Senate. His term is for a maximum period of 15 years and he is subject to removal from office only by Congress through joint resolution or by impeachment.

The major activities of GAO fall into the following categories: (a) providing direct assistance to the Congress (this function was expanded by the Legislative Reorganization Act of 1970); (b) performing audits and reviews; (c) prescribing accounting principles and standards for all agencies of the federal government under the Budget and Accounting Procedures Act of 1950; (d) rendering legal decisions as to the authority and appropriateness of contracts, procurements, and disbursements by all federal agencies; (e) settling claims for and against the United States, including claims for salary and other compensation under the Federal Claims Collection Act of 1966; and (f) participating in the regulation of federal elections under the Federal Election Campaign Act of 1971. In the latter regard, GAO prescribes regulations on the use of communications media by candidates for federal elective office and on charges for using communications media. The law requires that GAO serve as a national clearinghouse for information on the administration of elections. Also, GAO is required to supervise, audit, and report on the election practices of the presidential and vice-presidential candidates.

REFERENCES

1. See U.S. Bureau of the Census, *Subject Reports—Occupation by Industry*, Publication C3.223/10.970/V.2/Pt.76, for overall occupational statistics, and *The '70's: A Decade for Decisions*, p. 42. The percentages on page 42 were applied to the total number of CPAs in 1970—119,000—as opposed to the Institute membership of 75,381.

2. State of California, Board of Accountancy, *California Accountancy Act with Rules and Regulations* (1971), pp. 20–21.

3. A discussion concerning whether or not CPA firms should issue their own financial statements is provided by H. JUSTIN DAVIDSON and THOMAS R. HOFSTEDT, "Published Financial Statements for CPAs," *Journal of Accountancy*, July 1972, pp. 31–45.

4. There is some difficulty in obtaining absolute data on public accounting firms. The data in this section were obtained from a number of sources, principally PAUL D. MONTAGNA, "The Public Accounting Profession," *American Behavioral Scien-*

tist, March–April 1971, pp. 475–491. See also HAL HIGDON, *The Business Healers* (New York: Random House, 1969); *Revenue and Expenses of Accounting Firms, map 14b* (New York: American Institute of Certified Public Accountants, 1963); JOHN L. CAREY, *The Rise of the Accounting Profession*, vols. 1, 2 (New York: American Institute of Certified Public Accountants, 1969); "The Very Private World of Peat, Marwick, Mitchell," *Fortune*, July 1, 1966, pp. 128–130; T. A. WISE, "The Auditors Have Arrived," *Fortune*, November, December 1960; "Are CPA Firms Taking Over Management Consulting?", *Forbes*, October 1, 1966, pp. 57–61; FELIX KAUFMAN, "Professional Consulting by CPAs," *The Accounting Review*, October 1967, pp. 713–720; and "Accounting's Big Eight Firms: A Capsule View," *Business Week*, April 22, 1972, pp. 54–60.

5. See MAURICE MOONITZ, ed., *Public Accounting: 1980* (Palo Alto, Ca.: California Certified Public Accountants Foundation for Education and Research, 1971), particularly the comments of ARTHUR M. SARGENT, pp. 5–11; LARRY A. JOBE, pp. 12–41; JAMES H. MACNEILL, pp. 42–55; DAVID F. LINOWES, pp. 70–81; and MICHAEL N. CHETKOVICH, pp. 86–97.

6. The dilemma posed by the non-CPA specialist who functions within the environs of the CPA firm is discussed by JOHN W. BUCKLEY, *In Search of Identity: An Inquiry Into Identity Issues in Accounting* (Palo Alto, Ca.: California Certified Public Accountants Foundation for Education and Research, 1972).

7. *The CPA*, September 1971, p. 1.

8. See, for example, *You as a Professional Accountant with the People of Price Waterhouse* (New York: Price Waterhouse & Co., 1973).

9. Ibid.

10. *The CPA*, January 1971, p. 11.

11. JOHN L. CAREY, *The Rise of the Accounting Profession*, vol. 2 (New York: American Institute of Certified Public Accountants, 1970), p. 339.

12. See CHARLES G. CARPENTER and ROBERT H. STRAWSER, "Displacement of Auditors When Clients Go Public," *Journal of Accountancy*, June 1971, p. 55.

13. Ibid.

14. CAREY, op. cit., (11), pp. 353–355.

15. CARPENTER and STRAWSER, op. cit., (12), p. 58.

16. JOHN C. BURTON and WILLIAM ROBERTS, "A Study of Auditor Changes," *Journal of Accountancy*, April 1967, pp. 31–38.

17. Changes in the registrant's certifying accounting was added as an additional item of information to Form 8-K (the so-called "current report") in 1971. Because of its unusual nature, the text of the requirement is quoted in full below:

> If an independent accountant has been engaged as the principal accountant to audit the registrant's financial statements who was not the principal accountant

for the registrant's most recently filed certified financial statements, state the date when such independent accountant was engaged. The registrant shall also furnish the Commission with a separate letter stating whether in the eighteen months preceding such engagement there were any disagreements with the former principal accountant on any matter of accounting principles and practices, financial statement disclosure, or auditing procedure, which disagreements if not resolved to the satisfaction of the former accountant would have caused him to make reference in connection with his opinion to the subject matter of the disagreement. The registrant shall also request the former principal accountant to furnish the registrant with a letter addressed to the Commission stating whether he agrees with the statements contained in the letter of the registrant and, if not, stating the respects in which he does not agree; and the registrant shall furnish such letter to the Commission together with his own.

Louis H. Rappaport, *SEC Accounting Practice and Procedure*, 3rd ed. (New York: Ronald Press, 1972), pp. 14-9, 14-10.

18. *The CPA*, January 1971, p. 11. Also, John W. Buckley, *In Search of Identity: An Inquiry into Identity Issues in Accounting* (Palo Alto, Ca.: California Certified Public Accountants Foundation for Education and Research, 1972), pp. 37–50, 66–74.

19. See "AICPA Council Opposes Licensing of Technicians," *Journal of Accountancy*, June 1970, pp. 10–12.

20. State of California, Board of Accountancy, *California Accountancy Act with Rules and Regulations* (1971), sections 75.1–75.11, article 11. Also, *Business and Professions Code*, sections 5010, 5011, 5018.

21. *Code of Professional Ethics* (New York: American Institute of Certified Public Accountants, March 1, 1973), pp. 28–29.

22. See, for example, *U.S. News and World Report*, October 15, 1973, pp. 86–87.

23. Richard C. Bradish, "Accountants in Top Management," *Journal of Accountancy*, June 1970, pp. 49–53. See also Austin J. Gerber and George L. Marrah, "How Our Key Executives Have Been Educated," *Business Horizons*, February 1969, p. 51; John Ashworth, "People Who Become Accountants," *Journal of Accountancy*, November 1968, p. 44; "Top Management Is Getting Tough," *Dun's*, May 1971, pp. 45–46; "Technology in the Manager's Future," *Harvard Business Review*, November–December, 1970, pp. 4–14, 165.

24. *CMA: Certificate in Management Accounting* (New York: Institute of Management Accounting, National Association of Accountants, 1973), p. 3.

25. *Report of the Committee on Education and Experience Requirements for CPAs* (New York: American Institute of Certified Public Accountants, March 1969).

26. U.S., Civil Service Commission, Salary Table #58 (January, 1973).

27. *Work with GAO for More Effective Government* (Washington, D.C.: U.S. General Accounting Office, 1970).

28. "GAO—Success Is a Problem," *Management Accounting*, April 1970, pp. 53–55.

29. *The General Accounting Office: Answers to Frequently Asked Questions* (Washington, D.C.: U.S. General Accounting Office, 1973).

TO BECOME
AN ACCOUNTANT

THE POSNAK EXPERIENCE

Robert L. Posnak has written a delightful little piece on how he became an accountant [1]. His "debut as an accountant was an improbable event. Clutching a degree in English literature," he notes, "I applied for a job as assistant to the chief accountant of a medium-sized firm. Much to my dismay, a dozen qualified accountants answered the same advertisement. Fortunately the chief accountant had a taste for Chaucer, so he took me on."

"Although able to write journal entries in the baroque style, I was not the world's best industrial accountant, and the annual audit bore witness to this sad fact." He proceeds then to tell us how he worked into "the wee hours of the morning to purge the books of the year's accumulation of errors and omissions." After three years of industrial accounting, Posnak decided to try his hand at public accounting. "Apparently the auditors had had enough of my creative bookkeeping," he observes. "With a sigh of pleasure at the prospect of never having to audit my work again, they accepted me into their ranks."

The study continues with his experiences as an auditor. With complete candor he recounts that "my first year in public accounting was a nightmare and remains so in retrospect. In the first place, I had little formal training in accounting and was ill-prepared for the work. In the second place, the night courses I took to supply this deficiency were in many cases drearily mechanistic, lacking the characteristics of a worthy academic discipline." He continues, "As I tested the ten thousandth transaction, statistically and otherwise, I still knew very little about the accounting profession and its role in society."

The situation improved significantly in the second year. "I began to work with little supervision and a great deal of latitude, and the work was suddenly exciting. Men worked for *me* on occasion, and it was with some glee that I assigned the test work to them. Mindful of my own recent experiences, however, and taken by the style of the partner with whom I worked, I tried to give them some insight into the nature and importance of the work."

Posnak soon learned that human factors vie with technical ability in creating the successful accountant. "With clients and with colleagues, personality dynamics soon came to be an important part of my job, but the problem was always the same: to reach someone. It was quickly apparent that accountants do not live by competence alone."

A lifetime commitment to learning also emerged as a cardinal need. Posnak observes that "accounting is a learned profession, but in a most peculiar way. Beyond a broad knowledge of accounting, auditing, and taxation, I soon realized that a successful accountant must somehow master a dozen other disciplines, and that a man who seeks the security of a discipline of limited proportions will find no sanctuary in public accounting."

"One day an auditor," he notes, "the next an accountant; tax planner; financial analyst; systems designer; executive recruiter; developer of plans of organization; general business adviser; profit planner; administrator; researcher; writer; statistical sampler; lecturer; salesman; fee-collector; arbiter of staff disputes; arbiter of client disputes; counselor to other tense accountants; Xerox mechanic; soothsayer, sage, seer and saint—the list is quite possibly endless. It became evident that in addition to having a host of technical skills, an accountant must be a generalist *par excellence*."

While Posnak's experiences in accounting are typical, his mode of entry into the profession is not! In common with other major professions, careers in accounting are generally preceded by formal studies in accounting which culminate in a college degree.

ROOTS IN EDUCATION

Accounting practice has been buttressed by formal education from the very beginning. Pacioli, recognized earlier as the inventor of double-entry accounting, was an academic. He taught mathematics and business in Perugia, Rome, Naples, Assisi, and the University of Pisa [2]. As already noted, auditing texts existed in Roman times and accounting has long been a respected academic discipline[3]. Professor Chatfield notes that accounting was part of the Oxford University's curriculum in the 13th century [4], and it is well-established that accounting studies in the United States were the springboard for schools of commerce and business administration.

"An attempt was made as early as 1851 to found a school of commerce at the university level," according to Professor Edwards. "This attempt was at the University of Louisiana but was apparently abandoned in 1857 [5]." Accounting was first taught on a commercial basis at the Bryant and Stratton School in 1853 [6]. Other commercial schools of accounting began to appear rapidly along the East Coast in the ensuing years [7].

The Wharton School of Finance and Economics,* established in 1881 through a contribution of $100,000 by Mr. Joseph Wharton, has the distinction of being the first collegiate school of business in the United States [8]. It has been a distinguished school since its founding. This pioneering effort bore fruit during the next twenty-five years in the establishment of departments of commerce and accounts in the universities and colleges listed in Exhibit 17.

EXHIBIT 17
Establishment of early schools of commerce and accounts, 1881–1917.

University of Pennsylvania		Pittsburgh	1908
(Wharton School)	1881	Marquette	1910
Agricultural College (Utah)	1891	St. Louis	1910
Montana	1895	Northeastern	1911
Indiana	1895	DePaul	1912
California (Berkeley)	1898	Boston University	1913
Louisiana	1899	Nebraska	1913
Ohio (Athens)	1899	Notre Dame	1913
Dartmouth (Amos Tuck)	1900	Duquesne	1913
New York University	1900	Oregon	1914
University of Chicago	1902	Tulane	1914
University of Denver	1908	Washington	1914
Harvard	1908	Illinois	1915
Iowa State	1908	Ohio State	1915
Northwestern	1908	North Dakota	1917

Today, accounting is taught in most institutions of higher learning which support professional education. The number of degrees conferred on students who major in accounting for the period 1960–1970 is noted in Exhibit 18 (bachelors and masters) and Exhibit 26 (doctoral). In addition, many hundreds of students take a variety of courses in accounting in support of their majors in other fields. It is estimated that up to a million students a year take the introductory accounting course.

* Its name was changed to the Wharton School of Commerce and Finance. The School is part of the University of Pennsylvania.

EXHIBIT 18
Supply of accounting graduates, 1967–1968 to
1974–1975.
SOURCE: Park E. Leathers and Howard P. Sanders, "The
Supply and Demand for Public Accountants," *Journal of Accountancy,* September 1971, p. 88.

Year	Educational level Bachelor's degrees	Master's degrees	Total supply	Growth index
1967–1968	18,100	1,500	19,600	93
1968–1969	19,400	1,500	20,900	99
1969–1970	21,300	1,400	22,700	108
1970–1971	22,700	2,000	24,700	117
1971–1972	24,300	2,500	26,800	127
1972–1973	26,200	3,000	29,200	139
1973–1974	28,100	3,700	31,800	151
1974–1975	29,800	4,300	34,100	162

Gone are the days to which Carey refers when the bulk of those admitted to membership had only high school training. Of those admitted to the profession during the period 1917–1926, 32% had not completed high school, 37% had been graduated from high school, and only 24% possessed a college degree [9].

Today, most states have adopted an educational requirement which serves as a prerequisite for entrance to the profession. California's educational requirement is typical in this respect [10]:

Each applicant must present evidence satisfactory to the board that he meets the requirements set forth in Section 5081 of the Accountancy Act. Satisfactory evidence as to education qualifications will usually take the form of transcripts or photostats thereof, of the applicant's high school and/or college record which should accompany the application. However, in unusual circumstances the board shall accept such other evidence as it deems appropriate and reasonably conclusive.

Section 5081 provides that one must either:

1.   Have a baccalaureate degree from a four year accredited university or college with a major in accounting, or if the major is not accounting, 45 semester units in accounting and related topics. The related subjects include but are not limited to the following subjects:

Economics   (credit allowed up to 12 units)
Finance and all business admin-
    istration subjects   (credit allowed up to 18 units)
Accounting and auditing   (a minimum of 10 units required)
Commercial law   (credit allowed up to 6 units)

         Computer sciences   (credit allowed up to 3 units)
         Mathematics & Statistics   (credit allowed up to 10 units)

or 2.   Have successfully completed two years at an accredited college or junior (community) college and have studied accounting and other subjects for at least four years (60 semester units in addition to the two years in college), of which 45 semester units have been in accounting and related subjects as in Number 1 above.

or 3.   Pass the appropriate test or tests as designated by the board in lieu of four years of college. Presently the board is using Educational Testing Service's "School and College Ability Test"—From UA(SCAT–UA) for this purpose.*

SUPPLY AND DEMAND

Leathers and Sanders [11] have studied the supply and demand characteristics for the public accounting sector during the period 1967–1975 (Exhibits 18 and 19). A trend toward postgraduate education in accounting is evident and it is at this level where the least disparity exists between supply and demand.

EXHIBIT 19
Demand for public accounting recruits, 1967–1968 to 1974–1975.
NOTE: Includes only those firms with 10 or more institute members. SOURCE: Park E. Leathers and Howard P. Sanders, "The Supply and Demand for Public Accountants," *Journal of Accountancy,* September 1971, p. 88.

	Educational level				
Year	Less than bachelor's	Bachelor's degree	Master's degree	Total demand	Growth index
1967–1968	200	6,600	1,500	8,300	78
1968–1969	200	9,600	1,800	11,600	109
1969–1970	300	9,900	1,900	12,100	113
1970–1971	100	6,400	1,800	8,300	78
1971–1972	100	8,600	2,300	11,000	103
1972–1973	100	9,500	2,800	12,400	116
1973–1974	100	10,200	3,500	13,800	129
1974–1975	100	11,300	4,200	15,600	146

* This latter provision is referred to as the "Abraham Lincoln" clause and is intended to permit self-educated people to sit for the CPA examination. This provision exists in all professional codes, but is exercised rarely.

EXHIBIT 20

The first placement of students majoring in
accounting, by decades.

SOURCE: The survey is summarized by Felix P. Kollaritsch in
"Job Migration Pattern of Accounting," *Management Accounting,* September 1968, p. 53.

Decade	Total number	Percent	Public	Industrial
1920's	6	0.5	–0–	16.7
1930's	99	8.1	29.3	29.4
1940's	387	31.7	39.7	25.4
1950's	416	34.1	34.2	28.6
1960's	312	25.6	43.9	27.8

Decade	Service	Government	Education	Other
1920's	–0–	–0–	33.3	50.0
1930's	6.0	1.0	3.0	31.3
1940's	7.8	5.9	3.6	17.6
1950's	6.7	3.1	5.5	21.9
1960's	4.7	8.1	8.1	7.4

EXHIBIT 21

The first placement of students majoring in
accounting, average 1920–1967.

(a) Includes banking, insurance, retail, transportation, hotels,
etc. (b) Includes those graduates going on to graduate schools.
(c) Includes military services, lawyers, and other work outside
the field of accounting. SOURCE: The survey is summarized by
Felix P. Kollaritsch in "Job Migration Pattern of Accounting,"
Management Accounting, September 1968, p. 53.

	Started	Present	Changes
Public accounting	37.9	22.4	– 15.5
Industrial accounting	27.3	42.3	+ 15.0
Service industry accounting [a]	6.5	14.4	+ 7.9
Governmental accounting	5.1	10.4	+ 5.3
Education [b]	5.5	3.5	– 2.0
Other [c]	17.7	7.0	– 10.7
	100.0	100.0	–0–

EXHIBIT 22
The major employers of MBAs, 1968–1970.
SOURCE: MBA Enterprises, Inc., *THE MBA* (Magazine), Spring 1970.

Year	1968	1969	1970
Total employed	1,250	1,301	1,320
Industry	Percent		
Banking	7.4	10.7	14.2
Management consulting	7.4	11.1	11.8
Public accounting	10.4	7.1	11.7
Computers, services	4.8	5.8	4.7
Investment banking	5.4	10.1	4.0
Food	4.7	3.8	4.0
Electrical goods, electronics	4.5	3.2	3.4
Real estate	1.5	2.8	2.7
Retailing	1.8	1.0	2.7
Government	2.7	1.0	2.7
Soaps, cosmetics	2.5	2.1	2.6
Oil	4.2	2.4	2.5
Lumber, pulp, paper	1.7	1.8	2.3
Brokerage	2.2	3.5	2.2
Chemicals	4.1	3.8	2.2
Insurance	1.3	1.1	2.2
Hardgoods manufacturing	—	1.4	2.0
Automotive	2.7	2.0	1.8
Education	3.1	2.8	1.8
Can, glass	0.4	1.0	1.6
Construction	—	1.3	1.5
Drugs	1.4	0.8	1.4
Office equipment	—	—	1.4
Advertising	1.7	1.4	1.0
Communications, telephone	1.6	1.1	0.9
Liquor, beverages	0.4	0.6	0.8
Steel, other metals	1.5	1.3	0.8
Textiles	0.5	0.8	0.8
Printing, publishing	—	1.7	0.7
Transportation	1.4	1.0	0.6
Aerospace	3.4	2.3	0.4
Agricultural equipment	—	0.2	0.3
Airlines	1.1	0.6	0.3
Television	0.3	0.5	0.3
Utilities	—	0.5	0.3
Rubber	0.4	0.2	0.2
Tobacco	0.2	0.2	—
Other	13.5	7.3	5.8

According to an Ohio State University survey [12], public accounting firms during the 1960's hired 43.9% of all accounting majors (Exhibit 20), or 37.9% for the overall period of the study, 1920–1967 (Exhibit 21).

Commenting further on the demand for accounting graduates with a master's degree, periodic surveys by MBA Enterprises, Inc. show that public accounting firms rank consistently among the top two or three major employers of MBAs nationally (Exhibit 22) [13]. A growing number of the MBAs who are hired in public accounting specialize in fields other than accounting and Professor McDonough argues for the acceleration of this trend [14]. His argument hinges in part on the need for a broadened perspective and more managerial—as opposed to technical—skill.

The annual salary survey conducted by the College Placement Council indicates a steady rise in the starting salaries for MBAs (Exhibit 23) [15]. Keller's study has shown that starting salaries for accounting majors with the master's degree averages 17% higher than with the baccalaureate degree [16]. Hence in 1973 starting salaries for accounting majors with the master's degree averaged about $14,000 versus $12,000 for those with the bachelor's degree. The com-

EXHIBIT 23
MBA starting salaries, 1968–1973.
SOURCE: "Salary Survey," The College Placement Council, June 1973, as reported in *THE MBA* (Magazine), August–September 1973, p. 22.

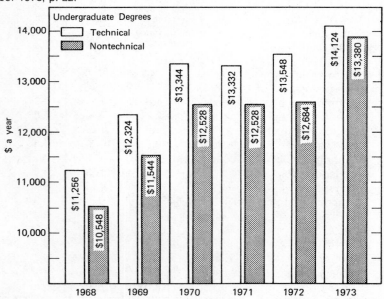

parable figures in 1966 were $8700 and $7500, respectively, which represents a compound growth rate of about 6.2% per annum.

LANDMARK STUDIES OF ACCOUNTING EDUCATION

The acquisition of a body of knowledge through organized means is a widely recognized attribute of a profession [17]. This principle has led to the development of professional schools as we know them today. But professional schooling goes beyond the acquisition of knowledge. These schools serve also as induction, screening, and acculturation centers [18]. In this sense, doctors, lawyers, nurses, or accountants become part of the profession during the years of formal education rather than upon graduation. The evolution from craft to profession is articulated succinctly by Roy and MacNeill [19]:

> In its evolution, each profession begins by providing, through self-taught practitioners, a service needed by society. Each then introduces apprenticeship procedures, by which accumulated experience is transmitted to novitiates. With sufficient accretion of knowledge, professional schools are established, but always the early history of these shows the same flavor of experience; the schools attempt to simulate the real world and their teachers impart their own experience to their pupils.

> Once established, the schools themselves evolve. Collective, repetitive experiences increasingly yield inductive knowledge, generalizations extracted from multiplicities of cases and, once extracted, (are made) applicable to cases yet to come. Research begins, from which there flows a yet higher order of knowledge through deduction, yielding laws, principles, postulates, theories, all applicable to the spectrum of the professional phenomena to which they apply.

> This progression of experience, induction and deduction is accompanied by continual increases in the total body of applicable knowledge. The professional schools respond to these growing accretions of relevant knowledge seriatim: by adding to the burdens of their students, by winnowing out subjects deemed less essential, by increasing the rigor of subjects retained and, ultimately, by insisting upon graduate training as a requirement for admission to the profession. Medicine, theology and law, defined as the "traditional learned professions," already require post-baccalaureate training, supplemented in the case of medicine by post–doctoral exposure as well. There are indications that engineering also is on the threshold of a graduate requirement.

Accounting, it will be noted, is also on the threshold of a graduate requirement. The prelude to the current thrust in accounting education is to be found in two historic inquiries into business education which are referred to commonly as the *Ford* [20] and *Carnegie* [21] studies. The studies were completed at approximately the same time, and their findings are surprisingly similar. They reported "widespread and acute" dissatisfaction with the quality of undergraduate education, and concluded that it was impossible to provide both general and specialized training in the management disciplines within the framework of four-year undergraduate programs [22].

Graduate education in business fared no better. One of the studies observed that "the majority of students currently studying for the master's degree in business are enrolled in make–shift programs which are generally unsatisfactory. This unhappy situation arises from the fact that most graduate business curricula were originally conceived as merely another year of specialization and electives for students whose undergraduate majors were in business [23]." Referring specifically to accounting the authors of the same study observed that "the most difficult problem exists in accounting, and it is this field that will probably require the longest transitional period [24]."

In the period since these findings were reported in 1959, strenuous efforts have been made to improve the quality of management and accounting education. These efforts have been most successful at the graduate level as seen (a) in the development of a growing number of graduate schools of management; (b) the quality of research; and (c) the quality of faculty.

Concern with the quality of accounting education in this same period led to the commissioning of a major study sponsored jointly by the Carnegie Corporation of New York and the American Institute of Certified Public Accountants [25]. Robert H. Roy of Johns Hopkins University and James H. MacNeill of Fordham University were selected to author the project which has come to be known briefly as the *Horizons* study.

Horizons called for a substantial improvement in accounting education, with increased attention to such subjects as mathematics, statistics, communications, and computer technology. It noted the difficulties of attempting to improve the substance of accounting education without increasing the years of schooling. It also noted that "tomorrow's beginning CPA must have mathematical facility beyond that possessed by his professional forebearers; he must also be given fundamental knowledge and skill to understand and use computers and to keep pace with their further development in the years to come. We further believe that these requirements, when added to the qualitative factors previously postulated, indicate that preparation for public accounting should come to include graduate study. These conclusions are fundamental to this report [26]."

Attempts to implement the recommendations of the *Horizons* study began soon after its publication. An AICPA Committee on Education and Experience Requirements for CPAs was formed under the chairmanship of Elmer G. Beamer in September 1966 to "restudy the Institute's policies pertaining to [education and experience] requirements, which set standards for admission to the accounting profession, and to recommend what the policies should be in the light of current and foreseeable conditions [27]."

The *Beamer Report* was published in March 1969. Its principal recommendations were as follows:

1. The CPA certificate is evidence of basic competence of professional quality in the discipline of accounting. This basic competence is demonstrated by acquiring the body of knowledge common to the profession and passing the CPA examination.

2. *Horizons for a Profession* [28] is authoritative for the purpose of delineating the common body of knowledge to be possessed by those about to begin their professional careers as CPAs.

3. At least five years of college study are needed to obtain the common body of knowledge for CPAs and should be the education requirement. For those who meet this standard, no qualifying experience should be required.

4. The states should adopt this five-year requirement by 1975. Until it becomes effective, a transitional alternative is four years of college study and one year of qualifying experience.

5. The college study should be in programs comparable to those described in "Academic Preparation for Professional Accounting Careers [29]." The transitional qualifying experience should be in public practice or equivalent experience in industry, government, or college teaching acceptable to state boards of accountancy.

6. Candidates should be encouraged to take the CPA examination as soon as they have fulfilled education requirements and as close to their college graduation dates as possible. For those graduating in June, this may involve taking the May examination on a provisional basis.

7. Student internships are desirable and are encouraged as part of the educational program.

8. The *Report of the Standing Committee on Accounting Education* [30], which provides that the accreditation of academic programs is the responsibility of the academic community, is endorsed.

9. Educational programs must be flexible and adaptive and this is best achieved by entrusting their specific content to the academic community. However, the knowledge to be acquired and abilities to be developed through formal education for professional accounting are proper and continuing concerns of the AICPA.

10. The AICPA should review periodically the standards of admission requirements for CPAs.

The Report also proceeded to develop a model program in accounting education while stressing "that the course designation and hours are prepared only for possible curriculum guidance and *not* for legislative prescription [31]." The model program appears in Exhibit 24 together with responses of a survey of opinion among accounting educators regarding the proposal. This model curriculum attempts to embody the recommendations of the *Horizons* study with

EXHIBIT 24

A survey of the opinions of a sample of accounting educators with regard to the "model curriculum."

SOURCE: Committee to Examine the 1969 Report of the AICPA Committee on Education and Experience Requirements for CPAs, supplement to vol. 47 of Accounting Review (1972), p. 257.

	AICPA recommendations (semester hours)	Number of responses	Your response to AICPA recommendations (% of responses)		
			Not enough	About right	Too much
General education					
Economics	6	123	11	89	0
Elementary accounting	3–6	122	3	96	1
Introduction to computer	2–3	122	5	93	2
Mathematics (modern algebra, calculus, statistics, probability)	12	123	2	78	20
Other general education	25–18	113	12	82	6
Total	60	120	8	88	4
General business					
Economics (intermediate theory and the monetary system)	6	123	1	76	23
The social environment of businesss	6	123	1	46	53
Business law	6	123	4	79	17
Production or operational systems	3	123	2	91	7
Marketing	3	123	2	96	2
Finance	6	123	2	84	14

Organization, group and individual behavior	9	123	0	43	57
Quantitative applications in business (optimization models, statistics, sampling, Markov chains, statistical decision theory, queueing, PERT, simulation)	9	123	3	58	39
Written communication	3	121	18	70	12
Business policy	3	121	3	90	7
Total	54	122	1	79	20
Accounting					
Financial reporting theory	9	124	14	81	5
Applied financial accounting problems					
Contemporary financial accounting issues					
Cost determination and analysis	6	124	5	87	8
Cost control					
Cost-based decision-making					
Tax theory and considerations	3	124	43	56	1
Tax problems					
Audit theory and philosophy	6	124	1	60	39
Audit problems					
Computers and information systems in business	6	124	2	73	25
Total	30	121	7	86	7
Electives	6	104	23	74	3
Total	150	121	5	86	9

increased emphasis on mathematics, statistics, communications, computer technology, and the behavioral sciences.

An indication of the general acceptance of the *Horizons* and *Beamer* reports has been provided through a survey of leading accounting educators [32]. The survey reported the level of responses to selected questions given in the table.

Question	Response %
1. Should the CPA certificate be evidence of basic competence of professional quality for	
(a) the entire discipline of accounting, or	45
(b) only the public accounting sector?	51
2. *Horizons* is authoritative for purposes of delineating the common body of knowledge for those entering	
(a) the entire discipline of accounting, or	42
(b) the public accounting sector?	44
3. How many years are necesary to acquire the common body of knowledge as set forth in *Horizons:*	
(a) 4 years?	34
(b) 5 years?	63
(c) 6 years or more?	3
4. Should state laws be amended to require the above as minimum?	
(a) Yes	72
(b) No	28

The cumulative effect of these studies, and the general agreement among educators which attends them, has brought about very significant changes in accounting education.

PROGRESS IN ACCOUNTING EDUCATION AND RESEARCH

Accounting education has come a long way in recent years toward shedding its vocational and bookkeeping images. The forces of change have affected all of the essential factors in education: subject matter, faculty, students, the learning environment, and the quality of research.

The accounting body of knowledge has been touched by a much broadened perspective of its mission, i.e., to that accounting is an information system geared to the utility of its users. In particular, mathematics, the behavioral sciences, and the computer have served to change accounting education radically. The computer places the burden of data processing on machines, allowing the accountant to shift his concern to systems planning and control. Mathematical and operations research models have been shown to be applicable to a wide variety of accounting problems and yield superior results to the routines which accountants have used traditionally for these purposes. Statistical sampling is now commonplace in auditing while statistical experimentation has burgeoned across the field of accounting research. The behavioral sciences lay focus on the human person as "the only real causal agent in society," for as Diesing observes, "numbers, laws, logics, are causal only as they enter into human acts [33]."

The doctoral degree has become a prerequisite to holding a faculty appointment in accounting in most four-year colleges and graduate schools of business administration. A 1968 study shows that 31.4% of all full-time accounting faculty held the doctorate and 59.7% held the CPA certificate at that time [34]. The former ratio will undoubtedly increase as nondoctorate faculty retire. As research training is stressed in most doctoral programs, it is understandable that the quality of research and the emphasis on a more rigorous and interdisciplinary approach to accounting education will rise proportionately.

The periodical literature in accounting is extensive. An index to 62 journals and periodicals appear in Appendix B [35]. The leading professional journals in order of circulation are listed in the table.

Professional journals	Circulation
1. Journal of Accountancy	132,000
2. Management Accounting	68,000
3. CPA Journal	25,000
4. Practical Accountant	20,000
5. Management Adviser	17,000
6. Journal of Taxation	15,600
7. National Public Accountant	15,500
8. Financial Executive	14,750
9. Taxes—The Tax Magazine	14,500
10. Hospital Financial Management	10,000

These journals are directed toward practitioners and contain articles of current interest, official statements and reports, and translations of research studies. Academic journals, on the other hand, cater to educators and others who share their interest in academic research. The principal research journals in order of circulation are:

Research journals	Circulation
1. *Accounting Review*	20,000
2. *Journal of Accounting Research*	2,500
3. *International Journal of Accounting Education and Research*	1,200

Accountants also contribute extensively to the literature in a variety of other fields. An abstract service on the literature in accounting is provided by Commerce Clearing House [36].

Ray Ball has indexed most of the empirical research in accounting through 1970 [37], and several other major efforts have been made to evaluate the overall quality of accounting research [38]. While there is much room for improvement it must be concluded that accountants have made excellent progress in closing the research gap in recent years, thus bringing the accounting discipline closer to academic acceptance and respectability than at any other time in its history.

An excellent barometer of change in accounting education is its textbook literature. Publishers are understandably reluctant to move faster than the market will support. We are entering what can be called the third generation of accounting texts. The first can be described as traditional texts for traditional courses, the second as new approaches to traditional courses, and the third as texts which substantially alter old courses and/or create new ones.

Traditional texts are descriptive and provide a heavy dosage of rules and procedures which stem from the conventional wisdom. The rationale for doing things is provided rarely, and often there is undue emphasis on laborious detail.

Second generation texts sample developments in other fields and the current state of art in accounting practice. They incorporate this new knowledge into the framework of existing courses. An analogy is pouring new wine into old bottles.

Third generation texts attempt to bring new content and structure to the accounting curriculum. One major effort of this type was a three-year study to examine and restructure the elementary accounting course. The study was sponsored by the Price Waterhouse Foundation [39]. All three generations of texts exist concurrently in accounting education at the present time.

While textbooks still occupy central stage in accounting education, a recent survey indicates a growing use of modern media such as computers, learning machines and television (Exhibit 25). A nationwide clearing house for computer programs in accounting teaching and research was established at Virginia Polytechnic Institute in 1973 [40]. These and other curricula developments are

EXHIBIT 25

Frequency in the use of modern media in accounting education, 1971.

Where media numbers are: 4=computers in problem-solving, 5=computers as learning machines, 6=games and simulations, 8=kinescopes, 9=movies (16mm), 11=overhead projectors, 14=rear-screen projectors, 15=slides, 16=tapes & cassettes, 17=TV—videotapes, 18=TV—closed circuit, 19=telephone answering (as an example of remote access), 22=programmed textbooks. SOURCE: *Report of Committee on Multi-Media Instruction in Accounting,* supplement to vol. 47 of *Accounting Review* (1972), p. 118.

Media	Elementary	Intermediate	Advanced	Cost	Tax	Auditing	Theory	Systems	Management	Total
4	6	2	0	3	0	10	0	9	19	49
5	2	1	0	0	0	2	0	2	19	26
6	4	3	1	1	3	1	0	1	5	19
8	1	0	0	0	0	0	0	0	0	1
9	0	1	0	0	0	0	0	1	0	2
11	58	20	11	13	4	4	2	5	15	132
14	0	1	1	0	0	0	0	0	0	2
15	3	2	0	0	1	0	0	0	0	6
16	0	0	0	0	1	0	0	0	0	1
17	1	0	0	0	0	0	0	1	0	2
18	2	0	0	0	0	0	0	0	0	2
19	0	0	0	0	0	0	0	0	0	0
22	5	3	0	0	0	0	0	1	2	11
Total	82	33	13	17	9	17	2	20	60	253
Population	980	472	219	296	208	207	106	112	407	3007
Ratio (%)	6.4	7.0	5.9	5.7	0.4	8.2	0.2	17.9	14.7	8.4

EXHIBIT 26

Survey of doctoral programs in accounting.

NOTE: NA=Figures not provided by school responding. SOURCE: William F. Crum, "The Second Survey of Doctoral Programs in Accounting," *Journal of Accountancy,* June 1971, p. 88.

University	Degree	Degrees granted					Estimate of degrees		Candidates currently in course work stage	Candidates in dissertation stage
		1966	1967	1968	1969	1970	1971	1972		
Alabama	Ph.D.	4	2	9	6	6	13	11	18	17
Arizona	Ph.D.	0	0	0	0	1	2	2	7	3
Arizona State	D.B.A.	0	0	2	0	3	3	4	6	8
Arkansas	Ph.D.	2	2	4	8	11	8	12	16	12
California, Berkeley	Ph.D.	0	4	4	4	3	10	5	5	14
California, Los Angeles	Ph.D.	2	3	1	3	5	6	6	6	4
Case-Western Reserve	Ph.D.	0	0	0	0	0	0	1	4	1
Chicago	Ph.D.	2	3	3	2	2	2	NA	14	5
City University of New York	Ph.D.	0	0	0	0	0	1	3	20	3
Colorado	D.B.A.	2	3	2	2	3	3	3	9	3
Columbia	Ph.D.	3	2	3	2	4	2	NA	13	8
Cornell	Ph.D.	0	0	0	1	0	2	2	4	2
Florida	Ph.D.	1	2	2	4	4	5	8	8	9
Florida State	D.B.A.	0	0	0	0	3	4	5	6	9
George Washington	D.B.A.	0	0	2	2	3	5	6	15	5
Georgia	Ph.D.	0	0	0	0	1	4	4	14	4
Georgia State	Both	0	0	0	0	1	3	4	20	9
Harvard	D.B.A.	3	7	4	2	4	9	9	3	18
Houston	Ph.D.	0	0	0	0	0	0	2	4	0
Illinois	Ph.D.	7	8	12	15	8	10	12	38	15
Indiana	D.B.A.	4	6	2	3	3	3	3	8	3
Iowa	Ph.D.	0	0	0	0	2	2	4	12	5
Kansas	Ph.D.	0	0	0	0	2	2	2	5	1

Institution	Degree									
Louisiana State	Both	5	5	2	2	7	7	6	8	9
Maryland	D.B.A.	0	0	0	1	3	4	4	16	4
Massachusetts	Ph.D.	0	0	0	0	0	2	3	5	2
Michigan	Ph.D.	1	NA	9	1	3	5	3	4	8
Michigan State	Both	NA	1	3	9	11	8	8	NA	14
Minnesota	Ph.D.	1	3	2	4	3	5	6	6	11
Missouri	Ph.D.	3	1	1	9	11	8	6	24	8
Nebraska	Ph.D.	4	3	0	0	2	2	5	7	3
New York University	Ph.D.	4	1	3	2	3	3	NA	38	5
North Carolina	Ph.D.	1	0	0	1	2	2	2	2	4
North Texas State	Ph.D.	0	1	1	1	0	3	3	7	4
Northwestern	Ph.D.	1	3	1	2	5	5	5	10	8
Ohio State	Ph.D.	4	1	0	4	4	5	5	15	6
Oklahoma	Both	0	0	2	1	2	1	4	11	4
Oklahoma State	Ph.D.	0	1	0	0	0	1	5	13	1
Oregon	D.B.A.	2	0	1	1	2	2	4	6	3
Pennsylvania	Ph.D.	0	1	0	0	0	1	2	3	1
Penn State	Ph.D.	0	2	3	2	0	5	6	11	5
Pittsburgh	Ph.D.	2	2	0	1	0	1	2	1	3
Purdue	Ph.D.	0	0	0	0	0	0	3	4	0
Rochester	Ph.D.	0	0	0	0	0	1	0	0	1
Southern California	D.B.A.	3	3	3	2	3	4	5	21	8
Stanford	Ph.D.	2	3	3	3	2	4	3	3	6
State University of New York, Buffalo	Ph.D.	0	0	0	1	0	1	2	2	4
Syracuse	Ph.D.	0	0	0	0	2	2	4	16	5
Texas	Ph.D.	3	4	3	4	2	5	4	25	14
Texas Tech	D.B.A.	0	0	0	2	2	3	4	12	6
Tulane	Ph.D.	0	0	0	0	0	1	2	1	1
Utah	Ph.D.	0	0	0	1	0	0	0	4	0
Washington	Ph.D.	2	2	5	3	0	6	8	12	9
Washington-St. Louis	Both	2	4	0	0	0	2	2	1	4
Wisconsin	Ph.D.	4	4	1	3	6	10	12	21	17
Totals		75	86	92	114	144	209	237	569	337

reported in an annual series of innovative accounting and information systems course outlines edited by Professor Thomas J. Burns of Ohio State under the title of *Accounting Trends* [41].

There is a growing emphasis on doctoral education in accounting, leading to either the Ph.D. or D.B.A. degree [42]. As noted in Exhibit 26, 56 universities now offer doctoral programs in accounting, and the number of degrees granted has risen from 75 in 1966 to an estimated 237 degrees in 1972.

Professor Paul Garner has studied the doctoral population in accounting and arrived at the following findings; based on a sample group of 272 doctoral candidates [43]:

1.   Only 11 of the 272 doctoral students (4%) are female.
2.   Of the 272, 231 (85%) are married. In the majority of cases the wife is employed while the husband pursues his doctoral studies.
3.   Age upon entering the doctoral program is: (*a*) 25 years or less (40%); (*b*) 26 to 30 years (37%); and (*c*) over 30 years (24%).
4.   Age of completing the doctoral program is: (*a*) 25 years or less (5%); (*b*) between 26 and 30 years (50%); (*c*) between 31 and 40 (38%); and (*d*) 41 years or more (7%).
5.   The 272 students in the sample undertook their undergraduate work in 156 different institutions, and the maximum number of doctoral students from a common undergraduate university or college was 5.
6.   Of the 272, 26 (10%) are foreign nationals.
7.   The dissertation or area of principal research is: (*a*) information systems (17%); (*b*) financial reporting and investment analysis (14%); (*c*) accounting principles and standards (13%); (*d*) financial and general accounting (19%); (*e*) auditing (10%); (*f*) professionalism and ethics (8%); (*g*) accounting history (6%); (*h*) taxation (6%); (*i*) the legal environment in accounting (5%); (*j*) education, governmental or cost accounting (4%); (*k*) international (3%); and (*l*) others (4%).

While doctoral programs traditionally have been geared to the production of future teachers, there is an increasing utilization of Ph.D.'s as researchers and staff specialists in public accounting, industry, and government.

As in most academic endeavors, some schools attain a higher degree of prestige and recognition than do others. In accounting as in other fields, most attempts at ratings rely heavily on the grapevine. Estes, however, employed a more formal survey of opinion to rank accounting programs [44]. His results are summarized in Exhibit 27. It is interesting to note how the categories differ in terms of evaluation.

PROFESSIONAL EXAMINATIONS

The most prestigious designation in accounting is the CPA certificate. We noted in Chapter 2 that the practice of accounting, in common with other pro-

EXHIBIT 27
Rankings of educational programs in accounting.
NOTE: *n*=213; (a) tie. SOURCE: Ralph W. Estes, "A Ranking of Accounting Programs," *Journal of Accountancy*, July 1970, p. 89.

Ranking	Deans (n=13)	Department heads (n=54)	Full professors (n=84)
1	Chicago	Illinois	Stanford
2	Stanford	Chicago	Illinois
3	Illinois	Stanford	Berkeley
4	Berkeley	Berkeley	Chicago
5	Michigan	Michigan	Michigan
6	Texas	Michigan State	Texas
7	Michigan State	Ohio State	Michigan State
8	Pennsylvania	Texas	Harvard
9	U.C.L.A.	Harvard	Ohio State
10	M.I.T.	Columbia	Columbia

Ranking	Other teachers (n=11)	Practitioners (n=42)	Panel of leaders (n=9)
1	Harvard	Chicago and Illinois [a]	Michigan
2	Pennsylvania		Illinois
3	Columbia	Stanford	Chicago and Harvard [a]
4	Stanford	Michigan	
5	Chicago	Michigan State	Stanford
6	Northwestern	Berkeley	Columbia
7	Texas	Harvard	Northwestern
8	Illinois	Texas	Ohio State
9	Berkeley	U.C.L.A.	Michigan State
10	U.C.L.A.	Columbia	Berkeley

fessions, is regulated by law. The first CPA legislation in the United States was enacted by the state of New York in 1896. It defined certified public accountant in legal terms and required an examination process incident to certification [45]. The law provided that the examination cover the theory of accounts, practical accounting, auditing, and commercial law [46]. The first examination was administered on December 15–16, 1896 [47]. After a long period in which each state administered its own examination the Uniform CPA Examination process evolved slowly to the point where in 1952 all states and jurisdictions of the United States were included in a common program administered by the Board of Examiners of the American Institute of Certified Public Accountants [48].

The CMA (Certificate in Management Accounting) is a new professional designation. It was established by the National Association of Accountants in 1971 to: "(1) foster higher educational standards in the field of management accounting; (2) to establish management accounting as a recognized profession by identifying the role of the management accountant and the underlying body of knowledge, and by outlining a course of study by which such knowledge can be acquired; and (3) assist employers and educators by establishing an objective measure of an individual's knowledge and competence in the profession of management accounting [49]."

The CPA Examination

The CPA examinations are administered twice a year in May and November throughout all states and jurisdictions of the United States. The educational prerequisites were discussed earlier in this chapter. The sequence of examination sections and their times is:

Accounting practice, part I	Wednesday	1:30– 6:00 PM
Auditing	Thursday	8:30–12:00 noon
Accounting practice, part II	Thursday	1:30– 6:00 PM
Business (commercial) law	Friday	8:30–12:00 noon
Accounting theory	Friday	1:30– 5:00 PM

A guide to the examination under the title *Information for CPA Candidates* is issued on a current basis by the AICPA [50]. It makes this observation concerning the general content of the examination [51]:

The content of the examination changes as conditions change in the discipline of accounting. It is possible, however, to indicate the general content of the examination, and the knowledge and skills which it is typically designed to test. Candidates may expect the examination to measure the extent of their knowledge of:

1. Accounting concepts, postulates, and principles
2. Generally accepted auditing standards, audit programs, and auditors' reports
3. Business organization and operation, including a knowledge of the basic laws governing such organization and operation
4. Use of accounting data for managerial purposes
5. Quantitative methods and techniques as they apply to accounting and auditing
6. Federal income taxation

7. Current professional literature and accounting issues receiving special attention at the time of the examination.

Candidates are expected to demonstrate their ability to apply to specific situations their knowledge of the foregoing areas with good judgment and logical reasoning, and to draw reasonable conclusions from such applications. In addition, the examination will determine the extent of their ability to:

1. Write precisely and concisely, and in good English
2. Organize accounting data and present them in acceptable form
3. Discriminate among data in a complex situation, and evaluate and classify such data
4. Apply appropriate accounting concepts and auditing procedures to given situations
5. Use mathematics with reasonable facility.

The grading of the examination is handled in New York under the supervision of 35 specialists. There is a four–stage grading process which ultimately establishes a score for each part of the examination. A passing grade is 75 or better, and if a candidate passes two parts he is entitled to sit for one or both of the remaining parts without repeating the sections that were completed before. Accounting practice parts I and II are considered as one section of the examination for this purpose.

Howard Sanders has studied the relationships between academic preparation and completion of the CPA examination. The results of his study are contained in Exhibits 28–30. As noted in Exhibit 28, 61% of the candidates are college graduates, while 9% are postgraduates. Exhibit 29 indicates that 87% of all candidates have completed 24 semester hours or more in accounting courses; however, the number of credit units in accounting appears to bear no major relationship to performance on the examination. In 1970, 54% of the candidates took a formal CPA coaching program in addition to their academic preparation. Correspondence courses rate low in effectiveness while in-house coaching couses sponsored by CPA firms achieved the greatest rate of success. In summary it appears that formal coaching courses—other than correspondence programs—do aid in passing the CPA examination.

In another study, Park E. Leathers has shown that students who do well on scholastic competence tests such as ACT (American College Testing) and SAT (Scholastic Aptitude Test) have enhanced prospects for passing the CPA examination [52]. The relationship between SAT scores and passage on the May 1970 examination is shown in Exhibit 31.

A number of accounting departments administer such tests as part of their student counseling programs. Timely guidance may provide alternative career tracks for students who demonstrate low aptitude for accounting. The AICPA

EXHIBIT 28
Percentage analysis of education of CPA candidates sitting for selected November examinations.

NOTE: November 1970 rather than May 1970 data are used for comparison because November data are available for 1946 and 1960. For 1946 data, see Norman Lee Buton, "Basic Information Concerning Candidates Writing the Uniform CPA Examination," *Challenges to the Accounting Profession* (American Institute of Certified Public Accountants, 1947), pp. 69–76. The 1960 data are from unpublished data compiled by the AICPA.

	One or more sittings (%)			
	1946	*1960*	*1966*	*1970*
High school graduate	8	1	—	—
Technical/business school or accounting correspondence course	25	10	5	2
College—less than degree requirement	20	12	7	3
College graduate—other than accounting major	18	7	10	25
College graduate—accounting major	25	66	70	61
Postgraduate work completed	4	4	8	9
Total	100	100	100	100

EXHIBIT 29
Percentage of undergraduate semester hours of accounting studied by candidates sitting for the CPA examination for the first time in May 1970.

Number of undergraduate accounting hours	*Percent of candidates*	*Cumulative percent*	*Percent receiving all or partial credit*
33 or more	27	27	47
30–32	24	51	51
27–29	20	71	51
24–26	16	87	46
21–23	6	93	47
18–20	3	96	44
15–17	1	97	56
12–14	1	98	42
Fewer than 12	2	100	74
Total	100		

EXHIBIT 30
Percentage analysis of formal CPA coaching
courses of candidates sitting for the CPA
examination in May 1970.
NOTE: Classroom course refers to a formal coaching course
given in a classroom, not to a college course taken for credit.
Staff course means any CPA coaching course given by the candidate's employer. SOURCE: Howard P. Sanders, "Factors in
Achieving Success on the CPA Examination," *Journal of Accountancy*, December 1972, pp. 85–88.

| | Two or more sittings | | First sitting | |
Type of course	Percent of candidates	Percent receiving all or partial credit	Percent of candidates	Percent receiving all or partial credit
Classroom	40	58	34	53
Correspondence	7	40	2	38
Staff	7	62	5	54
None	46	48	59	45
Total	100		100	

EXHIBIT 31
SAT scores and passage on the CPA examination.
SOURCE: Park E. Leathers, "Relationship of Test Scores to CPA
Examination Performance," *Journal of Accountancy*, September 1972, p. 102.

| | First-time CPA candidates receiving credit for | |
SAT scores	All parts (%)	No parts (%)
Verbal		
700–800	50	9
600–699	37	21
500–599	28	32
400–499	13	54
300–399	5	70
Mathematics		
700–800	47	15
600–699	29	31
500–599	14	50
400–499	7	67
300–399	2	80

encourages the use of these tests by making them available to accounting instructors.

The CMA Examination

The CMA examination is administered by the Institute of Management Accounting of the National Association of Accountants [53]. The examination is given in the first week of December in major cities throughout the United States. Candidates must satisfy one of the following admission requirements: (a) hold a baccalaureate degree in any field from an accredited college or university; (b) achieve a satisfactory score on the Admission Test for Graduate Study in Business (ATGSB), or (c) be a certified public accountant or hold a comparable professional qualification in a foreign country. The examination covers the following syllabus:

Part 1. *Economics and Business Finance*
   A. Enterprise economics
   B. Institutional environment of business
   C. National and international economics
   D. Working capital management
   E. Long-term finance and capital structure

Part 2. *Organization and Behavior, Including Ethical Considerations*
   A. Organization theory and decision-making
   B. Motivation and perception
   C. Communication
   D. Behavioral science application in accounting
   E. Ethical considerations

Part 3. *Public Reporting Standards, Auditing and Taxes*
   A. Reporting requirements
   B. Audit protection
   C. Tax accounting

Part 4. *Periodic Reporting for Internal and External Purposes*
   A. Concepts of information
   B. Basic financial statements
   C. Profit planning and budgetary controls
   D. Standard costs for manufacturing
   E. Analysis of accounts and statements

Part 5. *Decision Analysis, Including Modeling and Information Systems*
   A. Fundamentals of the decision process
   B. Decision analysis
   C. Nature and techniques of model building
   D. Information systems and data processing

The first CMA examination was offered in December 1972, and there is insufficient data at this point to develop a reliable profile of candidates. The Institute of Management Accounting expects a steady increase in demand for the examination and a continuing buildup in the prestige of the CMA certificate.

WHO BECOMES AN ACCOUNTANT?

Psychologist Selwyn W. Becker has described the accountant in less than serious terms as the "most likely to straighten a picture in a house where he was a visitor, and most likely to play a practical joke. And, after bankers, most likely to beat his children for disobeying. Compared with others, the accountant is also seen as most likely to run away and join a circus [54]."

More serious inquiries conclude otherwise. One study concludes that "the CPA's prestige is impressive. He seems to be regarded by business executives as an efficient professional man, highly respected for his technical competence, for his personal integrity, and for his genuine interest in promoting the financial success of his clients [55]."

Don T. DeCoster and John Grant Rhode have summarized many of the studies which relate to the accountant's stereotype as it exists in the minds of the general public and/or students [56]. They admit that while the stereotype exists, it is largely undeserved. Their conclusions rest on personality test scores for public accountants as contrasted with other occupational groups. The results appear in Exhibit 32. Significant differences between CPAs and other groups as measured by the two-tailed t score, are summarized in Exhibit 33. The occupation which scores significantly higher in a given category is listed first, e.g., architects have significantly higher capacity for status than CPAs, while CPAs exhibit more sociability than architects.

The personality test used in their study is the well-known California Psychological Inventory (CPI), of which the principal measures are described in the Appendix to this chapter. The accountant, according to the DeCoster and Rhode study, appears to score high, average, or low in relation to these other groups as follows:

Class I. *Measures of Poise, Ascendancy, Self-Assurance and Interpersonal Adequacy*

1.	Dominance	average
2.	Capacity for status	average
3.	Sociability	high
4.	Social presence	high
5.	Self-acceptance	average
6.	Sense of well-being	average

EXHIBIT 32

CPI scale mean scores and standard deviations of accountants and other selected occupations.

Source: (a) H. G. Gough, *Manual for the California Psychological Inventory* (Palo Alto, Ca: Consulting Psychologists Press, 1957). (Revised 1969). As reported in Don T. DeCoster and John Grant Rhode, "The Accountant's Stereotype: Real or Imagined, Deserved or Unwarranted," *Accounting Review*, October 1971, p. 659.

CPI scale	CPA firm employees [a] n=56		Salesmen [a] n=85		Bank managers [a] n=25		Business executives [a] n=107		City school superintendents n=144		Practicing dentists [a] n=59		Architects [a] n=124		Research scientists [a] n=45		Military officers [a] n=343	
	Mean	Standard Deviation	Mean	Standard Deviation	Mean	Standard Deviation	Mean	Standard Deviation	Mean	Standard Deviation	Mean	Standard Deviation	Mean	Standard Deviation	Mean	Standard Deviation	Mean	Standard Deviation
Measures of poise, ascendancy and self-assurance																		
Dominance (Do)	31.1	5.7	32.0	4.7	30.2	4.3	29.5	6.7	31.8	5.3	31.3	5.2	30.9	5.1	31.6	4.7	31.8	5.6
Capacity for status (Cs)	21.1	3.5	21.1	3.3	21.3	3.2	20.5	4.3	21.2	3.5	21.6	3.2	22.2	3.0	24.1	2.4	21.6	3.6
Sociability (Sy)	26.2	5.0	28.0	3.8	25.4	4.3	25.4	5.5	25.4	4.5	26.9	4.3	24.3	4.5	27.4	4.4	27.3	4.4
Social presence (Sp)	37.9	5.7	38.2	4.5	36.4	5.2	36.1	5.4	35.8	5.2	35.9	5.7	37.1	5.1	41.0	4.6	38.4	3.8
Self-acceptance (Sa)	22.7	3.9	23.2	2.4	19.6	3.3	20.7	4.4	21.8	3.6	21.8	3.3	22.5	3.8	23.1	3.5	23.0	3.4
Sense of well-being (Wb)	38.8	3.7	39.8	3.0	40.5	2.7	39.8	3.4	38.7	3.7	39.8	3.0	37.7	3.5	40.2	2.5	39.0	3.7
Measures of socialization, maturity and responsibility																		
Responsibility (Re)	31.8	4.6	31.6	4.4	33.2	3.6	31.5	5.7	33.9	3.5	34.1	3.8	32.6	3.8	34.1	3.2	32.2	4.4
Socialization (So)	38.2	4.8	38.3	4.4	39.0	5.1	37.5	5.1	37.7	4.3	38.8	4.5	36.6	4.6	36.1	4.5	36.3	4.7
Self-control (Sc)	32.1	5.9	32.0	6.2	34.8	6.9	32.9	7.1	30.7	7.5	33.1	6.3	30.0	6.2	32.7	5.3	29.6	7.5
Tolerance (To)	24.7	4.3	24.1	4.1	25.2	4.0	24.5	5.1	25.0	4.0	25.5	3.9	23.9	3.7	27.1	3.3	23.5	6.3
Good impression (Gi)	19.3	5.7	20.7	5.6	21.2	7.2	20.0	6.8	19.1	5.9	20.5	5.9	17.4	5.7	19.4	5.1	19.2	1.5
Communality (Cm)	25.7	2.4	27.1	1.1	26.5	1.3	26.3	1.4	26.6	1.3	26.5	1.5	25.4	1.7	25.7	1.4	26.5	1.5
Measures of achievement, potential and intellectual efficiency																		
Achievement via conformance (Ac)	30.3	3.7	30.1	4.0	30.6	4.0	28.7	5.2	30.1	4.0	30.9	3.9	29.0	4.1	31.0	3.3	29.3	4.4
Achievement via independence (Ai)	22.6	3.8	17.9	3.6	22.1	3.3	19.7	4.8	21.3	3.6	20.6	3.5	22.4	3.6	25.1	2.7	20.0	3.6
Intellectual efficiency (Ie)	39.6	4.2	40.3	4.3	41.2	4.2	40.1	6.3	40.5	4.8	41.8	3.6	40.4	4.0	44.2	3.0	40.7	4.4
Measures of intellectual and interest modes																		
Psychological-mindedness (Py)	13.4	2.4	12.1	2.4	12.1	2.5	12.2	3.1	11.8	2.7	12.9	2.3	13.6	2.4	16.6	2.5	11.9	2.5
Flexibility (Fx)	9.7	3.9	6.9	3.1	8.7	3.6	9.3	3.6	9.7	3.4	8.1	3.7	10.6	4.2	13.3	3.9	8.5	3.5
Femininity (Fe)	16.4	3.6	16.3	3.1	16.4	3.4	16.2	3.5	16.6	3.6	17.2	3.6	18.5	3.2	17.3	2.6	14.6	3.3

EXHIBIT 33

Significant t tests for CPA firm employees and select occupational group CPI scale mean differences.

NOTE: The comparison group with the largest mean score is listed first. On the capacity for status scale, architects would accordingly have a higher mean score than the CPA firm employee. CPA firm employees are listed within the table as CPAs. (a) $P < .05$, two-tailed t score (b) $P < .01$, two-tailed t score. (c) $P < .001$, two-tailed t score. SOURCE: Don T. DeCoster and John Grant Rhode, "The Accountant's Stereotype: Real or Imagined, Deserved or Unwarranted," *Accounting Review*, October 1971, p. 660.

CPI scale	Comparison groups [a]	t score
Capacity for status	Architects/CPAs	2.15 [a]
	Research scientists/CPAs	4.85 [c]
Sociability	Salesmen/CPAs	2.41 [a]
	CPAs/architects	2.52 [a]
Social presence	CPAs/city school superintendents	2.48 [a]
	Research Scientists/CPAs	2.93 [b]
Self-acceptance	CPAs/bank managers	3.42 [c]
	CPAs/business executives	2.85 [b]
Sense of well-being	Bank managers/CPAs	2.04 [a]
	CPAs/city school superintendents	3.59 [c]
Responsibility	City school superintendents/CPAs	3.46 [c]
	Practicing dentists/CPAs	2.90 [b]
	Research scientists/CPAs	2.82 [b]
Socialization	CPAs/architects	2.12 [a]
	CPAs/research scientists	2.22 [a]
	CPAs/military officers	2.79 [b]
Self-control	CPAs/architects	2.12 [a]
	CPAs/military officers	2.37 [a]
Tolerance	Research scientists/CPAs	3.05 [b]
	CPAs/architects	2.06 [a]
Good impression	Salesmen/CPAs	4.65 [c]
Communality	City school superintendents/CPAs	3.38 [c]
	Practicing dentists/CPAs	2.14 [a]
	Military officers/CPAs	3.34 [c]

CPI scale	Comparison groups [a]	t score
Achievement via conformance	CPAs/architects	2.02 [a]
Achievement via independence	CPAs/salesmen	7.37 [c]
	CPAs/business executives	3.90 [c]
	CPAs/city school superintendents	2.25 [a]
	CPAs/practicing dentists	2.91 [b]
	Research scientists/CPAs	3.69 [c]
	CPAs/military officers	4.96 [c]
Intellectual efficiency	Practicing dentists/CPAs	2.99 [b]
	Research scientists/CPAs	6.13 [c]
Psychological-mindedness	CPAs/salesmen	3.12 [b]
	CPAs/bank managers	2.20 [a]
	CPAs/business executives	2.51 [a]
	CPAs/city school superintendents	3.86 [c]
	Research scientists/CPAs	6.47 [c]
	CPAs/military officers	4.18 [c]
Flexibility	CPAs/salesmen	4.70 [c]
	CPAs/practicing dentists	2.24 [a]
	Research scientists/CPAs	4.56 [c]
Femininity	CPAs/military officers	2.33 [a]
	Architects/CPAs	3.90 [c]
	CPAs/military officers	3.73 [c]

Class II. *Measures of Socialization, Maturity, Responsibility, and Intrapersonal Structuring of Values*
  7. Responsibility   average
  8. Socialization   average
  9. Self-control   high
  10. Tolerance   average
  11. Good impression   average
  12. Communality   low

Class III. *Measures of Achievement Potential and Intellectual Efficiency*
  13. Achievement via conformance   average
  14. Achievement via independence high
  15. Intellectual efficiency   average

Class IV. *Measures of Intellectual and Interest Modes*
  16. Psychological-mindedness   high
  17. Flexibility   high
  18. Femininity   average

Several studies indicate that accounting students do better scholastically, despite a more rigorous curriculum, than students majoring in other business fields [57]. A 1956 study by the U.S. Department of Labor has rated 4000 occupations and concluded that "accountants are perceived as being in the upper 10 per cent of the working population in the aptitudes of intelligence and numerical skills, and in the upper 20 per cent of the working population in verbal skills, with the exception of public accountants who are in the upper 10 per cent [58]."

J. T. Gray, utilizing the Edwards Personal Preference Schedule (EPPS) and Miller Occupational Values Indicator (OVI), compares secondary teachers, accountants, and mechanical engineers and arrives at this descriptive statement of the accountant [59]:

The single factor which seems to be most distinguishing for accountants is the high level of striving; it is of extreme importance to workers in this group to do things well, particularly difficult tasks that will bring recognition . . . Accountants are hard workers, they insist on closure and will remain at a task until it is finished . . . The primary value accountants place on an occupation is that of the intrinsic rewards to be gained from it. Prestige is also important to accountants, while social rewards mean little to this occupational group.

C. Richard Baker has shown that accounting versus nonaccounting majors exhibit significant differences with respect to the following values, as measured by the Rokeach Values Scale (RVS) [60]:

Terminal Values
  1. Accountants were less concerned with a "comfortable life" than nonaccounting majors.

2. Accountants placed greater value on a "world of beauty" than nonaccounting majors.

Instrumental Values

3. Accountants were less "ambitious" than nonaccounting majors.
4. Accountants were more "imaginative" than nonaccounting majors.
5. Accountants had less sense of "responsibility" than nonaccounting majors, particularly in terms of "public responsibility."

Rhode and others have conducted a longitudinal study of accounting majors from the point where they decide on an accounting career through induction into the profession and during the first three years as staff accountants [61]. Their studies show that instructors in accounting play the prominent role in attracting students toward accounting careers, as opposed to the role of parents, friends, or other sources of influence. Accounting majors develop high expectations regarding their future careers, and these expectations are met for the most part in the actual work experience. The ten qualities about the work experience in accounting which appealed most (and least) to the respondents in the study, following the first year of experience in the job, were (in rank order):

The Ten Best Qualities About Careers in Public Accounting

1. Contact with a wide range of people, firms, accounting systems—diversity or variety of work situations.
2. Personal development, learning and work experience, training.
3. Challenging work—enjoyable work.
4. Responsibility—recognition.
5. Professionalism.
6. Working with high calibre, intelligent, competent, interesting colleagues and clients.
7. Salary.
8. Opportunity to use technical skills and personal abilities, e.g., those learned in school.
9. Freedom and independence.
10. Opportunity for advancement.

The Ten Least-Liked Qualities About Careers in Public Accounting

1. Dull work—which does not require brains or education.
2. Long or irregular hours.
3. Time constraints and budgets—pressures.
4. Firm attitudes toward personnel, attitudes required of personnel, unprofessionalism.
5. Salary and salary increases.
6. Travel (too much).
7. Job insecurity.

APPENDIX

California psychological inventory scale descriptions.

SOURCE: Harrison G. Gough, *Manual for the California Psychological Inventory* (Consulting Psychologists Press, 1957), pp. 10–11. Reproduced by special permission from The California Psychological Inventory by Harrison G. Gough, Ph.D. Copyright 1956. Published by Consulting Psychologists Press Inc.

High scorers tend to be seen as	Scale and purpose	Low scorers tend to be seen as
Class I. Measures of poise, ascendancy, self-assurance, and interpersonal adequacy		
Aggressive, confident, persistent, and planful; as being persuasive and verbally fluent; as self-reliant and independent; and as having leadership potential and initiative.	1. Do (dominance) To assess factors of leadership ability, dominance, persistence, and social initiative.	Retiring, inhibited, commonplace, indifferent, silent and unassuming; as being slow in thought and action; as avoiding of situations of tension and decision; and as lacking in self-confidence.
Ambitious, active, forceful, insightful, resourceful, and versatile; as being ascendant and self-seeking; effective in communication; and as having personal scope and breadth of interests.	2. Cs (capacity for status) To serve as an index of an individual's capacity for status (not his actual or achieved status). The scale attempts to measure the personal qualities and attributes which underlie and lead to status.	Apathetic, shy, conventional, dull, mild, simple, and slow; as being stereotyped in thinking; restricted in outlook and interests; and as being uneasy and awkward in new or unfamiliar social situations.
Outgoing, enterprising, and ingenious; as being competitive and forward; and as original and fluent in thought.	3. Sy (sociability) To identify persons of outgoing, sociable, participative temperament.	Awkward, conventional, quiet, submissive, and unassuming; as being detached and passive in attitude; and as being suggestible and overly influenced by others' reactions and opinions.

Clever, enthusiastic, imaginative, quick, informal, spontaneous, and talkative; as being active and vigorous; and as having an expressive, ebullient nature.	4. Sp (social presence) To assess factors such as poise, spontaneity, and self-confidence in personal and social interaction.	Deliberate, moderate, patient, self-restrained, and simple; as vacillating and uncertain in decision; and as being literal and unoriginal in thinking and judging.
Intelligent, outspoken, sharp-witted, demanding, aggressive, and self-centered; as being persuasive and verbally fluent; and as possessing self-confidence and self-assurance.	5. Sa (self-acceptance) To assess factors such as sense of personal worth, self-acceptance, and capacity for independent thinking and action.	Methodical, conservative, dependable, conventional, easygoing, and quiet; as self-abasing and given to feelings of guilt and self-blame; and as being passive in action and narrow in interests.
Energetic, enterprising, alert, ambitious, and versatile; as being productive and active; and as valuing work and effort for its own sake.	6. Wb (sense of well-being) To identify persons who minimize their worries and complaints, and who are relatively free from self-doubt and disillusionment.	Unambitious, leisurely, awkward, cautious, apathetic, and conventional; as being self-defensive and apologetic; and as constricted in thought and action.

Class II. Measures of socialization, maturity, responsibility, and intrapersonal structuring of values

Planful, responsible, thorough, progressive, capable, dignified, and independent; as being conscientious and dependable; resourceful and efficient; and as being alert to ethical and moral issues.	7. Re (responsibility) To identify persons of conscientious, responsible, and dependable disposition and temperament.	Immature, moody, lazy, awkward, changeable, and disbelieving; as being influenced by personal bias, spite, and dogmatism; and as undercontrolled and impulsive in behavior.
Serious, honest, industrious, modest, obliging, sincere, and steady; as being conscientious and responsible; and as being self-denying and conforming.	8. So (socialization) To indicate the degree of social maturity, integrity, and rectitude which the individual has attained.	Defensive, demanding, opinionated, resentful, stubborn, headstrong, rebellious, and undependable; as being guileful and deceitful in dealing with others; and as given to excess, exhibition, and ostentation in their behavior.

APPENDIX (Continued)

High scorers tend to be seen as	Scale and purpose	Low scorers tend to be seen as
Calm, patient, practical, slow, self-denying, inhibited, thoughtful, and deliberate; as being strict and thorough in their own work and in their expectations for others; and as being honest and conscientious.	9. Sc (self-control) To assess the degree and adequacy of self-regulation and self-control and freedom from impulsivity and self-centeredness.	Impulsive, shrewd, excitable, irritable, self-centered, and uninhibited; as being aggressive and assertive; and as overemphasizing personal pleasure and self-gain.
Enterprising, informal, quick, tolerant, clear-thinking, and resourceful; as being intellectually able and verbally fluent; and as having broad and varied interests.	10. To (tolerance) To identify persons with permissive, accepting, and nonjudgmental social beliefs and attitude.	Suspicious, narrow, aloof, wary, and resentful; as being passive and overly judgmental in attitude; and as disbelieving and distrustful in personal and social outlook.
Cooperative, enterprising, outgoing, sociable, warm, and helpful; as being concerned with making a good impression; and as being diligent and persistent.	11. Gi (good impression) To identify persons capable of creating a favorable impression, and who are concerned about how others react to them.	Inhibited, cautious, shrewd, wary, aloof, and resentful; as being cool and distant in their relationships with others; and as being self-centered and too little concerned with the needs and wants of others.
Dependable, moderate, tactful, reliable, sincere, patient, steady, and realistic; as being honest and conscientious; and as having common sense and good judgment.	12. Cm (communality) To indicate the degree to which an individual's reactions and responses correspond to the modal ("common") pattern established for the inventory.	Impatient, changeable, complicated, imaginative, disorderly, nervous, restless, and confused; as being guileful and deceitful; inattentive and forgetful; and as having internal conflicts and problems.

Class III. Measures of achievement potential and intellectual efficiency

13. Ac (achievement via conformance) To identify those factors of interest and motivation which facilitate achievement in any setting where conformance is a positive behavior.

Capable, cooperative, efficient, organized, responsible, stable, and sincere; as being persistent and industrious; and as valuing intellectual activity and intellectual achievement.

Coarse, stubborn, aloof, awkward, insecure, and opinionated; as easily disorganized under stress or pressures to conform; and as pessimistic about their occupational futures.

14. Ai (achievement via independence) To identify those factors of interest and motivation which facilitate achievement in any setting where autonomy and independence are positive behaviors.

Mature, forceful, strong, dominant, demanding, and foresighted; as being independent and self-reliant; and as having superior intellectual ability and judgment.

Inhibited, anxious, cautious, dissatisfied, dull, and wary; as being submissive and compliant before authority; and as lacking in self-insight and self-understanding.

15. Ie (intellectual efficiency) To indicate the degree of personal and intellectual efficiency which the individual has attained.

Efficient, clear-thinking, capable, intelligent, progressive, planful, thorough, and resourceful; as being alert and well-informed; and as placing a high value on cognitive and intellectual matters.

Cautious, confused, easygoing, defensive, shallow, and unambitious; as being conventional and stereotyped in thinking; and as lacking in self-direction and self-discipline.

Class IV. Measures of intellectual and interest modes

16. Py (psychological-mindedness) To measure the degree to which the individual is interested in, and responsive to, the inner needs, motives, and experiences of others.

Observant, spontaneous, quick, perceptive, talkative, resourceful, and changeable; as being verbally fluent and socially ascendant; and as being rebellious toward rules, restrictions, and constraints.

Apathetic, peaceable, serious, cautious, and unassuming; as being slow and deliberate in tempo; and as being overly conforming and conventional.

APPENDIX (Continued)

High scorers tend to be seen as		Scale and Purpose	Low scorers tend to be seen as
Insightful, informal, adventurous, confident, humorous, rebellious, idealistic, assertive, and egoistic; as being sarcastic and cynical; and as highly concerned with personal pleasure and diversion.	17.	Fx (flexibility) To indicate the degree of flexibility and adaptability of a person's thinking and social behavior.	Deliberate, cautious, worrying, industrious, guarded, mannerly, methodical, and rigid; as being formal and pedantic in thought; and as being overly deferential to authority, custom, and tradition.
Appreciative, patient, helpful, gentle, moderate, persevering, and sincere; as being respectful and accepting of others; and as behaving in a conscientious and sympathetic way.	18.	Fe (femininity) To assess the masculinity or femininity of interests. (High scores indicate more feminine interests, low scores more masculine.)	Outgoing, hard-headed, ambitious, masculine, active, robust, and restless; as being manipulative and opportunistic in dealing with others; blunt and direct in thinking and action; and impatient with delay, indecision, and reflection.

8. Lack of proper personal development opportunities—inadequate supervision and training by seniors and above—supervisors who will not listen to problems or are insensitive.

9. Off-season uselessness—too much unassigned time—unassigned time.

10. Office politics and rules.

By and large these studies show that accounting attracts a high calibre student, and that careers in accounting are rewarding and challenging.

A final comment can be made about the occupational prestige ratings which are compiled periodically by the National Opinion Research Center (NORC) [62]. Unfortunately, the survey makes no provision for the CPA engaged in the public practice of accounting, nor is there reference to the independent auditor or controller. Instead, reference is made to the "accountant for a large business" who, in the June 1963 ratings, ranked 29.5 out of 90 occupational categories. Economists rated 34.5, architects 14, and physicians 2 on the scale. Perhaps future NORC ratings will provide for a wider variety of accounting occupations and give particular recognition to the role of the professional public accountant.

Without question, however, the accountant is playing a greater role in community and social affairs. While the quality of education and research are gaining academic recognition for accounting, the involvement of practicing accountants in a variety of problems and situations of mounting significance to industries, communities, and nations, serves to increase their visibility across the social spectrum.

REFERENCES

1. ROBERT L. POSNAK, "The Decline and Fall of Cratchit," *Journal of Accountancy*, May 1970, pp. 59–63.

2. WILMER L. GREEN, *History and Survey of Accounting* (Brooklyn, N.J.: Standard Text Press, 1930), pp. 88–105.

3. See References for Chapter 1, #14, 15.

4. MICHAEL CHATFIELD, *Contemporary Studies in the Evolution of Accounting Thought* (Belmont, Ca.: Dickenson, 1968).

5. JAMES DON EDWARDS, *History of Public Accounting in the United States* (East Lansing: MSU Business Studies, Michigan State University, 1960), p. 60.

6. NORMAN E. WEBSTER, "Early Movements for Accountancy Education," *Journal of Accountancy*, May 1941, p. 441.

7. JAMES B. LOVETTE, "History of Accounting in the United States" (New York:

American Institute of Accountants Library,), p. 14, and in EDWARDS, op. cit., p. 60.

8. WEBSTER, op. cit., p. 443.

9. JOHN L. CAREY, *The Rise of the Accounting Profession*, vol. 1 (New York: American Institute of Certified Public Accountants, 1969), p. 270.

10. State of California, Board of Accountancy, "Information for Candidates for the CPA Examination," a document furnished to students who propose to sit for the CPA examination in California.

11. PARK E. LEATHERS and HOWARD P. SANDERS, "The Supply and Demand for Public Accountants," *Journal of Accountancy*, September 1971, pp. 88.

12. FELIX P. KOLLARITSCH, *Opinions, Scholastic Rankings, and Professional Progress of Accounting Graduates* (Columbus, Ohio: College of Administrative Science, 1968). The study is summarized by the author in "Job Migration Pattern of Accounting," *Management Accounting*, September 1968, pp. 52–55.

13. See, for example, *The MBA*, Spring 1970.

14. JOHN J. McDONOUGH, "The M.B.A. and the Accounting Profession," *CPA Journal*, April 1973, pp. 292–296.

15. Salary Survey Committee, *Salary Survey*, College Placement Council, June, 1973.

16. DONALD E. KELLER, *A Research Study of Some Aspects of Accounting Education in California* (Palo Alto, Ca.: Certified Public Accountants Foundation for Education and Research, 1968), p. 25.

17. MARIE R. HAUG and MARVIN B. SUSSMAN, "Professional Autonomy and the Revolt of the Client," *Social Problems*, Fall 1969, p. 153, define a profession "as an occupation based on a unique scientific body of knowledge, whose practitioners have a service orientation, and autonomy in the performance of their work." MORRIS L. COGAN, "Toward a Definition of Profession," *Harvard Educational Review*, Winter 1953, pp. 33–50, provides this definition: "A profession is a vocation whose practice is founded upon an understanding of the theoretical structure of some department of learning or science, and upon the abilities attending such understanding." See also A. M. CARR-SAUNDERS and P. A. WILSON, *The Professions* (Oxford: Clarendon Press, 1964), pp. 137–158; HOWARD M. VOLLMER and DONALD L. MILLS, eds., *Professionalization* (Englewood Cliffs, N.J.: Prentice–Hall, 1966), pp. 3, 5, 157; EVERETT C. HUGHES, "Professions," *Daedalus*, Fall 1963, pp. 655–668; and J. E. STERRETT, "The Profession of Accountancy," *Annals of the American Academy of Political and Social Science*, July–December 1906, pp. 16–27.

18. See, for example, "The Priesthood of the Law," *Harper's Magazine*, December 1938–May 1939, pp. 515–526; BRONISLAW MALINOWSKI, *Magic, Science and Religion* (New York: Doubleday, 1948); ELVI WHITTAKER and VIRGINIA OLESEN,

"The Faces of Florence Nightingale: Functions of the Heroine Legend in an Occupational Subculture," *Human Organizations*, Summer 1964, pp. 123–130; ERNEST GREENWOOD, "Attributes of a Profession," *Social Work*, July 1957, pp. 44–55; HOWARD S. BECKER and BLANCHE GEER, "The Fate of Idealism in Medical Schools," *American Sociological Review*, February 1958, pp. 50–56; and A. D. WHITING, "The Professional Organization, Training, and Ethical Codes of Physicians, Dentists, Nurses and Pharmacists," *Annals of the American Academy of Political and Social Science*, May 1922, pp. 51–67.

19.   ROBERT H. ROY and JAMES H. MACNEILL, *Horizons for a Profession: The Common Body of Knowledge for Certified Public Accountants* (New York: American Institute of Certified Public Accountants, 1967), pp. 3–4.

20.   ROBERT A. GORDON and JAMES E. HOWELL, *Higher Education for Business* (New York: Columbia University Press, 1959).

21.   FRANK C. PIERSON, et al., *The Education of American Businessmen* (New York: McGraw–Hill, 1959).

22.   GORDON and HOWELL, op. cit., p. 132.

23.   Ibid., p. 131.

24.   Ibid., p. 214.

25.   ROBERT H. ROY and JAMES H. MACNEILL, *Horizons for a Profession: The Common Body of Knowledge for Certified Public Accountants* (New York: American Institute of Certified Public Accountants, 1967).

26.   Ibid., p. 5.

27.   *Report of the Committee on Education and Experience Requirements for CPAs* (New York: American Institute of Certified Public Accountants, 1969), pp. 6, 7.

28.   ROY and MACNEILL, op. cit.

29.   AICPA Committee on Education and Experience Requirements for CPAs, "Academic Preparation for Professional Accounting Careers," *Journal of Accountancy*, December 1968.

30.   Standing Committee on Education, *Report of the Standing Committee on Accounting Education* (New York: American Institute of Certified Public Accountants, 1966).

31.   *Report of the Committee on Education and Experience Requirements for CPAs*, op. cit., p. 43.

32.   *Report of the Committee to Examine the 1969 Report of the AICPA Committee on Education and Experience Requirements for CPAs*, supplement to vol. 47 of *The Accounting Review* (1972), pp. 237–257.

33.   PAUL DIESING, *Patterns of Discovery in the Social Sciences* (New York: Aldine–Atherton, 1971), p. 287.

34.   DOYLE Z. WILLIAMS, "A Survey of Accounting Education," *Journal of Accountancy*, February 1970, pp. 85–89.

35. A summary of publications in accounting is also provided by RICHARD J. VARGO, *The Author's Guide to Accounting and Financial Reporting Publications* (Williamsburg, Va.: College of William and Mary, 1971).

36. The abstract service is known as *Accounting Articles;* it classifies and describes accounting articles, books and pamphlets. The publisher is Commerce Clearing House, Inc., 4025 West Peterson Avenue, Chicago, Ill. 60646.

37. RAY BALL, "Index of Empirical Research in Accounting," *Journal of Accounting Research,* Spring 1971, pp. 1–31.

38. For example, NICHOLAS DOPUCH and LAWRENCE REVSINE, eds., *Accounting Research 1960–1970: A Critical Evaluation,* Monograph 7 (Urbana, Ill.: University of Illinois, 1973); and ROBERT R. STERLING, ed., *Research Methodology in Accounting* (Lawrence, Ks.: Scholars Book Co., 1972).

39. Study Group on Introductory Accounting, *A New Introduction to Accounting* (New York: Price Waterhouse Foundation, 1971). For comments on the study see MARTIN L. GOSMAN, "An Assessment of the Recommendations of the Study Group on Introductory Accounting," *Accounting Review,* July 1971, pp. 158–162; and CHARLES H. SMITH, "A New Introduction to Accounting: Some Explanations," *Accounting Review,* January 1973, pp. 148–157.

40. PAUL E. DASCHER and ROBERT H. STRAWSER, "A 'Clearing House' for Computer Programs Used in Accounting Instruction and Research," *Journal of Accountancy,* April 1973, pp. 90–92.

41. THOMAS J. BURNS, *Accounting Trends* (New York: McGraw–Hill, published annually since 1967).

42. WILLIAM F. CRUM, "The Second Survey of Doctoral Programs in Accounting," *Journal of Accountancy,* June 1971, pp. 86–89.

43. PAUL GARNER, "Some Reflections on Research by Doctoral Candidates in Accounting," *Monograph Series No. 2* (Center for Business and Economic Research, University of Alabama, 1973).

44. RALPH W. ESTES, "A Ranking of Accounting Programs," *Journal of Accountancy,* July 1970, pp. 86–90. For a commentary on the study see JOHN GRANT RHODE and STEPHEN A. ZEFF, "Comments on 'A Ranking of Accounting Programs,' " *Journal of Accountancy,* December 1970, pp. 83–86.

45. JAMES DON EDWARDS, *History of Public Accounting in the United States* (East Lansing: Michigan State University, 1960), pp. 68–69.

46. Ibid., p. 70.

47. Ibid., p. 73. The text of the first examination is contained in Appendix A. Ibid., pp. 328–335.

48. JOHN L. CAREY, *The Rise of the Accounting Profession,* vol. 1 (New York: American Institute of Certified Public Accountants, 1969), pp. 272–273.

49. "Certificate in Management Accounting," *Management Accounting*, March 1972, pp. 13, 14, 64.

50. *Information for CPA Candidates* (New York: American Institute of Certified Public Accountants, published periodically).

51. Ibid., 1970 edition, p. 3.

52. PARK E. LEATHERS, "Relationship of Test Scores to CPA Examination Performance," *Journal of Accountancy*, September 1972, pp. 101–103. See also LE-BRONE HARRIS, "Personality Traits of Accountants," *Journal of Accountancy*, April 1972, pp. 87–89; and FRANK K. REILLY and HOWARD F. STETTLER, "Factors Influencing Success on the CPA Examination," *Journal of Accounting Research*, Autumn 1972, pp. 308–321.

53. Institute of Management Accounting, CMA: *Certificate in Management Accounting* (New York: National Association of Accountants, [n.d.]).

54. SELWYN W. BECKER, "The Accountant as Others See Him," *The Newsletter of the Graduate School of Business, University of Chicago*, Spring 1969, pp. 16–19. The paper is based on Dr. Becker's remarks to the American Accounting Association's annual meeting in San Diego, August 28, 1968. Also see JOHN ASHWORTH, "People Who Become Accountants," *Journal of Accountancy*, November 1968, pp. 43–49; JOHN ASHWORTH, "The Pursuit of High Quality Recruits," *Journal of Accountancy*, February 1969, pp. 53–56; ELMO ROPER, "As Others See You," *Journal of Accountancy*, January 1964, pp. 32–36; JOHN L. COBBS, "How the Business Press Views the Accounting Profession," *Journal of Accountancy*, August 1969, pp. 48–52; KEN SOLOMON, "The CPA's Public Image," *Bulletin of the National Association of Hotel–Motel Accountants*, April 1970, pp. 3–11; D. D. O'DOWD and D. C. BEARDSLEE, "College Student Images of a Selected Group of Professions and Occupations" (Wesleyan University and U.S. Office of Education, April 1960), pp. 38–39; and ALBERT NEWGARDEN, "A Little Anthology of Words and Pictures About Accounting and Accountants from Antiquity to the Present Day," *The Arthur Young Journal*, Spring–Summer 1969, pp. 47–62.

55. *Small Business Looks at the CPA*, Bulletin No. 2, Economics of Accounting Practice (New York: American Institute of Certified Public Accountants, 1957).

56. DON T. DeCOSTER and JOHN GRANT RHODE, "The Accountant's Stereotype: Real or Imagined, Deserved or Unwarranted," *Accounting Review*, October 1971, pp. 651–664.

57. See JOHN ASHWORTH, "People Who Become Accountants," *Journal of Accountancy*, November 1968, p. 48.

58. As reported in DON T. DeCOSTER, "Mirror, Mirror on the Wall . . . The CPA in the World of Psychology," *Journal of Accountancy*, August 1971, p. 43.

59. Ibid., p. 43.

60. CHARLES R. BAKER, "Accounting Majors versus Non-Majors: A Comparison of Values," *Working Paper 73–25* (Los Angeles: Accounting-Information Systems Research Program, UCLA, January 1973).

61. JOHN GRANT RHODE, et al., "Pre-Employment Expectations vs. Actual Work Experience in Public Accounting," *Working Paper 74–10* (Los Angeles: Accounting–Information Systems Research Program, UCLA, October 1973); EDWARD E. LAWLER III, JOHN GRANT RHODE, and JAMES SORENSON, "Study on Sources of Professional Staff Turnover in Public Accounting Firms," (research project reports, American Institute of Certified Public Accountants, circa 1970).

62. See ROBERT W. HODGE, PAUL M. SIEGEL, and PETER H. ROSSI, "Occupational Prestige in the United States, 1925–1963," vol. 70, *American Journal of Sociology* (1964), pp. 286–302.

4

POLICING THE
PROFESSION

HALLMARKS OF PROFESSIONALISM

From the seemingly endless discussions as to what constitutes a profession [1], four characteristics appear to be indisputable. Two are causative and two are effective; the relationship among these factors is illustrated in Exhibit 34.

In seeking professional recognition, aspirants offer a unique knowledge set (often represented by skills) and affirm that it will be used in the public interest (service ideal). The public responds by granting autonomy (self-regulation) to the profession. This exchange leads to an authority situation in which the state or government grants privileges, such as the need for licensing, to the profes-

EXHIBIT 34
Four essential characteristics of a profession.
SOURCE: John W. Buckley, *In Search of Identity: An Inquiry into Identity Issues in Accounting* (Palo Alto, Ca.: Certified Public Accountants Foundation for Education and Research, 1972), p. 39.

Causative		*Effective*
(A profession offers)	(A profession receives)	(The outcome is)
Expertise $\longrightarrow$	$\longleftarrow$ Autonomy	$\longrightarrow$ Authority
Altruism $\longrightarrow$		
(A service ideal)		

sion. However, government retains the final authority with respect to professional activity and intervenes legislatively or through the legal system to correct neglect and abuse. Thus, a profession's domain must be viewed as a mandate rather than a natural prerogative, for professions can and do lose autonomy and authority where they fail in their responsibility to the public.

Through observation we know that some professions have more status than others. The range is vast, beginning with illegitimate "professions" such as prostitution and thieving, passing through some presently dubious candidates such as management and labor, and moving upward until we reach the zenith professions of medicine, law, and the ministry [2].

Given that scholars are able to rank professions in very nearly the same order (at least in general categories), it is surprising that the principles of differentiation have not been drawn with greater clarity.

The search for commonalities is elusive. Licensing, for example, does not appear to be a critical variable. Physicians are licensed but so are plumbers. Economists, on the other hand, are not licensed, yet in most quarters are viewed as distinguished professionals, as are sociologists and scientists generally.

Or take codes of ethics. Medicine has a most abbreviated one [3]; accountants have an elaborate one, as do engineers [4]; but other professions have none. Management consultants [5] have developed a rather detailed code of ethics, yet suffer from professional agenesis.

Consider the question of organization. Again, certain prestigious professions have tight organizations (law, medicine, accounting) while others are less structured (architects, engineers, scientists). Labor unions and some other groups with tight organizations do not place high on the professional ladder.

Glossed-over intangibles such as deportment and erudition are more powerful discriminators than the foregoing. Culture, propriety, and even a little detachment go further toward promoting the status of a profession than is admitted to in the literature [6].

Exclusivity is an important discriminator. By regulating inflow into the profession, membership always appears desirable. Exclusivity serves the additional purpose of maintaining full employment and an income level commensurate with the profession's aspired social status. The volatile nature of careers such as engineering and science in recent years cannot help but lower the perceived social status of these professions.

Attempts to improve status involve changing the public image of the profession. This generally is done in one of two ways: (*a*) changing the name of the group, or (*b*) drawing a tighter boundary, such as raising the entrance requirements to those with advanced education. As examples of the former we have seen hospital superintendents transmute into hospital administrators, relief investigators into social workers, newspaper reporters into journalists, undertakers into funeral directors, and garbage collectors into refuse workers. An example

EXHIBIT 35
The distinction between a bureaucratic and professional environment.
SOURCE: James E. Sorensen, "Professional and Bureaucratic Organization in the Public Accounting Firm," *Accounting Review,* July 1967, p. 555.

Bureaucratic	Professional
High ⟵⟶ *Low*	*High* ⟵⟶ *Low*

I. Authority
  A. *Basis of authority*
    1. Rules sanctioned by organizational hierarchy | 1. Rules sanctioned by powerful and legally created professions
    2. Authority from office | 2. Authority from personal competence

  B. *Use of knowledge in decision-making*
    3. Decisions applying rules to routine problems | 3. Decisions relating to professional policy and unique problems

  C. *Direction of loyalty*
    4. Loyalty to organization and superiors | 4. Loyalty to professional colleagues, clients, and community

II. Standardization
  A. *Approach to the problem*
    1. Emphasis on uniformity: client's problems; personnel | 1. Emphasis on uniqueness: client's problems; personnel
  B. *Latitude of rules*
    2. Rules stated as categoricals/specifics | 2. Rules stated as alternatives/multiples
  C. *Initiative in work*
    2. Emphasis on stability (e.g., records and files) | 3. Emphasis on creativity (e.g., research, change)

III. Specialization
  A. *Functional objective*
    1. Efficiency of technique for specific task | 1. Satisfaction of specific client needs
  B. *Depth and breadth of knowledge*
    2. Specific tasks based primarily on practice of narrow range of technical skills | 2. Variety of activities based primarily on generalized knowledge

of the latter is the attempt to define the boundaries of accounting such that bookkeepers are excluded [7], or the emerging demand for five years of education as the prerequisite for certification.

Many professionals act as individuals or in small groups in rendering services to the public. Medical and legal practice is essentially in this mode. Some professionals, however, work in large industrial and governmental organizations. Corporate doctors, lawyers, and accountants are cases in point. Then, in some professional organizations such as the major accounting firms, individuality yields to the interests of the firm. Maintaining professionalism within the context of bureaucratic organizations is a matter of concern to sociologists. Professor Sorenson distinguishes between a bureaucratic and professional environment (Exhibit 35) and notes that the behavior in large accounting firms tends toward the bureaucratic rather than the professional [8]. The preservation of professionalism in the large accounting firm is of concern to many thoughtful persons in the profession and, indeed, afflicts all large organizations. Remedies should follow the growing awareness which attends this problem.

ETHICS

The service ideal of most professions is exhibited in the form of a code of ethics. The Concepts of Professional Ethics, and Rules of Conduct which currently apply to the practice of public accounting are contained in Appendix C. The current code of ethics was approved by a referendum held on November 15, 1972. It represents the latest in a series of codes of ethics which date from 1906 when the by–laws of the American Association of Public Accountants (which was a predecessor organization to the American Institute of Certified Public Accountants) were extended to provide for rules of professional conduct [9].

As noted in Appendix C the principal areas covered by the current rules of conduct are: (a) independence, integrity, and objectivity; (b) competence and technical standards; (c) responsibilities to clients, (d) responsibilities to colleagues, and (e) other responsibilities and practices.

Independence is a cardinal principle in public accounting. As Louis H. Rappaport observes, "public accountants know that their reputation for independence and integrity is their principal stock in trade and the justification for their existence as a profession. They are impelled by enlightened self-interest, and admonished by rules of ethics and professional conduct to maintain their independence at all costs, since it is obvious as can be that independence is the very foundation of the public accounting profession [10]."

Independence is crucial in that the public accountant occupies a position of trust and mutual confidence which is necessary to the orderly conduct of business relationships, whether they are between management and investors, borrowers and lenders, or purchasers and sellers. As the Executive Committee of the American Institute of Certified Public Accountants noted in 1947, "It has become of great value to those who rely on financial statements of business enterprises that they be reviewed by persons skilled in accounting whose judgment is uncolored by any interest in the enterprise, and upon whom the obligation has been imposed to disclose all material facts. With the growth of business enterprises, the public accountant makes a vital contribution in meeting the need for independent, impartial, and expert opinions on the financial position and results of operations. This is his unique contribution, a service for which no one else offers or is qualified to perform [11]."

Allied to the principle of independence is the requirement of competence, i.e., that a CPA should only undertake engagements which he or she is qualified to perform by reason of education or experience. The test of competence is measured by the degree of judgment and skill that would be applied in a given situation by a typical, well-trained accountant.

Most codes of professional conduct distinguish between *efferent* and *afferent* ethics. The former prescribes the relationship between the profession and its client, such as confidentiality or service above fees; the latter promotes harmony within the profession by reducing competition and other disruptive behavior. The accountant's code of ethics addresses both areas of concern. Confidentiality with respect to the client's information is the major efferent ethic, while professional courtesy and nonencroachment are the principal factors in terms of responsibilities to colleagues.

Setting accounting standards and policing the code of ethics are functions which vest partially in the public and private sectors under the jurisdiction of these organizations: (*a*) Securities and Exchange Commission (SEC); (*b*) American Institute of Certified Public Accountants (AICPA); (*c*) Financial Accounting Standards Board (FASB); and (*d*) Cost Accounting Standards Board (CASB). While a number of other public and private organizations contribute to these matters, we will concentrate attention on the four organizations which assume the essential responsibility for policy and professional affairs.

SECURITIES AND EXCHANGE COMMISSION

The SEC is an independent regulatory agency of the U.S. government, created by the Securities and Exchange Act of 1934 [12]. It administers the following statutes: (*a*) Securities Act of 1933; (*b*) Securities Exchange Act of 1934; (*c*) Public Utility Holding Act of 1935; (*d*) Trust Indenture Act of 1939; (*e*) Investment Company Act of 1940; (*f*) Investment Advisers Act of 1940; (*g*) Chapter

X of the Bankruptcy Act; and (*h*) functions under the Securities Investor Protection Act of 1970. Its role in terms of these statutes is described briefly as follows:

1. *Securities Act of 1933:*   Requires a registration statement with the Commission on the part of those who intend to issue securities to the public. Exemptions include federal and local agencies, certain common carriers such as interstate railroads, and offerings not exceeding $500,000 which comply with the Commission's Regulations A and E.

2. *Securities Exchange Act of 1934:*   Requires the filing of registration statements, annual financial statements, and other reports for companies whose securities are listed on the exchanges. Over-the-counter securities are included where the company has $1,000,000 in assets and 500 or more shareholders.

3. *Public Utility Holding Act of 1935:*   Requires regulation by the Commission of the purchase and sale of securities, properties and other assets by holding companies in the utility system. The authority extends to distribution of voting power and to reorganizations, mergers, and consolidations of public utility holding companies.

4. *Trust Indenture Act of 1939:*   Requires compliance with SEC regulations pertaining publicly offered debt securities issued under trust indentures. The Act also provides for the independence of indenture trustees.

5. *Investment Company Act of 1940:*   Provides for the registration of investment companies and subjects their activities to regulation in accordance with standards prescribed to protect investors. It may file court actions to enjoin acts and practices of management officials involving gross misconduct or abuse of trust and to disqualify such persons from holding office.

6. *Investment Advisers Act of 1940:*   Requires that persons who, for compensation, engage in the business of advising others with respect to their security transactions to register with the Commission. This requirement extends to security brokers and dealers, as well as to accountants who practice before the SEC.

7. *Bankruptcy Act:*   Provides that the Commission advise the federal courts regarding the reorganization of insolvent corporations.

8. *Securities Investor Protection Act of 1970:*   Prescribes a role for the Commission in guarding investors against losses of cash and securities where brokerage firms fail or merge. This Act followed in the wake of the widespread financial instability among brokerage houses in the period 1969–1971, in which period 110 firms either failed or merged [13].

The organization chart for the SEC appears in Exhibit 36. The Commission comprises five members appointed by the President with the consent of the Senate. One member is designated by the President to serve as chairman. Generally, commissioners are appointed for five-year terms, and not more than three commissioners can belong to the same political party.

The Office of the Chief Accountant, currently occupied by Dr. John C.

EXHIBIT 36
Organization of the Securities and Exchange
Commission.
SOURCE: *U.S. Government Organization Manual, 1972–1973,*
p. 595.

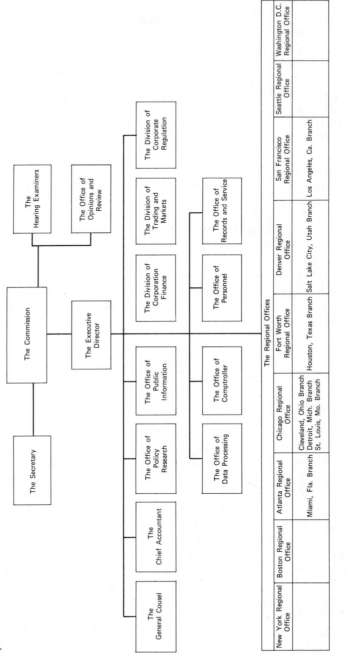

Burton, is of particular interest to us. The Chief Accountant is the principal adviser to the Commission on all matters relating to accounting and auditing. He is also responsible for executing Commission policy with respect to accounting principles, auditing practices, the form and content of financial statements filed with the Commission, uniform systems of accounts, and the interpretation and application of accounting principles in unusual situations.

He initiates and supervises research and studies, drafts policies and regulations, answers questions from registrants or their public accountants dealing with matters affecting the SEC, and publishes his opinions in what is known as the "Accounting Series Releases."

An important part of the Chief Accountant's job is liaison with other policy and enforcement groups, together with judicious prodding where these groups fail to make adequate progress in resolving matters which require definitive action. Also, he is responsible for dealing with questions of independence, qualifications, and malpractice of public accountants who perform services for clients who are registered with the SEC.

The role of governmental agencies in promulgating accounting policy cannot be minimized. The Securities and Exchange Act of 1934 empowered the SEC "to prescribe the form and content of financial statements filed by reporting companies, and to specify the methods to be followed in their preparation [14]." However, in carrying out its functions over the years, the SEC has sought to work closely with the accounting profession in setting accounting policy. In reporting to a Congressional committee in 1964, the SEC stated [15]:

> Much improvement in financial reporting practices has occurred since the enactment of the first Federal securities law in 1933. The Commission believes that its policy of working with and supporting the accounting profession in the development of accounting principles has directly influenced this progress and is the best means for assuring continuing improvement of accounting practices.

At the annual meeting of the American Institute of Certified Public Accountants which convened in Atlanta, October 16, 1973, Ray Garrett, Jr., the current chairman of the Securities and Exchange Commission, reaffirmed the Commission's "historical policy of reliance on the private sector for solving financial measurement problems." He noted that the SEC and the Financial Accounting Standards Board can meet the needs of investors by bringing their cumulative expertise to bear on the problems [16].

In more cases than not, policy generated in the private sector becomes embodied in the policy of the SEC, thereby giving it the status of federal law. SEC policy is exhibited in a series of regulations, rules, and releases. *Regulation S–X* is the principal administrative document of the SEC and is updated periodically. This regulation (together with the Accounting Series Releases

[ASR] *) states the requirements applicable to the form and content of all financial statements required to be filed under the various acts which the SEC administers [17].

The *Ash Report* [18] (after its chairman Roy L. Ash) was issued in January 1971 and dealt with problems facing several independent agencies of the federal government, including the SEC. The Report noted major changes in the nature of the securities markets since the 1930's, including these items: (a) in the period 1962–1968, trading volume on the New York Stock Exchange quadrupled, and in 1970 reached the staggering volume of 2.937 billion shares (or 11.7 million shares daily); (b) the excessive trading volume in late 1968, for example, caused the brokerage industry to default on the delivery of $4.1 billion of securities by the settlement date; (c) 110 brokerage firms, as noted earlier, failed or merged in the two-year period, 1969–1971; (d) institutional investors now dominate the markets, representing 62% of the volume on the New York Stock Exchange, and registered investment companies (including mutuals) have grown from $2.5 billion in assets and 400,000 shareholders in 1940 to $70 billion in assets and 8 million shareholders in 1969; and (e) despite the rapidly expanding workload, the SEC's budget has remained essentially unchanged since 1965, and the number of personnel has actually declined. The *Ash Report* concluded with the recommendation that a new Securities and Exchange Agency replace the existing Commission, but at the time this is written no action has been taken to effect this change.

AMERICAN INSTITUTE OF CERTIFIED PUBLIC ACCOUNTANTS

Private sector regulation of accounting has been centered in the activities of the AICPA and its predecessor organizations which are listed in Exhibit 37 [19].

We noted in Chapter 2 that the AICPA is the membership organization of certified public accountants throughout the United States, with approximately 88,200 members in 1972. There are also fifty-three state and other jurisdictional (District of Columbia, Puerto Rico, and the U.S. Virgin Islands) societies of CPAs, as detailed in Appendix D. There is close cooperation between the local societies and the national organization, with policy matters resident in the latter. However, the state societies actively engage in research, promotion and public relations, continuing education for CPAs, and lobbying on behalf of legislation by the states as it affects the welfare and development of the profession.

---

* The issuance of ASR's and discussions of their relevance to practice are summarized periodically in the *Journal of Accountancy.*

EXHIBIT 37
Chronology of the American Institute of Certified Public Accountants and its predecessor organizations.

American Association of Public Accountants	1887–1916
Federation of Societies of Public Accountants in the U.S.	1903–1906
The Institute of Accountants in the United States of America	1916–1917
American Institute of Accountants	1917–1956
American Institute of Certified Public Accountants	1956–present

Exhibit 38 contains the present organizational chart for the staff of the American Institute of Certified Public Accountants and its office holders.

An executive vice-president heads the staff organization and in turn reports to the president of the Institute, who is assisted by other officers and the AICPA Council.

Being concerned with policy, however, our attention rivets on two principal functions of the AICPA: (*a*) its role in generating policy with respect to financial reporting; and (*b*) its role in defining auditing standards. These areas of concern have come to be called "generally accepted accounting principles" and "generally accepted auditing standards," respectively.

Generally Accepted Accounting Principles

Reed Storey has written a delightful account of the long and arduous search for accounting principles [20]. Particularly, he notes the inherent conflict between the ideal and pragmatic, hope and reality, and the prescriptive versus feasible in the pilgrimage toward truth in accounting. Perfection is hindered in part by the democratic nature of the process, and hence the words *generally accepted* take on added meaning.

What is known as *generally accepted accounting principles* consists of fifty-one *Accounting Research Bulletins* [20a] issued by the Committee on Accounting Procedure in the period 1939–1959, and *Opinions of the Accounting Principles Board* issued between 1959 and 1973. These bodies, which are referred to more commonly by the acronyms of CAP and APB, have been the policy arms of the AICPA since 1939. In addition, established practices among CPAs which have substantive support may be considered to be generally accepted accounting principles.

The Council of the American Institute of CPAs issued a Special Bulletin in

EXHIBIT 38

Staff organization structure of the American Institute of Certified Public Accountants.

SOURCE: *Committee Handbook 1972–73* (New York: American Institute of Certified Public Accountants, 1972), p. 152.

Executive Vice President	W.E. Olson
General Counsel	D. Schneeman
Director of Planning	R. Crum, Jr.

V.P. Government Relations — G. Simonetti, Jr.
- Federal Taxation Div. — J. Forster, Director
- Federal Technical Liaison Div. — T. Hanley, Director

Administrative V.P.—Security — J. Lawlor
- Accounting and Official Service Div. — G. Taylor, Director
- Member Relations Div. — D. Lanman, Director
- Publication Div. — W. Doherty, Director
- Public Relations Div. — S. Schackne, Director
- State Social Regulations Div. — N. Myers, Director

V.P.—Education — G. Trump
- Examinations Div. — D. Sweeney, Director
- Personnel Div. — A. Grunwald, Director
- Professional Development Div. — R. Schlosser, Director

V.P.—Professional Regulation — W. Bruschi
- Trial Board Div. — (   )
- Professional Ethics Div. — (W. Bruschi)
- Regulation Div. — (   )

- Accounting Standards Div. — R. Lytle, Director
- Auditing Standards Div. — J. Fitzmayer, Director
- Management Advisory Services Div. — J. Mitchell, Director
- Technical Research Div. — D. Carmichael, Director
- Information Retrieval Div. — R. Stone, Director
- International Practice Div. — R. Sampler, Director

October 1964 which defined generally accepted accounting principles. Its essential passages are [21]:

> The Council of the Institute, at its meeting October 2, 1964, unanimously adopted recommendations that members should see to it that departures from Opinions of the Accounting Principles Board (as well as effective Accounting Research Bulletins issued by the former Committee on Accounting Procedure) are disclosed, either in footnotes to financial statements or in the audit report of members in their capacity as independent auditors.
>
> "Generally accepted accounting principles" are those principles which have substantial authoritative support.
>
> Opinions of the Accounting Principles Board constitute "substantial authoritative support."
>
> "Substantial authoritative support" can exist for accounting principles that differ from Opinions of the Accounting Principles Board.
>
> If an accounting principle differs materially in its effect from one accepted in an opinion of the Accounting Principles Board as applied in financial statements, the reporting member must decide whether the principle has substantial authoritative support and is applicable in the circumstances.
>
> If he concludes that it does not, he would either qualify his opinion, disclaim an opinion or give an adverse opinion as appropriate . . .
>
> If he concludes that it does have substantial authoritative support:
> (1)   he would give an unqualified opinion and
> (2)   disclose the fact of departure from the opinion in a separate report or see that it is disclosed in a footnote to the financial statements, and where practicable, its effects on the financial statements.

For most practical purposes official policy supersedes convention and makes it difficult to support alternative strategies in a given area. Accordingly, the bulletins and opinions of the AICPA have had the effect of law as it applies to principles and practices in accounting.

An improved understanding of the policy-making process in accounting can be obtained by studying the sequential steps set forth in Exhibit 39.

The need for policy may stem from a number of quarters. For example, litigation through the courts has often led to changes in accounting policy, as has the passage of federal laws. Practitioners may bring problems to light as they encounter them in practice. Educators, and especially those engaged in academic research, play an important role in extending the state of the art, such that policy becomes possible in areas that were held previously to be beyond the pale of formalization.

Research has always accompanied policy in accounting, but a major step

EXHIBIT 39
The process underlying accounting policy.

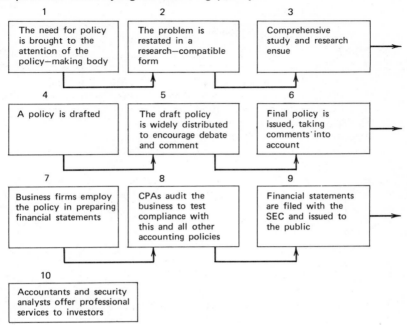

forward occurred in 1959 when, following the report of a special committee on research under the chairmanship of Weldon Powell, a Division of Research was formed within the AICPA. Dr. Maurice Moonitz became its first director. This action was taken in recognition of the fact that some problems require more extensive research than others, necessitating that formal research projects be commissioned in certain instances. Formal research studies completed by the Division of Research of the AICPA are listed in Exhibit 40.

In 1972 the Division of Research was replaced with the office of Technical Research and Dr. Douglas R. Carmichael was appointed as its director. This change occurred because of the creation of the Financial Accounting Standards Board which then assumed policy-related research within its organization.

We have noted that policy statements of the Committee on Accounting Procedure was output in the form of fifty-one *Accounting Research Bulletins*. Since 1959, the policy statements which have emanated from the *Accounting Principles Board* have been titled *Opinions* and *Statements*. There have been thirty-one opinions and four statements, as listed in Exhibits 41 and 42, respectively.

EXHIBIT 40
Research studies of the American Institute of Certified Public Accountants.

1. *The Basic Postulates of Accounting*, Maurice Moonitz, 1961
2. *"Cash Flow" Analysis and the Funds Statement*, Perry Mason, 1961
3. *A Tentative Set of Broad Accounting Principles for Business Enterprises*, Robert N. Sprouse and Maurice Moonitz, 1962
4. *Reporting of Leases in Financial Statements*, John H. Myers, 1962
5. *A Critical Study of Accounting for Business Combinations*, Arthur R. Wyatt, 1963
6. *Reporting Financial Effects of Price-Level Changes*, Staff, 1963
7. *Inventory of Generally Accepted Accounting Principles for Business Enterprises*, Paul Grady, 1965
8. *Accounting for the Cost of Pension Plans*, Ernest L. Hicks, 1965
9. *Interperiod Allocation of Corporate Income Taxes*, Homer Black, 1966
10. *Accounting for Goodwill*, George R. Catlett and Norman O. Olson, 1968
11. *Financial Reporting in the Extractive Industries*, Robert E. Field, 1969
12. *Reporting Foreign Operations of U.S. Companies in U.S. Dollars*, Leonard Lorensen, 1972
13. *The Accounting Basis of Inventories*, Horace G. Barden, 1973
14. *Accounting for Research and Development Expenditures*, Oscar S. Gellein and Maurice S. Newman, 1973
15. *Stockholders' Equity*, Beatrice Melcher, 1973.

EXHIBIT 41
Opinions of the Accounting Principles Board, 1959–1973.

1. *New Depreciation Guidelines and Rules*, November 1962
2. *Accounting for the "Investment Credit,"* December 1962
3. *The Statement of Source and Application of Funds*, October 1963
4. *Accounting for the "Investment Credit,"* March 1964 (Amending No. 2)
5. *Reporting of Leases in Financial Statements of Lessee*, September 1964
6. *Status of Accounting Research Bulletins*, October 1965
7. *Accounting for Leases in Financial Statements of Lessors*, May 1966
8. *Accounting for the Cost of Pension Plans*, November 1966
9. *Reporting the Results of Operations*, December 1966

10. *Omnibus Opinion—1966,* December 1966
11. *Accounting for Income Taxes,* December 1967
12. *Omnibus Opinion—1967,* December 1967
13. *Amending Paragraph 6 of APB Opinion No. 9, Application to Commercial Banks,* March 1969
14. *Accounting for Convertible Debt and Debt Issued with Stock Purchase Warrants,* March 1969
15. *Earnings Per Share,* May 1969
16. *Business Combinations,* August 1970
17. *Intangible Assets,* August 1970
18. *The Equity Method of Accounting for Investments in Common Stock,* March 1971
19. *Reporting Changes in Financial Position,* March 1971
20. *Accounting Changes,* July 1971
21. *Interest on Receivables and Payables,* August 1971
22. *Disclosure of Accounting Policies,* April 1972
23. *Accounting for Income Taxes—Special Areas,* April 1972
24. *Accounting for Income Taxes—Investments in Common Stock Accounted for by the Equity Method (Other than Subsidiaries and Corporate Joint Ventures*), April 1972
25. *Accounting for Stock Issued to Employees,* October 1972
26. *Early Extinguishment of Debt,* October 1972
27. *Accounting for Lease Transactions by Manufacturer or Dealer Lessors,* November 1972
28. *Interim Financial Reporting,* May 1973
29. *Accounting for Nonmonetary Transactions,* May 1973
30. *Reporting the Results of Operations—Reporting the Effects of Disposal of a Segment of a Business, and Extraordinary, Unusual and Infrequently Occurring Events and Transactions,* June 1973
31. *Disclosure of Lease Commitments by Lessees,* June 1973

EXHIBIT 42
Statements of the Accounting Principles Board, 1959–1973.

1. *Statement of Accounting Principles Board re Accounting Research Studies Nos. 1 and 3,* 1962
2. *Disclosure of Supplemental Financial Information by Diversified Companies,* 1967
3. *Financial Statements Restated for General Price-Level Changes,* 1969
4. *Basic Concepts and Accounting Principles Underlying Financial Statements of Business Enterprises,* 1970

Opinions carry greater authority than *Statements*, with the former being obligatory and the latter recommendatory in nature.

Generally Accepted Auditing Standards

It is the task of CPAs acting in the capacity of independent auditors to audit their clients' financial affairs and express opinions on the extent to which a client's financial statements conform with generally accepted accounting principles. He must also express an opinion on the extent to which the statements are a fair representation of the financial condition and operations of the firm for the specified period. This role, known as "the attest function," is pivotal to the professional status of the CPA and therefore earns the close attention of the AICPA as well as the SEC and other regulatory agencies.

The general auditing framework is depicted in Exhibit 43. This framework is purposive in that all observations are directed to the fundamental questions of fair presentation. These questions include the following [22]:

I. **Values:** Are the figures accurate?
   A. *Rules:* Have generally accepted accounting principles (specifically APB *Opinions*), and other legal and regulatory procedures (or well-established industry practices) been followed?
      1. *Consistently*
         (a) On an interperiod basis—specifically in accordance with those used in the preceding year?
         (b) On an intraperiod basis—have similar events been treated in a similar manner?
      2. *Applied correctly*
         Have the principles and procedures been applied correctly?
   B. *Timing:* Are the figures in their proper time-frame?
      1. Was there a proper cut-off?
      2. Was there a proper matching?
         (a) Were time-related (period) costs matched with their proper time periods?
         (b) Were activity-related (product) costs matched with their appropriate revenues?
   C. *Realization:* As financial statements are prepared on a "going-concern" basis, certain key figures imply certain assumptions about future value. An audit objective is to evaluate the reasonableness of these expectations.
      1. *Payability:* What is the probability of having to make certain payments, e.g., refunds or payments against warranties?
      2. *Salability:* Are inventory items actually salable, or are they damaged, obsolete, or otherwise unmarketable?

EXHIBIT 43
The auditing framework.
SOURCE: John W. Buckley and Kevin M. Lightner, *Accounting: An Information Systems Approach* (Belmont, Ca.: Dickenson, 1973), p. 1191.

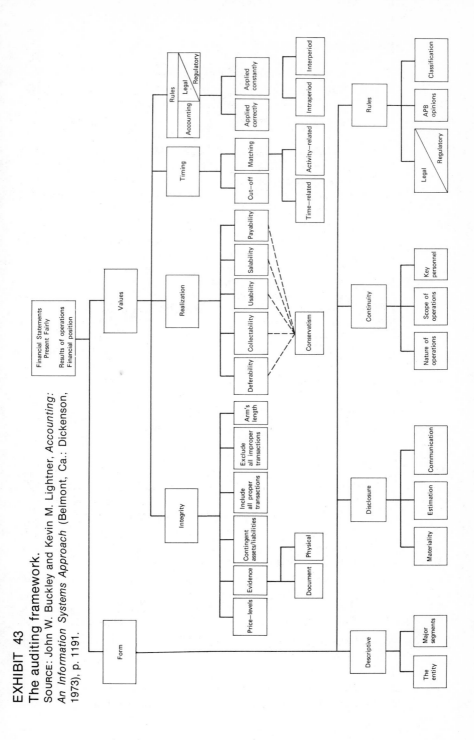

3. *Usability:* Does plant and equipment have future utility?
4. *Collectibility:* Are accounts receivable as shown (net of the allowance for doubtful accounts) actually collectable?
5. *Deferability:* Is there proper cause to defer prepaid expenses and similar accruals to future accounting periods?

> In assessing management's assumptions of realization, the auditor relates to past and present conditions—not to speculative future ones such as the probability of collecting receivables should a major depression occur in the following year, or the continued utility of a machine that is rendered prematurely obsolete by a revolutionary invention.
>
> Because future events are of the nature of probabilities rather than certainties, there is room for error. This "room for error" is expressed by a confidence-level/reliability relationship covering a reasonable range of expected values. It is here that the much-maligned conservatism of the auditor can be applied with justification—his preference is for expected values in the low range with respect to future receipts, and in the high range for future payments. Figures generated in this manner give the user an assurance that matters will likely turn out better than stated, but it is unlikely that they will worsen, i.e., there should be a pleasant (or at least satisfying) rather than an unpleasant outcome to realization prognoses.

D. *Integrity:* Do the figures represent reality and what actually happened?

1. *Arm's-length:* Were sales and other transactions consummated at arm's-length, or do the figures represent certain undisclosed "discounts," "gifts," or "kickbacks"?
2. *Exclude all improper transactions:* Do the figures include transactions that are improper from the viewpoint of generally accepted accounting principles, e.g., "puffing" sales or the cost balance to make things look better, or valuing fixed assets at market value?
3. *Include all proper transactions:* Do the figures represent a complete account of all proper transactions—have all sales been recorded, have all receipts been deposited, and so forth?
4. *Contingent liabilities:* Has the firm honestly disclosed contingent liabilities arising out of past or present transactions, such as pending lawsuits, warranties and guarantees, tax liability arising out of differences between income reported for tax versus financial purposes?
5. *Evidence:* Can the integrity of the financial data be substantiated by independent means?
   (a) By direct physical examination?
   (b) Or by examining the system of documents and records?
6. *Price-levels:* Do the financial statements imply real increases in sales

and earnings on the basis of stable or constant dollars in the presence of a changing purchasing power—without some effort to alert the users to the significance of constant versus current dollar reporting?

II. **Presentation:** Are the financial statements in good form and do they communicate with clarity to the average user?

A. *Rules:* Are the various rules and regulations relating to presentation being followed?

   1. *Classification:* Are items in the right place, such as extraordinary gains and loss that should appear in the income statement rather than in the statement of retained earnings?

   2. *APB:* Are disclosure rules of APB *Opinions* being followed, such as "fully diluted" earnings per share?

   3. *Other rules, regulations, and practices:* Are other rules, regulations, and practices with respect to form and presentation being followed?

B. *Continuity:* Do the financial statements reveal any major known changes that may influence realization expectations, such as:

   1. *Nature of operations:* A major switch from one line of business to another?

   2. *Scope of operations:* A major change in the size of operations, such as doubling capacity?

   3. *Key personnel:* Has the top salesman resigned, taking his top customers with him?

     While the case may be made that management ought to attempt a prediction as to the consequences of major changes on future financial earnings and position, the auditor's responsibility is limited to seeing that the statements do not imply continuity when major change is already committed. A disclosure of the change is sufficient for the auditor's purposes, while he may encourage the client to go further.

C. *Disclosure:* Is there sufficient disclosure?

   1. *Materiality:* Of all facts and figures of a material nature?

   2. *Estimation:* Of the rules and degree of estimation used in arriving at certain figures?

   3. *Communication:* Of an understandable and unequivocal nature so that the financial statements, and especially their footnotes, communicate with clarity with respect to "the average user"?

D. *Descriptive of Reality:* Do the financial statements in their form and presentation reflect the reality of what the business is all about as:

   1. *Economic entity:* An economic entity that has production, buying, and selling cycles?

   2. *Major segments:* Are the major economic segments (industries, markets, domestic versus foreign) of the business identified with suf-

ficient clarity to enable the average user to make discriminative judgments about the scope and nature of business operations?

The audit process culminates in the auditor's report [23]. The *short-form report* or *unqualified opinion* is used customarily in connection with financial statements in which fair presentation and conformance are present. The text of the short-form report has been standardized and follows the format in Exhibit 44.

EXHIBIT 44
The standard short-form report.

We have examined the balance sheet of X Company as of December 31, 19—, and the related statements of income and retained earnings and changes in financial position for year then ended. Our examination was made in accordance with generally accepted auditing standards, and accordingly included such tests of the accounting records and such other auditing procedures as we considered necessary in the circumstances.

In our opinion, the aforementioned financial statements present fairly the financial position of X Company at December 31, 19—, and the results of its operations and the changes in its financial position for the year then ended, in conformity with generally accepted accounting principles applied on a basis consistent with that of the preceding year.

The short-form report consists of a representation as to the work performed in an opening, or *scope*, paragraph, while the auditor's conclusions appear in the closing, or *opinion*, paragraph. Note the reference in the scope paragraph to generally accepted auditing standards. These standards are given in Exhibit 45.

These auditing standards are of a general nature and refer to matters of competence, integrity, and independence. The standards are supported by specific policy statements which aim at the work of the auditor, and are called *Statements on Auditing Procedure* (SAPs). The current statements in the SAP series (numbers 33–54) have been consolidated and incorporated into one policy document called the *Statement on Auditing Standards No. 1: Codification of Auditing Standards and Procedures* [24]. Presumably, forthcoming auditing policy will appear as Statements on Auditing Standards No. 2, No. 3, etc.

Until 1972 the responsibility for auditing standards has rested with the Committee on Auditing Procedure of the AICPA. This committee began its work in 1939 under the chairmanship of Samuel J. Broad. Following the general reorganization of the staff of the AICPA in 1972, auditing policy has become the function of the Auditing Standards Executive Committee, under the chair-

EXHIBIT 45
Generally accepted auditing standards.

General standards

1. The examination is to be performed by a person or persons having adequate technical training and proficiency as an auditor.
2. In all matters relating to the assignment, an independence in mental attitude is to be maintained by the auditor or auditors.
3. Due professional care is to be exercised in the performance of the examination and the preparation of the report.

Standards of field work

1. The work is to be adequately planned and assistants, if any, are to be properly supervised.
2. There is to be a proper study and evaluation of the existing internal control as a basis for reliance thereon and for the determination of the resultant extent of the tests to which auditing procedures are to be restricted.
3. Sufficient competent evidential matter is to be obtained through inspection, observation, inquiries and confirmations to afford a reasonable basis for an opinion regarding the financial statements under examination.

Standards of reporting

1. The report shall state whether the financial statements are presented in accordance with generally accepted principles of accounting.
2. The report shall state whether such principles have been consistently observed in the current period in relation to the preceding period.
3. Informative disclosures in the financial statements are to be regarded as reasonably adequate unless otherwise stated in the report.
4. The report shall either contain an expression of opinion regarding the financial statements, taken as a whole, or an assertion to the effect that an opinion cannot be expressed. When an overall opinion cannot be expressed, the reasons therefor should be stated. In all cases where an auditor's name is associated with financial statements, the report should contain a clear-cut indication of the character of the auditor's examination, if any, and the degree of responsibility he is taking.

manship of Ernest L. Hicks. The objective of the committee is succinct and to the point, i.e., "to continue the development of auditing and reporting standards [25]."

In addition to policy statements, the AICPA furnishes broad–based support, including an updated list of guides and technical publications.

FINANCIAL ACCOUNTING STANDARDS BOARD

While the AICPA retains authority for auditing standards, the forum for setting accounting standards shifted in 1973 to a newly created organization known as the Financial Accounting Standards Board (FASB). Accordingly, the Accounting Principles Board completed its work in 1973.

The impetus for this historic transition in accounting policy began in March 1971, when Marshall Armstrong, as President of the AICPA, appointed a seven–man group "to study the establishment of accounting principles and to make recommendations for improving the process [26]." Francis M. Wheat, a Los Angeles attorney and former Commissioner with the SEC (1964–1969), chaired the study group. The appointment of the study group was made at a time of mounting criticism of the work of the Accounting Principles Board and with a keen awareness of the need to extend participation in accounting policy to interest groups other than certified public accountants [27].

The study group rendered its report in March 1972 [28]. It bore the title *Establishing Financial Accounting Standards* but is referred to informally as the *Wheat Report*, after its chairman. The principal recommendation of the Report was to create an independent organization for setting accounting standards to be known as the Financial Accounting Foundation. Its organization structure appears in Exhibit 46.

The Financial Accounting Foundation is governed by nine trustees who serve without pay. One of them is the president of the AICPA, ex officio, and the other eight are selected by the Institute's Board of Directors—four certified public accountants in public practice, two financial executives, one financial analyst, and one accounting educator. Selection in the last three categories is done on the basis of lists submitted by organizations in the fields represented. The primary duties of the Foundation's trustees are these [29]:

1. To appoint the members of the Financial Accounting Standards Board.
2. To select the members of the Financial Accounting Advisory Council.
3. To arrange for financing the new structure.
4. To approve the annual budget of the Financial Accounting Standards Board.
5. To review periodically the basic structure of the standard–setting function.

EXHIBIT 46
Organization structure of the Financial Accounting Foundation.

NOTE: Four of nine trustees are to be appointed from lists of nominees submitted, respectively, by the Financial Executives Institute, National Association of Accountants, Financial Analysts Federation, and American Accounting Association.
SOURCE: *Report of the Study on Establishment of Accounting Principles, Establishing Financial Accounting Standards* (New York: American Institute of Certified Public Accountants, March 1972), p. 103.

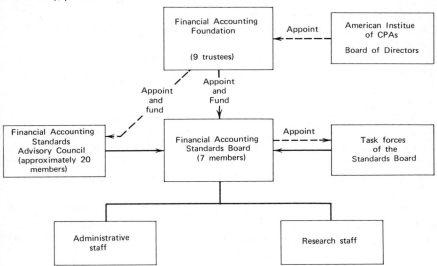

The first trustees of the Financial Accounting Foundation are given in Exhibit 47.

The Financial Accounting Standards Board consists of seven full-time members who are independent of other responsibilities. Four members of the Board are to be certified public accountants drawn from public practice, while the remaining three members need not be CPAs but must have extensive experience in financial reporting matters.

The Board is responsible for issuing accounting standards and interpretations of those standards. In conducting its work the Board acts independently of the Foundation. The Board's *Rules of Procedures* are designed "to encourage the participation of all groups and to create effective channels for the communication of all points of view. Every effort will be made to keep the public

EXHIBIT 47
First Financial Accounting Foundation Board of
Trustees.

John C. Biegler, senior partner of Price Waterhouse & Co.
Ivan O. Bull, managing partner of McGladrey, Hansen, Dunn & Co.
Samuel A. Derieux, partner of Derieux & Watson
James Don Edwards, Distinguished Professor of Accounting, University of
    Georgia
William H. Franklin, Chairman of the Board of Caterpillar Tractor Co.
Ralph E. Kent, senior partner of Arthur Young & Company
LeRoy Layton, senior partner of Main Lafrentz & Co.
Thomas A. Murphy, Vice-Chairman of the Board of General Motors Cor-
    poration
Thomas C. Pryor, Senior Vice-President and Chairman of the Investment
    Policy Committee of White Weld & Co., Inc.

fully informed about the Board's activities. Pronouncements usually will be preceded by thorough research, by public hearings addressed to the substance of a question as well as possible alternative solutions, and by broad public exposure of proposed statements [30]."

The first members of the Financial Accounting Standards Board are listed in Exhibit 48 [31].

Under the FASB rules of procedure, the work of the Board is assigned to task forces who are responsible for refining the definition of a problem and its financial accounting and reporting issues, defining the nature and extent of the

EXHIBIT 48
First members of the Financial Accounting
Standards Board.

Marshall S. Armstrong, Chairman, formerly managing partner of George S.
    Oliver & Co., Indianapolis
John W. Queenan, Vice-Chairman, formerly managing partner of Haskins &
    Sells and member of the U.S. Price Commission (1971–1973)
Donald J. Kirk, formerly partner with Price Waterhouse and Co.
Arthur L. Litke, formerly Chief of the Office of Accounting and Finance of
    the Federal Power Commission
Robert E. Mays, formerly Controller of Exxon Corporation
Walter P. Schuetze, formerly partner with Peat, Marwick, Mitchell & Co.
Robert T. Sprouse, formerly professor of Accounting, Stanford University,
    and President of the American Accounting Association, 1972–1973

research to be performed, and preparing discussion memoranda. A discussion memorandum will include alternative solutions and the arguments and implications relevant to each solution as the basis for a public hearing.

Each task force is chaired by a member of the Board, but task force membership usually extends beyond the members of the Board or Advisory Council to include other persons who are aware of the responsibilities of issuers and the needs of users of financial statements, or possess expertise relevant to the subject. The Board began its work with an agenda of seven items—each assigned to a task force under the direction of a member of the Board. The first task force assignments can be found in Exhibit 49 [32].

EXHIBIT 49
First task force assignments of the Financial
Accounting Standards Board.

	Topic	Task force chairman
1.	Accounting for foreign currency translation	Donald J. Kirk
2.	Reporting by diversified companies	Arthur L. Litke
3.	Criteria for determining materiality	John W. Queenan
4.	Accounting for leases by lessees and lessors	Walter P. Schuetze
5.	Accruing for future losses	Walter P. Schuetze
6.	Accounting for research and development, start-up and relocation	Robert T. Sprouse
7.	Broad qualitative standards for financial reporting	Marshall S. Armstrong

Research is designed to play a significant role in the promulgation of standards by the Board, with technical and research personnel assigned to each task force. Coordinating the research efforts of the Board is Ronald J. Patten, Director of Research, who was formerly professor and head of the accounting faculty at Virginia Polytechnic Institute [33].

The Financial Accounting Standards Advisory Council, with about twenty members, serves as a vehicle for contact and communication between the Board and individuals and groups in business and the professional associations. The Council also assists the Board in identifying problems in financial reporting, setting agenda priorities, establishing task forces to work on specific projects, and reacting to proposed financial accounting standards [34].

The new policy structure in accounting incorporates five attributes which distinguish it from its predecessor organizations, as noted in a statement issued by the trustees of the Foundation [35]:

1. It is more broadly based than any former standard–setting body. It represents the financial community as a whole and the points of view of all who contribute to and rely upon such standards.
2. The insulation of the Board from all other organizations gives assurance of its independence both in fact and in appearance. This independence—and its concomitant, objectivity—will confirm the authority of its pronouncements and thus enhance their acceptance.
3. Because of its compact size and its full-time character, the Standards Board is able to devote undivided attention to its tasks and, when necessary, to move expeditiously to resolve urgent problems.
4. Because of its ties with both the accounting profession and the financial community, the Standards Board will command the support essential to effective enforcement of its standards.
5. The existence of the Board will help to retain the standard-setting function in the private sector where it will be responsive to the needs of the public.

As this book went to press, the Board had issued its first statement—on accounting for foreign currency translations—in draft form as the basis for public hearings and circulation for comments among interested parties [36]. The statement proposes to require that companies disclose the methods used in reporting the effect of changes in currency values on their operations.

The accounting profession has placed great faith in the FASB as being an effective policy-making body which preserves the private sector tradition of regulation in this important area of the economy. As a recent issue of the Price Waterhouse & Co. *Review* observes, "what the FASB does in the next few years could spell the difference between progress or decline for the accounting profession [37]."

COST ACCOUNTING STANDARDS BOARD

While efforts are being made to strengthen the private-sector role in setting accounting standards, government agencies also continue to increase their regulation of the profession. Various governmental agencies participate in accounting regulation. Some agencies such as the Federal Communications Commission (FCC) and Civil Aeronautics Board (CAB) permit industries within their jurisdiction to follow generally accepted accounting principles in lieu of establishing separate policy; separate policy does exist, however, for industries which come under the jurisdiction of the Interstate Commerce Commission (ICC) and the Public Utilities Commission (PUC). The Internal Revenue Service (IRS) administers the tax law, with its many ramifications for financial reporting, and the Federal Trade Commission (FTC) has moved into the arena in requiring line of business disclosures in financial reports. We have already discussed the role of the Securities and Exchange Commission.

Government regulation of accounting has been strengthened in recent years by the creation of the *Cost Accounting Standards Board* (CASB). The CASB is the creation of *Public Law 91–379 (84 Stat. 796)* which extends and amends the *Defense Production Act of 1950.* The CASB mandate under the law is "to promulgate uniform cost accounting standards for use in connection with all defense-related negotiated contracts and subcontracts in excess of $100,000 [38]." Further, *Public Law 91–379* requires, "defense contracts and subcontractors as a condition of contracting to disclose in writing their cost accounting principles, including methods of distinguishing direct costs and the basis used for allocating indirect costs, and to agree to a contract price adjustment, with interest, for any increased costs caused the government by a contractor's failure to comply with any promulgated standards or to follow consistently his disclosed practices [39]."

Its by-laws provide that the CASB will be composed of the Comptroller General of the United States and four members appointed by him. The founding and present members of the Board are given in Exhibit 50 [40].

EXHIBIT 50
Founding members of the Cost Accounting Standards Board.

Elmer B. Staats, Ex Officio Chairman, Comptroller General of the United States
Charles A. Dana, Manager of Government Accounting Controls, The Raytheon Company
Robert C. Moot, Assistant Secretary and Controller, Department of Defense
Herman K. Bevis, retired partner, Price Waterhouse & Co.
Robert K. Mautz, partner, Ernst & Ernst and formerly Professor of Accounting, University of Illinois

Unlike the FASB, the members of the CASB serve on a part-time and largely supervisory basis. The work of the committee vests with a full-time professional staff directed by Arthur Schoenhaut, executive secretary [41]. The process followed in setting cost accounting standards is depicted in Exhibit 51.

To date the CASB has issued four standards, a disclosure statement [42], a variety of regulations, definitions, and related items. As an agent of the Congress, the promulgations of the CASB are published in the *Federal Register* and become law. The four standards issued to date are [43]:

EXHIBIT 51
The process in setting cost accounting standards.
SOURCE: David H. Li, "Cost Accounting Standards Board: A Progress Report," *Management Accounting*, June 1973, p. 13.

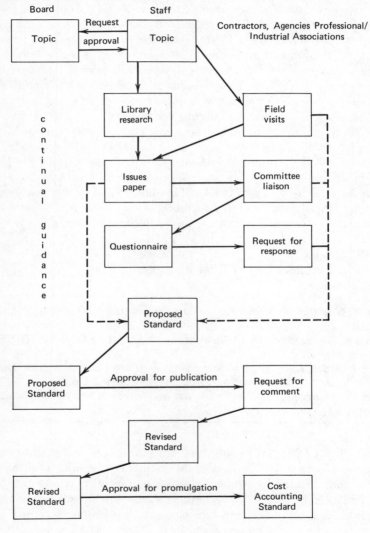

Standard 401:   consistency in estimating, accumulating and reporting costs
Standard 402:   consistency in allocating costs incurred for the same purpose
Standard 403:   allocation of home office expenses to segments
Standard 404:   capitalization of tangible assets

While the CASB's initial authority was limited to defense contracting, David H. Li observes that "the General Services Administration, which has jurisdiction over nondefense contracts entered into by governmental agencies, has incorporated the cost accounting standards into its Federal Procurement Regulations. This voluntary adoption by nondefense agencies renders cost accounting standards applicable to most government contracts and makes the work of the Board that much more important [44]."

The wide labyrinth of federal government contracts, the desire on the part of business to reduce the multiplicity of reports and standards, and the close interplay between cost and financial accounting standards, create the need for close cooperation between the CASB and other federal agencies on the one hand, and with the FASB and other private sector policy groups on the other. Elmer B. Staats has a keen awareness for the delicate environment in which accounting standards are formulated and of the need for continuing articulation among the groups concerned. He noted, in a recent address before the Financial Executives Institute that "coordination with other accounting authorities is perhaps the most topical issue facing the Board [45]." He stressed the need for close cooperation with other federal authorities and then turned his attention to coordination with the FASB in these words [46]:

The Board's coordination with the Financial Accounting Standards Board has, as we all know, been underway only a short time. Increasingly we are being asked: Will these two Boards follow the same paths? Will they be in conflict? Will they issue conflicting standards on the same subject? Should financial accounting, as some believe, provide a point of departure for cost accounting. Or is cost accounting the foundation for financial accounting and reporting?

Marshall Armstrong and I and members of our Boards have had several meetings to discuss areas of mutual interest, and the staffs of the two Boards also have had several meetings. We have every reason to believe that in the future the two Boards will work cooperatively and will coordinate their efforts. If it requires faith on your part to regard the members and the staffs of the two Boards as reasonable men, surely you can assume that both organizations clearly recognize that the public interest would not be served by issuing differing requirements concerning the same subject.

To summarize this point, let me assure you that discussions of the implications on the business community have preceded every decision by our Board. It has tried to encourage actions to reduce to the smallest degree the problem of differing regulations and differing accounting principles for the diverse business community.

THE UNHERALDED POLICY-MAKERS

While we have focused, appropriately, on the role of the principal policy-making bodies, the roots of accounting standards and procedures penetrate the entire fabric of our socioeconomic system. Grass-roots momentum has traditionally had at least as much influence on change as has dictum from above. The investor's desire for more complete and accurate information, the firm's desire to tell its message in its own terms, or the demand of conservationists that business render a better accounting of its use of scarce resources and how they affect the environment—these and many other pressures are the imperatives of policy-making.

Certain interest groups which are affected vitally by accounting standards can now for the first time participate actively in policing the profession. We refer specifically to the Financial Executives Institute, Financial Analysts Federation, National Association of Accountants, and the American Accounting Association. All of these groups have formed liaison committees to work with the FASB, the CASB, or both.

Policing has never been an easy task—for any profession—but accounting has now moved closer to representative and participative rule-making than at any other point in its history.

REFERENCES

1. For some standard definitions of professions see ERNEST GREENWOOD, "Attributes of a Profession," *Social Work*, July 1957, p. 51 and MARIE B. HAUG and MARVIN B. SUSSMAN, "Professional Autonomy and the Revolt of the Client," *Social Problems*, Fall 1969, pp. 153–161. The latter define a profession on page 153 "as an occupation based on a unique scientific body of knowledge, whose practitioners have a service orientation, and autonomy in the performance of their work." MORRIS L. COGAN, "Toward a Definition of Profession," *Harvard Educational Review*, Winter 1953, pp. 33–50, provides this definition:

   A profession is a vocation whose practice is founded upon an understanding of the theoretical structure of some department of learning or science, and upon the abilities attending such understanding. This understanding and these abilities are applied to the vital practical affairs of man. The practices of the profession are modified by knowledge of a generalized nature and by the accumulated wisdom and experience of mankind, which serve to correct the errors of specialism. The profession, serving the vital needs of man, considers its first ethical imperative to be altruistic service to the client.

A definitive work on professions is that of A. M. CARR–SAUNDERS and P. A. WIL-SON, *The Professions* (Oxford: Clarendon Press, 1933); also see HOWARD M. VOLLMER and DONALD L. MILLS, *Professionalization;* and in accounting J. E. STERRETT, "The Profession of Accountancy," *Annals of the American Academy of Political and Social Science,* July–December 1906, pp. 16–27; W. A. PATON, "Earmarks of a Profession and the APB," *Journal of Accountancy,* January 1971, pp. 37–45; and JOHN W. BUCKLEY, *In Search of Identity: An Inquiry into Identity Issues in Accounting* (Palo Alto, Ca.: California Certified Public Accountants Foundation for Education and Research, 1972), pp. 37–50.

2.   Classifications of professions have been attempted by ALEXANDER MORRIS CARR-SAUNDER, "Metropolitan Conditions and Traditional Professional Relationships," in ROBERT M. FISHER, ed., *The Metropolis in Modern Life* (New York: Double-day, 1955), pp. 280–281; by ALBERT J. REISS, JR., "Occupational Mobility of Pro-fessional Workers," *American Sociological Review,* December 1955, pp. 693–700; and HAROLD L. WILENSKY, "The Professionalization of Everyone?," *American Journal of Sociology,* September 1964, pp. 137–158, among others. Thieving is viewed as a profession by EDWIN H. SUTHERLAND, *The Professional Thief* (Chicago: University of Chicago Press, 1937); prostitution by KINGSLEY DAVIS, "Prostitu-tion," in MERTON and R. NISBETT, eds., *Contemporary Social Problems* (New York: Harcourt, Brace & World, 1961); the military by MORRIS JANOWITZ, *The Professional Soldier* (New York: Free Press of Glencoe, 1960); teaching by MYRON LIEBERMAN, *Education as a Profession* (Englewood Cliffs, N.J.: Prentice-Hall, 1956); librarianship by WILLIAM GOODE, "The Librarian: From Occupation to Profession?," *The Library Quarterly,* October 1961, pp. 306–318; business as a profession by F. M. FEIKER, "The Profession of Commerce in the Making," *Annals of the American Academy for Political and Social Science,* May 1922, pp. 203–207, and L. D. BRANDEIS, *Business—A Profession* (Boston: Small, Maynard, 1914); labor by N. FOOTE, "The Professionalization of Labor in Detroit," *Ameri-can Journal of Sociology,* January 1953, pp. 371–380; hospital administration by *Hospital Administration: A Life's Profession* (Chicago: American College of Hospi-tal Administrators, 1948); pharmacy by T. H. McCORMACK, "The Druggists' Di-lemma: Problems of a Marginal Occupation," *American Journal of Sociology,* January 1956, pp. 308–315; and many others. CECIL C. NORTH and PAUL K. HATT, "Jobs and Occupations: A Popular Evaluation," *Opinion News,* September 1, 1947, pp. 3–13, attempt to rank 80 major occupational and professional groups. Also see TALCOTT PARSONS, "The Profession and Social Structure," *Social Forces,* vol. 17, (1939), pp. 457–467, and T. H. MARSHALL "The Recent History of Pro-fessionalism in Relation to Social Structure and Social Policy," *Canadian Journal of Economics and Political Science,* August 1939, pp. 325–340.

3.   Essentially, the Hippocratic oath.

4.   Engineers agreed on "principles of professional conduct" in the 1920's as discussed

in *Annals of the American Academy of Political and Social Science,* May 1922, but these "principles" were not codified until 1947; see "Canons of Ethics for Engineers," *Annals of the American Academy of Political and Social Science,* January 1955, pp. 56–58—but the code lacks muscle due to the lack of organization which is present in engineering. References to other codes of ethics include: A. D. WHITING, "The Professional Organization, Training, and Ethical Codes of Physicians, Dentists, Nurses and Pharmacists," *Annals of the American Academy of Political and Social Science,* May 1922, pp. 51–67; "Code of Ethics for the Teaching Profession," in T. M. STINNETT, *The Teacher and Professional Organizations* (Washington, D.C.: The National Education Association, 1956), pp. 164–166. CHAUNCEY LEAKE, ed., probes the ancient foundations of codes of ethics (as early as 4000 B.C.) in *Percival's Medical Ethics* (Baltimore: William & Wilkins, 1927), pp. 11, 18.

5. *Professional Practices in Management Consulting* (New York: American Association of Consulting Management Engineers, 1959), and *How the Management Consulting Profession Serves Business Enterprise* (New York: American Association of Consulting Management Engineers, 1961), pp. 20–23.

6. It is interesting to note that the first association of lawyers (founded 1739) incorporated the name "gentlemen" in its title: *The Society of Gentlemen Practicers in the Courts of Law and Equity,* referenced by VOLLMER and MILLS, op. cit. (1), p. 155. For reference to these values in the training of accountants see R. K. MAUTZ and JOHN C. MARTIN, *Duties of Junior and Senior Accountants* (New York: American Institute of Accountants, 1953), where this comment appears on page 54:

   A clean hat, neat business suit, harmonizing ties and socks are expected.

   And this comment on page 57:

   As a professional accountant the junior should avoid any appearance of being overly friendly. This does not mean that he must be aloof or unfriendly. A dignified friendliness with the client's staff is desirable. Anything more than this should be avoided.

   And this comment on page 115:

   An important requirement in dealing with the client or his representatives is the exercise of tactfulness, saying or doing what is appropriate without giving offense. Friction should never be allowed to develop. If in the discussion of unpleasant subjects, the client becomes angry or unreasonable, the senior should courteously suggest that the matter be deferred until they both have time to think further about the matter.

7. Bookkeepers are viewed as nonmembers of the profession in *Prospects* (published by The Daily Princetonian, circulated by the American Institute of Certified Public Accountants, as part of its promotional literature, 1969), p. 3 (n.):

Strictly speaking, however, there is a world of difference between the book-keeper who posts the figures in the daily journal and the accountant who sets up the system and organizes these figures into concise statements of what the company owns, owes, and ought to do. *The former is not a professional and his career is emphatically not what this article is concerned with.*

8. JAMES E. SORENSON, "Professional and Bureaucratic Organization in the Public Accounting Firm," *Accounting Review*, July 1967, pp. 553–565.

9. For a history and contemporary discussion of the ethics of public accountants see ALAN R. CERF, *Professional Responsibility of Certified Public Accountants* (Palo Alto, Ca.: California Certified Public Accountants Foundation for Education and Research, 1970). For a summary of the major changes underlying the new code of ethics see *Restatement of the Code of Professional Ethics* (New York: American Institute of Certified Public Accountants, background information provided for the November 15, 1972 referendum). Also, THOMAS G. HIGGINS, "Professional Ethics: A Time for Reappraisal," *Journal of Accountancy*, March 1962, p. 30; DARWIN J. CASLER, *The Evolution of CPA Ethics: A Profile of Professionalization*, occasional paper no. 12, (East Lansing: Graduate School of Business Administration, Michigan State University, 1964), and STEPHEN E. LOEB, "A Survey of Ethical Behavior in the Accounting Profession," *Journal of Accounting Research*, Autumn 1971, pp. 287–306.

10. LOUIS H. RAPPAPORT, *SEC Accounting Practice and Procedure*, 3rd edition (New York: Ronald Press, 1972), p. 26.2.

11. *Journal of Accountancy*, vol. 51, (1947).

12. The definitive work on the SEC is by LOUIS H. RAPPAPORT, op. cit. (10).

13. Ibid., p. 1.21.

14. "Report of the Study on Establishment of Accounting Principles," *Establishing Financial Accounting Standards* (New York: American Institute of Certified Public Accountants, March 1972), p. 48.

15. "Statement of the SEC to the Subcommittee on Commerce and Finance of the Committee on International and Foreign Commerce," House of Representatives, February 19, 1964.

16. See report in the *Journal of Accountancy*, November 1973, p. 3.

17. Regulation S–X can be obtained from, among other sources, Bowne of Los Angeles, Inc., 1706 Maple Avenue, Los Angeles, Ca. 90015.

18. A summary of the Ash Report with respect to its findings on the SEC is provided by LOUIS H. RAPPAPORT, op. cit. (10), pp. 1.20–1.23.

19. A comprehensive history of the development of the accounting profession in the United States is provided by JOHN L. CAREY, *The Rise of the Accounting Profession*, vol. 1,2 (New York: American Institute of Certified Public Accountants, 1970). Chronologies appear in the appendices to both volumes.

20. REED STOREY, *The Search for Accounting Principles* (New York: American Institute of Certified Public Accountants, 1964).

20a. *Accounting Research and Terminology Bulletins* (New York: American Institute of Certified Public Accountants, 1961).

21. See "Report on the Study on Establishment of Accounting Principles," *Establishing Financial Accounting Standards,* (New York: American Institute of Certified Public Accountants, March 1972), pp. 41–42.

22. From JOHN W. BUCKLEY and KEVIN M. LIGHTNER, *Accounting: An Information Systems Approach* (Belmont, Ca.: Dickenson, 1973), pp. 1192–1194.

23. *Statement on Auditing Standards No. 1: Codification of Auditing Standards and Procedures* (New York: American Institute of Certified Public Accountants, 1973), p. 5.

24. Ibid.

25. *Committee Handbook 1972–73* (New York: American Institute of Certified Public Accountants), pp. 123–124.

26. As announced in *The CPA,* February 1971, p. 1.

27. For a view of the pressures that existed in the time period in which the group was appointed see "A Report to Change the Accounting Profession," *Business Week,* March 25, 1972, pp. 86–87. Also see the essence of the comments made by RICHARD T. BAKER, managing partner of Ernst & Ernst, before the 1971 annual convention of the American Accounting Association, as reported in the *New York Times,* August 25, 1971, p. 49. As the *Times* notes, "he urged the establishment of a new single body, including such nonaccountants as economists, securities analysts and other financial analysts to be selected by a committee."

28. "Report on the Study on Establishment of Accounting Principles, *Establishing Financial Accounting Standards* (New York: American Institute of Certified Public Accountants, March, 1972).

29. As noted in *Financial Standards in a Free Society* (Stamford, Conn.: Financial Accounting Foundation, 1972), pp. 7–8.

30. Ibid., pp. 8–9.

31. See "Status Report," *Financial Accounting Standards Board,* June 18, 1973.

32. Ibid., pp. 1, 4.

33. Ibid., p. 3.

34. *Financial Accounting Standards in a Free Society* (Stamford, Conn.: Financial Accounting Foundation, 1972), p. 9.

35. Ibid., pp. 9–10.

36. As reported in the *Wall Street Journal,* December 14, 1973, p. 7.

37. *Review,* Price Waterhouse & Co., vol. 18, no. 1, (1973), p. 30.

38. See *Cost Accounting Standards Guide* (New York: Commerce Clearing House, 1972).

39. Ibid., Foreword.

40. See announcement in *Journal of Accountancy*, March 1971, p. 14.

41. See PAUL R. McCLENON, "Operations of the Cost Accounting Standards Board," *Journal of Accountancy*, April 1973, pp. 58–62.

42. The disclosure statement appears in Commerce Clearing House, *Cost Accounting Standards Guide*, (1972), pp. 51–115. Also, the *Federal Register*, (72–3001 Field 2–28–72, 8:54 AM).

43. As reported in DAVID H. LI, "Cost Accounting Standards Board: A Progress Report," *Management Accounting*, June 1973, pp. 11–15.

44. Ibid., p. 14.

45. ELMER B. STAATS, "The Role of the General Accounting Office and the Cost Accounting Standards Board in the Evolution of Accounting Principles and Standards," (remarks at the International Conference of the Financial Executives Institute, New York, October 22, 1973), p. 4.

46. Ibid., p. 6.

5
THE LIVING PROFESSION

ACCOUNTABLE ACCOUNTING

Abraham Briloff, who wears the cloak of Ralph Nader within the narrower circle of financial reporting, calls periodic attention to the wrongs in accounting. His recent diatribe bears the title *Unaccountable Accounting* [1] and points to the shortcomings in such colorful language as "2 Plus 2 Equals . . . ?," "Alice in GAAP * Land," "Dirty Pooling and Polluted Purchase," "Inflated Bosoms and Big Busts," and "Riding Two Horses with One Backside." Such allure itself commands attention, but even at the substantive level Briloff's criticisms are as well-founded as they are well-documented. His proddings are taken seriously if not willingly by authorities in accounting.

Critics such as Nader and Briloff arise because of perceived inadequacies in social regulation. Briloff's work should be viewed in the context of the turbulent financial environment which developed in the 1960's. Financial practices began to outpace policy and created many opportunities for innovations in accounting procedures which led to unscrupulous conduct on the part of a number of promoters. During this period, for example, such practices as pooling of interests, the use of convertible bonds for acquisition purposes, and new franchising arrangements emerged. These and other practices in a number of cases were used to deceive investors, and accounting policy-makers were seen as being slow to respond to the need for improved regulation. It was in this climate that Briloff found the impetus for his crusade against inadequate accounting standards.

* GAAP is the acronym for "generally accepted accounting princples."

The trouble with Briloff's work, as with many critics, is that it suffers from what David H. Fischer refers to as the "fallacies of factual significance [2]." In particular, two such fallacies afflict the work of Briloff. The first is the *prodigious* fallacy whereby a few monstrous events are selected and assigned an absurd standard of significance when viewed against the sweeping hindsight of history. Says Fischer, "in the genre called popular history, many prodigious fallacies are perpetrated by historians who have mistaken their muse for Miss Dorothy Kilgallen, and their mission for the titillation of illiterate thrill-seekers [3]."

The second is the *furtive* fallacy which posits "that facts of special significance are dark and dirty things and that history itself is a story of causes mostly insidious and results mostly invidious. It begins with the premise that reality is a sordid, secret thing; and that history happens on the back stairs a little after midnight, or else in a smoke-filled room, or a perfumed boudoir, or an executive penthouse or somewhere in the inner sanctum of the Vatican, or the Kremlin, or the Reich Chancellery, or the Pentagon. It is something more, and something other than merely a conspiracy theory, though, that form of causal reduction is a common component. The furtive fallacy is a more profound error, which combines a naive epistemological assumption that things are never what they seem to be, with a firm attachment to the doctrine of original sin [4]."

"He who is deficient in the art of selection," wrote Macaulay, "may, by showing nothing but the truth, produce the effect of the grossest falsehood [5]."

While there is some truth to the observation that "facts, like sinners, gain something from an unsavory reputation [6]," the true history of the accounting profession in this period when weaned of sensationalism, will be revealed as purposive, highly sensitive to its environments, and strongly motivated toward the future. Indeed, we share the view expressed earlier of sociologist Paul Montagna, that accountants, "because of their unique position as auditors and advisers in financial and related areas to major American and world institutions, are destined to plan an increasingly important role in social policy and planning [7]." Accounting is a living profession! It has accommodated to our changing times with greater perception and activation than many of our contemporary institutions.

FORCES OF CHANGE

This is a turbulent period along all dimensions. Most of our institutions, including the most venerable ones, are being called into question. New social structures will emerge from this milieu, and the values that mark this era will undoubtedly differ from those which preceded it. The role of accounting in society will be redefined one way or the other.

A realignment, in fact, has been under way for some time, but the changes are so subtle that we can read the signals and monitor the course only by taking a macroview and analyzing long-term trends. The alignment is largely de facto. No grand policy statement or planning document has emerged to mark the path of accounting in a changing world. But by assembling the scattered evidence we can begin to construct the mosaic of the accounting profession reborn to the present age.

It would be a profound error to view the thrust in accounting as something which does or should emanate from the top. As Lerner observes, "the great dramas of societal transition occur through individuals involved in solving their personal problems and living their private lives [8]." In this, as in other periods in the development of the profession, real progress hails not so much from the generals but from the infantry in practice and education who continually wage war against the tideforces of convention. Indeed, the giant steps of mankind are marked not by power groups or supermen but by pedestrian feet!

These closing pages diagnose briefly the syndrome of adaptation in accounting and invite you to take part in shaping and improving the profession. For this period is pregnant with meaning to the profession. It looms as a pivotal era in the long history of accounting. As accountants we are privileged to be part of a strategic change process which is at least as significant as the emergence of record-keeping in the fifth millenium BC, double-entry in the early Renaissance, or corporate financial reporting and cost accounting as spin-offs of the Industrial Revolution over the past century.

The imperatives for accounting have never been clearer. As a society and world community we face the necessity for conserving scarce resources, protecting the natural environment within which we live and breathe, waging war against social injustice and inequity, and improving the quality of life for people everywhere. Against these needs the profit motive becomes servant to the more primitive instinct of survival. Great moments are born by the confluence of needs and the willingness and ability to respond. The needs are apparent and the profession is willing and able to respond.

IMPROVING FINANCIAL REPORTS

We noted at the outset that the accounting function in the final analysis is an arbiter of wealth and power—determining who gets rich or poor. This is true because the data contained in financial reports dictates the flow of capital toward efficient enterprises. While there is a constant effort to improve financial reports we stand on the threshold of major developments in this area.

At one level the accountant's preoccupation with historical data is yielding to a concern for the future. This change in focus is seen most clearly in the growing resolve to include forecast data in financial reports. The United Kingdom has already taken this step [9]. In the United States, the SEC announced on February 2, 1973 that it planned to relax its prohibition against earnings forecasts in published financial statements. In making the announcement the SEC noted that forecast data was being distributed on a selective basis and that publication would result in a more equitable distribution of this type of information. The announcement followed public hearings on the subject which were held between November 20 and December 12, 1972 [10]. Douglas Carmichael has surveyed attitudes on forecast information in financial statements and reports that while "little sentiment exists for requiring the publications of forecasts," there is support for a voluntary approach [11]. In a talk before the New York State Bar Association, January 27, 1972, William J. Casey, as chairman of the SEC, noted that the "securities markets are essentially markets for discounted future incomes and that investors are future oriented [12]." Obviously the forces of change are moving in favor of forecasts in financial reports.

Change beckons in other areas of financial reporting which have long eluded measurement. Current value reporting is one such area. Fifty years have slipped by since Henry W. Sweeney and later Joel Dean brought attention to the distortions which result from ignoring the impact of price-level changes (inflation and recession) on earnings and financial position [13]. In 1969 the Accounting Principles Board issued its Statement No. 3 entitled *Financial Statements Restated for General Price–Level Changes* [14], which recommended that price-level statements be issued as supplements to the regular financial reports. But even the achievement of price-level adjustments is but a bus stop on the road to the more elusive objective of reporting financial affairs on the basis of current values [15]. The distinction between the two is that the former excludes price appreciation and other factors which impact on values beyond changes in the general purchasing power.

For the first time in history, we have reached the point where a majority of the working population in the United States and other advanced countries is delivering services rather than producing goods, thereby creating an economic condition which has been characterized widely as the post-industrial society [16]. With respect to the future development of this type of society, Toffler notes [17]:

We can thus sketch the dim outlines of the super-industrial economy . . . Agriculture and the manufacture of goods will have become economic backwaters, employing fewer people . . . The service sector, as defined today, will be vastly enlarged, and once more the design of psychological rewards will occupy a growing percentage of corporate time, energy and money.

Human inventory is critical in service industries, and accountants have been foremost in attempts to measure and report on the effective utilization of persons within work organizations. From these efforts has emerged the specialty of human resources accounting [18]. Exhibit 52 refers to the financial statements of R.G. Barry Corporation, which has established the practice of reporting on its utilization of human resources.

Years may pass before human resources accounting is an integral part of financial statements. But many of the ingredients in financial reports which we now take for granted had such humble beginnings. A few firms appear willing to give more information than is required—to venture beyond the requirements of disclosure. As the utility of the new information is proven, more firms subscribe to the procedure. Ultimately the demand for such information is strong enough to prompt action by regulatory bodies.

At a more basic level, the objectives of financial reporting have been the subject of extensive deliberation by a select study group operating under the aegis of the AICPA. In fact, this study group was set in motion in March 1971 as a parallel effort to the "Wheat group" on establishing financial accounting standards. The latter effort, as noted in Chapter 4, resulted in the creation of the Financial Accounting Standards Board. The study group on the objectives of financial statements under the chairmanship of Robert Trueblood rendered its findings on October 1973 [19]. The *Trueblood Report* will not have the immediate impact of the *Wheat Report* but its effects will be felt over the long term.

The report recognizes that the basic objective of financial reporting is "to provide information useful for making economic decisions [and that it] applies within a broad economic environment." "An economy," the study notes, "is organized to strive for efficient allocation of resources. This allocation is affected by government action and by private actions in the marketplace, or some combination of the two. Both kinds of actions involve economic decisions and require financial information [20]."

The supporting objectives of financial statements, according to the report, include the following [21]:

1. to serve primarily those users who have limited authority, ability or resources to obtain information and who rely on financial statements as their principal source of information about an enterprise's economic activities.
2. to provide information useful to investors and creditors for predicting, comparing, and evaluating potential cash flows to them in terms of amount, timing, and related uncertainty.
3. to provide users with information for predicting, comparing, and evaluating enterprise earning power.
4. to supply information useful in judging management's ability to utilize enterprise resources effectively in achieving the primary enterprise goal (of in-

EXHIBIT 52
R. G. Barry Corporation: financial and human
resource accounting.
SOURCE: From the 1969 *Annual Report* of R. G. Barry Corporation.

	1969 *financial and* *human resource*	*1969* *financial* *only*
BALANCE SHEET		
Assets		
Total current assets	$10,003,628	$10,003,628
Net property, plant and equipment	1,770,717	1,770,717
Excess of purchase price of subsidiaries over net assets acquired	1,188,704	1,188,704
Net investments in human resources	986,094	—
Other assets	106,783	106,783
	$14,055,926	$13,069,832
Liabilities and stockholders' equity		
Total current liabilities	$ 5,715,708	$ 5,715,708
Long term debt, excluding current installments	1,935,500	1,935,500
Deferred compensation	62,380	62,380
Deferred federal income taxes as a result of appropriation for human resources	493,047	—
Stockholders' equity		
Capital stock	879,116	879,116
Additional capital in excess of par	1,736,253	1,736,253
Retained earnings		
Financial	2,740,875	2,740,875
Appropriation for human resources	493,047	—
Total stockholders' equity	5,849,291	5,356,244
	$14,055,926	$13,069,832
STATEMENT OF INCOME		
Net sales	$25,310,588	$25,310,588
Cost of sales	16,275,876	16,275,876
Gross profit	9,034,712	9,034,712
Selling, general and administrative exp.	6,737,313	6,737,313
Operating income	2,297,399	2,297,399
Other deductions, net	953,177	953,177
Income before federal income taxes	1,344,222	1,344,222
Human resource expenses applicable to future periods	173,569	—
Adjusted income before federal income taxes	1,517,791	1,344,222
Federal income taxes	730,785	644,000
Net income	$ 787,006	$ 700,222

creasing its monetary wealth over time to maximize the amount of cash flow to its owners).

5. to provide factual and interpretive information about transactions and other events which is useful for predicting, comparing, and evaluating enterprise earning power. Basic underlying assumptions with respect to matters subject to interpretation, evaluation, prediction, or estimation should be disclosed.

6. to provide information useful for the predictive process. Financial forecasts should be provided when they will enhance the reliability of users' predictions.

7. With respect to governmental and not-for-profit organizations—"to provide information useful for evaluating the effectiveness of the management of resources in achieving the organization's goals. Performance measures should be quantified in terms of identified goals [22].

8. to report on those activities of the enterprise affecting society which can be determined and described or measured and which are important to the role of the enterprise in its social environment.

In reaching these objectives the report stated a strong preference for a professional as opposed to political process, i.e., continued active involvement by the private sector in establishing accounting policy. A number of the conclusions if not premises of the *Trueblood Report* would have been heresy to many accountants a few years ago but they are now received with general acclamation. Yes, accountants are continuing to make progress in the never-ending process of improving the institutions of financial reporting.

SOCIAL ACCOUNTING AND RESPONSIBILITY

The accountant's involvement in social measurement relates to the basic drive toward improving financial reporting, but is also indicative of a growing desire to raise the profession to a new level of social consciousness. Not only is the accountant anxious to apply his models and technology toward the solution of pressing social problems, but a personality change is occurring in favor of greater external perception—of a willingness on the part of accountants individually and collectively to ride and influence the currents in the social mainstream.

A recent publication by Ralph W. Estes, *Accounting and Society* [23], is a microcosm of the broader phenomenon of the socialized accountant. Its contents report on such activities as accounting aid societies; the role of accountants in the renaissance of our cities; improving the efficiency of our criminal justice systems; the accountant's participation in environmental management; and his or her role in labor relations, political campaigns, and divorce litigation. One item propositions "Accountants: The Arts Need You," while another shows "How Accountants Can Fight Organized Crime [23]." And this book is

EXHIBIT 53

The incidence in reporting on corporate social responsibilities in a selected sample of fifty-five major U.S. corporations in the period 1960–1970.

Source: Sidney L. Jones, "Reporting Corporate Social Responsibility Activities," in a paper presented at the Financial Management Association's National Convention, October 8, 1971.

	1960	1961	1962	1963	1964	1965	1966	1967	1968	1969	1970
Financial statement entries											
Financial statement entries											
Contingent liabilities involving social responsibilities										1	7
Qualitative references											
Special section devoted to social issues							1	1	2	6	14
Pollution control—air		2	2	3	2	11	18	24	21	35	39
Pollution control—water		2	1	3	3	8	16	17	15	32	31
Pollution control—noise									1	3	3
Pollution control—visual (billboards, plant, office)											
Internal organization for social responsibility						1	2	2	6	4	19
Community involvement—civic	5	5	5	4	1	1	1	1	2	1	7
Community involvement—aid to disadvantaged						6	5	6	14	12	16
Community involvement—urban development	1				1	1	1	1	5	9	6
Employee—education and training programs	12	8	9	18	12	14	16	3	8	12	9
Employee—fair employment practices		1	3	6	7	7	6	20	16	12	10
Employee—disadvantaged worker hiring			1	1			1	9	20	8	17
Safety	10	13	15	12	13	17	15	10	26	26	21
Support of education and basic research	15	11	11	9	15	13	15	16	17	13	19
Support of arts	1	1				5		15	15	13	15
Institutional advertising	2	1	1	2	3	2	4	1	1	1	2
Political	2	1		1	1	3	1	4	3	2	2
Education for disadvantaged				1	1			1	1	1	6
Charities	3	2	4	1	2	5	5	3	5	6	8
International	2	1	1	1		1	1	4	7	8	8
Recycling of materials								2	1	2	3
Use of company facilities for recreation										2	3
Total	53	48	53	62	61	95	108	140	186	209	264

but one volume in the growing library on social accounting [24].

The U.S. business firm, voluntarily and through compulsion, is exhibiting a greater responsiveness to the need for social reporting. Professor Sidney Jones has examined the annual reports of fifty-five major corporations from *Fortune's* list of 500, over the ten-year period 1960–1970, and tabulated the growing number of comments on corporate social responsibility (Exhibit 53). Abt Associates Inc. have devised examples of what income statements (Exhibit 54) and balance sheets (Exhibit 55) might look like within a comprehensive schema of social financial reporting. Their format extends the audience for financial statements beyond the investor to include employees (the staff), the community, and the general public.

Social reporting will be accompanied by social auditing, and the foundation for the latter is being laid now within the profession and on the part of a variety of other interest groups, including the Ralph Nader organization [25]. Underlying all of the activities in this important area is the need for better measures, particularly those which distinguish between positive and negative social action [26].

The need for better measures is urgent. Not only are qualitative factors virtually absent in existing measures, but the quantitative ones which do exist often measure the wrong thing. Thus, for example, vast sums are spent on curing disease but little on preventing it. Law enforcement budgets rise in proportion to the crime rate—a correlative which raises questions as to which way the cause and effect flows [27]. Federal programs involving billions of dollars are started, limp along, or are abruptly canceled without solid indication at any point as to their effectiveness. The need for better measures is as crucial to the executive suite as it is to the government bureau. Business enterprises still are unable to assess with accuracy the benefits of advertising or research and development, not to mention such esoteric areas as goodwill or contribution to social welfare. Even such primitive needs as the gauging of clerical and administrative efficiency await solution [28].

The confluence of social reporting and improved measurement will result in macromodels of accounting which will raise the accountant's perspective above the immediate client situation to an appreciation for the systemic world in which one firm's activities are seen to impinge on those of others in the industry, and that industry with other industries, and so forth to interaction among national accounts [29]. Kenneth S. Most gives us a glimpse into the world of macro-accounting in Exhibit 56 [30].

From humble beginnings, the accounting function has progressed from accounts of men to those of nations, and soon to resource flows within societies and among nations.

EXHIBIT 54
Abt Associates Inc. social income statements, year
ended December 31, 1971, with comparative
figures for 1970.
SOURCE: Abt Associates Inc., Annual Report and Social Audit,
1971.

	1971	1970
Social benefits and costs to staff		
Social benefits to staff		
Health insurance, life insurance, sick leave $	93,492	$ 67,271
Career advancement (note a)	345,886	173,988
Company school and tuition reimbursement	6,896	—
Vacation, holidays, recreation	207,565	163,994
Food services, child care, parking	57,722	41,292
Quality of life (space and its quality)	61,002	70,551
Total benefits to staff	772,563	517,096
Social costs to staff		
Layoffs and involuntary terminations (note b)	9,560	7,560
Overtime worked but not paid (note c)	645,000	474,000
Inequality of opportunity (note d)	—	3,600
Total costs to staff	663,560	485,160
Net social income to staff $	109,003	$ 31,936
Social benefits and costs to community		
Social benefits to community		
Local taxes paid (note e) $	38,952	$ 31,091
Environmental improvements	10,100	8,367
Local tax worth of net jobs created	20,480	15,750
Total benefits to community	69,532	55,208

(continued on page 135)

FUTURISM

The dynamics of change are guided by a sense of the future and, accordingly, the rapid changes within the accounting profession in recent years have been accompanied by a growing interest in futurism. The future can be approached conceptually in one of two ways: teleologically or ontologically. The teleological view conforms with such notions as manifest destiny, fatalism, or predestination, which would hold that the accounting function is being guided and shaped by forces essentially beyond its control. By contrast, Robert U. Ayres

	1971	*1970*
Social costs to community		
Local taxes consumed in services (note e)	55,700	34,400
	$ 13,832	$ 20,808
Social benefits and costs to general public		
Social benefits to general public		
Federal taxes (notes e and f)	$ 165,800	$ —
State taxes paid (notes e and f)	55,500	9,830
Contributions to knowledge (publications, etc.)	14,100	8,300
Federal and state tax worth of net jobs created	69,800	34,800
Total benefits to public	305,200	52,930
Social costs to general public		
Federal services consumed (notes e and f)	83,000	77,000
State services consumed (notes e and f)	31,100	23,500
Total costs to public	114,100	100,500
Net social income (cost) to general public	$ 191,100	$ (47,570)
Net social income (cost) to staff, community and public	$ 313,935	$ 4,174
Social benefits and costs to clients		
Social benefits to clients		
Added value to previous contracts to clients (note g)	$22,337,500	$12,870,000
Social costs to clients		
Contract revenues as opportunity costs (note h)	4,572,459	3,254,541
Net social income to clients	$17,765,041	$ 9,615,459

notes that the "ontological view is that invention and innovation are visible manifestations of a self-generating process or an institution having a dynamism and life of its own [31]." The latter view looks primarily to intrinsic motivators as the determinants of change. Probably the truth lies between these extremes such that external and intrinsic forces combine to make institutions more compatible with their environments. The compromise position is most descriptive of the way in which the accounting profession appears to relate to the future.

John L. Carey's book *The CPA Plans for the Future* [32] ranks among the first formal efforts in accounting to part the veil and peer curiously into years

EXHIBIT 55
Abt Associates Inc. social balance sheet, year
ended December 31, 1971, with comparative
figures for 1970.
SOURCE: Abt Associates Inc., Annual Report and Social Audit,
1971.

	1971	1970
Social assets available		
Staff		
Available within 1 year (note i)	$2,594,390	$ 2,312,000
Available after 1 year (note j)	6,368,511	5,821,608
Training investment (note k)	507,405	305,889
	9,470,306	8,439,497
Less accumulated training obsolescence (note k)	136,995	60,523
Total staff assets	9,333,311	8,378,974
Organization		
Social capital investment (note l)	1,398,230	1,272,201
Retained earnings	219,136	—
Land	285,376	293,358
Building at cost	334,321	350,188
Equipment at cost	43,018	17,102
Total organization assets	2,280,081	1,932,849
Research		
Proposals (note m)	26,878	15,090
Child care research	6,629	—
Social audit	12,979	—
Total research	46,486	15,090
Public services consumed net of tax payments (note e)	152,847	243,399
Total social assets available	$11,812,725	$10,570,312

(continued on page 137)

ahead. As the study was published in 1965 it is possible for us to look back from our position in the 1970's and note that Carey's perspective into the future was right in more instances than it was wrong. A bolder effort at futurism was made in California in 1970 when Arthur M. Sargent gathered together some seers in accounting and asked them for a scenario of public accounting in 1980 [33].

Emboldened by these efforts, Professor Charles T. Horngren has extended

	1971	1970
Social commitments, obligations, and equity		
Staff		
Committed to contracts within 1 year (note n)	$ 43,263	$ 81,296
Committed to contracts after 1 year (note o)	114,660	215,459
Committed to administration within 1 year (note n)	62,598	56,915
Committed to administration after 1 year (note o)	165,903	150,842
Total staff commitments	386,424	504,512
Organization		
Working capital requirements (note p)	60,000	58,500
Financial deficit	—	26,814
Facilities and equipment committed to contracts and administration (note n)	37,734	36,729
Total organization commitments	97,734	122,043
Environmental		
Government outlays for public services consumed, net of tax payment (note e)	152,847	243,399
Pollution from paper production (note q)	1,770	770
Pollution from electric power production (note r)	2,200	1,080
Pollution from automobile commuting (note s)	10,493	4,333
Total environmental obligations	167,310	249,582
Total commitments and obligations	651,468	876,137
Society's equity		
Contributed by staff (note t)	8,946,887	7,874,462
Contributed by stockholders (note u)	2,182,347	1,810,800
Generated by operations (note v)	32,023	8,907
Total equity	11,161,257	9,694,175
Total commitments, obligations, and equity	$11,812,725	$10,570,312

the horizon even further—to 1999, in fact [34]. He foresees that accounting occupations will become more attractive with much of the drudgery handled by computers and by paraprofessionals who do not expect to be promoted without further education. In education, he predicts that accounting will become a first class citizen in the university, attracting students of superior quality. "Of special satisfaction to me," he notes, "is the thought that our status is higher

EXHIBIT 56

A system of social accounts within a
macroframework of accounting.
SOURCE: Kenneth S. Most, "Another Look at Socio-Economic
Accounting," *The Accountant,* December 30, 1971.

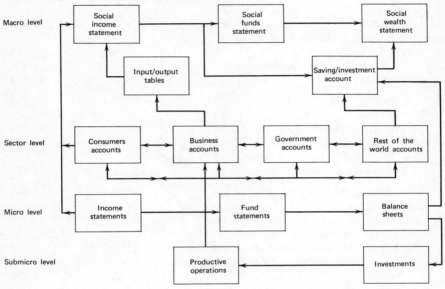

because we responded positively to the demands to broaden our scope and ele-
vate our rigor. We removed the insular walls that would have eventually
trapped us in oblivion. At no time was accounting more essential and exciting
than it is today [35]."

The cornerstones of the future are hewn from appreciation and self-image.
Appreciation is not casual sensations, but disciplined perception and judgment,
as we have noted already. Self-image, in turn, is the most influential factor in
determining how we appreciate and respond to the changing world about us
[36].

From these points of departure, accountants will embrace existing methodologies which deal with the future in formal ways and contribute to the development of new ones. These methodologies range from traditional forecasting to
more sophisticated techniques such as Delphi, scenario formulation, systems
dynamics, morphological analysis and synectics [37].

Briefly, Delphi employs a formal procedure for arriving at a concensus
among a panel of experts [38]. A scenario consists of a hypothetical sequence of
events which lead to an envisioned outcome. Herman Kahn is the leading ex-

EXHIBIT 57

A morphology for establishing accounting standards.

NOTE: Combinatorially there are $5^3 \times 3^2 \times 4^2 = 18{,}000$ possible schema for establishing accounting standards.

Parameters	States of the world for each parameter				
	1	2	3	4	5
A. Principal beneficiary	Government/public sector	Investors/analysts	Capital/credit markets	Management	Accountants
B. Climate	Laissez-faire	Uniformity	Circumstantial variables	—	—
C. Rationale	Inductive theoretic (empirical)	Deductive theoretic	Pragmatic	Authoritarian	Plebiscite (poll)
D. Where authority vests	Private—accounting profession	Private—consortium	Public (government)	Quasi-public	—
E. Primary objective	Conformity	Curb abuses	Power	Authority	Abstract-theoretic
F. Sociological rationale	Public—protection	Public service	Private rights	Profession's welfare	—
G. Impetus	Internal	Regulatory	Societal	—	—

EXHIBIT 58

A morphology for establishing the objectives of financial reporting.

NOTE: Combinatorially there are $5^2 \times 3^3 \times 4^5 = 692,600$ ways in which to look at the objectives of financial reporting.

Parameter	States of the world for each parameter				
	1	2	3	4	5
A. Principal beneficiary (user)	Government/ public sector	Investors/ analysts	Capital/ credit markets	Management	Accountants
B. Proprietorship	Issuer	Attestor	Regulator	—	—
C. Scope (cumulative)	Tangible economic	Intangible economic	Noneconomic	Societal	Global
D. Value basis	Money	Real	Current	Psychic	—
E. Primary time frame	Past	Present	Future	—	—
F. Communication level	Novice	Working knowledge	Expert	—	—
G. Timing	Periodic	Continuous	Impromptu	When accessed	—
H. Medium	Formal— hard copy	Formal— soft	Informal	On-line	—
I. Validity	Surveyed	Reviewed	Confirmed	Guaranteed	—
J. Payee	Investors/ analysts	Government	Client	Client assocation	—

ponent of this approach, and a number of his studies have enjoyed wide publicity [39].

Systems dynamics, the brain child of Jay W. Forrester, uses the power of the computer to analyze what Ashley refers to as "richly joined subsystems [40]." While Forrester's conclusions have been criticized because of his doomsday projection of trends based on the limitations of current technology, systems dynamics as a technique has proved to be highly useful [41].

Morphological analysis attempts to list and enumerate combinatorially an exclusive and total set of solutions to a given problem. A morphology for establishing accounting policy, for example, is illustrated in Exhbit 57, while Exhibit 58 illustrates the morphology of the objects of financial reporting [42].

Synectics is a "creative problem-solving technique" which uses analytic group discussions and brainstorming sessions to force, monitor, and replicate the unique solutions which often emerge from communal decision processes [43].

These and many other methods will be integral to accounting in the years ahead. To probe the future, accountants will join hands with futurists, management scientists, computer experts, and many other specialists.

COPING WITH CHANGE

Expanding horizons in accounting create problems as well as opportunities. The true mark of a living profession is measured not solely by its ability to seize opportunities but also by its willingness to assess its strengths and weaknesses in a spirit of objectivity and complete candor. A living profession is catalytic of change but also demonstrates an ability to listen and learn. When convinced that it is right it will press forward and accept risks; but it also knows when to back-track gracefully when it is shown to be wrong.

There are five areas in which the profession's ability to cope with change has been tested with the greatest severity: (*a*) the legal environment, (*b*) technological change (especially the computer), (*c*) obsolescence, or the need to continue to learn, (*d*) equality of opportunity, and (*e*) organizational adaptation.

Coping with the Legal Environment

The courts have taught the profession some harsh lessons [44]. While many legal actions brought against public accountants lack merit, some have proved to be beneficial to the profession over the long term, even though the medication was intolerable at the point of administration. More importantly, while some spokesmen call for the retrenchment of accounting practices in order to avoid exposure to litigation, the majority viewpoint supports continued progress and expansion. The prevailing mood among CPAs is to push forward with the work of the profession, to defend strongly against litigation, to be less willing to settle out of court to avoid adverse publicity, and to change accounting and auditing practices to conform to meritorious standards and procedures which sometimes emerge from these legal cases.

The McKessons & Robbins case in 1938 was among the first major lawsuits against a CPA in the United States. By the time the case had run its course the president of McKesson & Robbins had committed suicide [45], the auditing firm of Price Waterhouse & Co. had settled out of court in the amount of $522,402 [46] and two new procedures in auditing became standardized: the physical observation of inventories and the confirmation of receivables [47].

Other cases have established precedent in other areas. In its 1972 decision on *Rhode Island Hospital Trust National Bank v. Swartz* [48], the U.S. Court of Appeal held that AICPA rules constitute minimum standards for the profession. *National Surety Corp. v. Lybrand* [49] defined the auditor's responsibility to uncover fraud in cases where the auditor's negligence is involved. In *1136 Tenants' Corp. v. Max Rothenberg & Co.* [50], the so-called "robot case," the accountants were held liable in matters involving undiscovered fraud even though they were engaged only in "write-up" work and did not audit or attest to the financial statements of the client.

Ultramares v. Touche [51] established that public accountants are liable to third parties for deceit but cannot be liable to unidentified third parties for negligence. *Escott v. Barchris Construction Corporation* [52] and *SEC v. Texas Gulf Sulphur Co.* [53] have helped to shape the principle of materiality in terms of the effects of nondisclosure on the average prudent investor and the market price of the security respectively. In *United States v. Benjamin* [54], criminal liability was assessed where grossly misleading statements were found to exist. The court rejected the AICPA position which held that accountants can be held liable only for failure to adhere to generally accepted accounting principles as determined by *expert* witnesses. The court ruled that lay jurors are in a position to evaluate the liability of accountants (and, presumably, other professionals). Judge Friendly's observations on this case are worth noting [55]:

> In our complex society the accountant's certificate and the lawyer's opinion can be instruments for inflicting pecuniary loss more potent than the chisel or the crowbar. Of course, Congress did not mean that any mistake of law or misstatement of fact should subject an attorney or an accountant to criminal liability simply because more skillful practitioners would not have made them. But Congress equally could not have intended that men holding themselves out as members of these ancient professions should be able to escape criminal liability on a plea of ignorance when they shut their eyes to what was plainly to be seen or have represented a knowledge they knew they did not possess.

The recent case of *Equity Funding* [56], which featured computerized fraud involving millions of dollars of phony insurance policies and went undetected by the auditors over a time period of several years, may well direct the profession toward more definitive auditing procedures as applied to computerized management information systems [57]. While litigation is never pleasant—and there is no intention here of making it appear glamorous—the profession has been able to cope and even benefit from its interactions with the legal environment.

Coping with Technological Change

Keeping abreast of technological change has posed serious problems for the profession at several points in its development. Computed technology in particular is impacting strongly on accounting education and practice. Accountants were slow to recognize the potential if not the threat of the computer [58]. But the hiatus is over! Education is incorporating the tools of modern technology, as are most CPA firms, in rendering tax, auditing, and management services. For example, not content with auditing around or through the computer, CPA firms now audit *with* the computer [59]. The trade deficit in computer skills may well have shifted to a net export balance in the early 1970's. The accounting profession is coping with technological change.

Coping with Obsolescence

Accountants are caught up in the vortex of the knowledge explosion which Alvin Toffler and others have portrayed so vividly [60]. The half-life in accounting knowledge today is around five years. This high rate of potential obsolescence necessitates a heavy emphasis on educational renewal.

In *Training by Objectives* [61], George Odiorne emphasizes that continuing education is the major agent of change in organizations. Accordingly, most major CPA firms have extensive professional development programs ranging vertically from junior staff to senior partners (Exhibit 59), and horizontally across a variety of different fields of specialization. Both large and small CPA firms participate actively in the extensive continuing education programs offered by the AICPA and many of the state societies. Continuing education for accountants is also provided by the American Management Association, National Association of Accountants, American Accounting Association, and National Industrial Conference Board. among others [62].

Colleges and universities are assuming a greater share of the mounting burden of continuing education and offer selected courses and seminars in addition to degree programs geared to the fully employed [63].

EXHIBIT 59
The professional development program of a major
CPA firm.
SOURCE: *Modern Auditing: The Arthur Young Approach* (New York: Arthur Young & Co., 1973), p. 17.

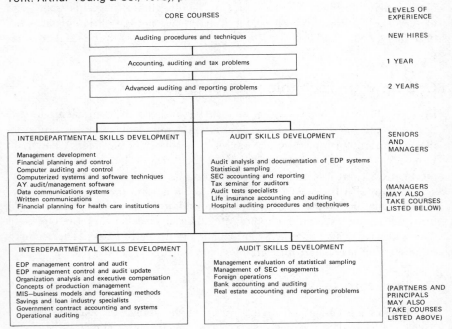

CORE COURSES

LEVELS OF EXPERIENCE

Auditing procedures and techniques	NEW HIRES
Accounting, auditing and tax problems	1 YEAR
Advanced auditing and reporting problems	2 YEARS

INTERDEPARTMENTAL SKILLS DEVELOPMENT	AUDIT SKILLS DEVELOPMENT	SENIORS AND MANAGERS
Management development Financial planning and control Computer auditing and control Computerized systems and software techniques AY audit/management software Data communications systems Written communications Financial planning for health care institutions	Audit analysis and documentation of EDP systems Statistical sampling SEC accounting and reporting Tax seminar for auditors Audit tests specialists Life insurance accounting and auditing Hospital auditing procedures and techniques	(MANAGERS MAY ALSO TAKE COURSES LISTED BELOW)

INTERDEPARTMENTAL SKILLS DEVELOPMENT	AUDIT SKILLS DEVELOPMENT	
EDP management control and audit EDP management control and audit update Organization analysis and executive compensation Concepts of production management MIS—business models and forecasting methods Savings and loan industry specialists Government contract accounting and systems Operational auditing	Management evaluation of statistical sampling Management of SEC engagements Foreign operations Bank accounting and auditing Real estate accounting and reporting problems	(PARTNERS AND PRINCIPALS MAY ALSO TAKE COURSES LISTED ABOVE)

The accounting profession was among the first to institute a requirement of continuing education. This requirement springs from the *Beamer Report* of 1969 [64], which led in turn to the following resolution by the Council of the AICPA in the same year [65]:

WHEREAS, the explosion of knowledge and the increasing complexity of practice make it essential that certified public accountants continue to develop their competence, and

WHEREAS, the public interest requires that certified public accountants provide competent service in all areas of their practice, and

WHEREAS, formal programs of continuing education provide certified public accountants with the opportunity to maintain and improve their competence

THEREFORE BE IT RESOLVED that the Council of the American Institute of Certified Public Accountants urges each of the several states to institute a requirement, by legislation or regulation as may be appropriate, that certified public accountants demonstrate that they are continuing their professional education as a condition precedent to the reregistration, renewal of permit to practice, or other validation of a CPA's designation.

FURTHER BE IT RESOLVED that the National Association of State Boards of Accountancy be asked to consider this resolution with a view to lending its support.

FURTHER BE IT RESOLVED that in the interest of uniformity the Council urges each of the several states to adopt the guidelines attached to the report of the committee on continuing education.

The uniform guidelines referred to in the last paragraph are contained in Exhibit 60. Compulsory continuing education is now law in eight states (Alabama, California, Iowa, Kansas, Nebraska, North Dakota, South Dakota, and Washington), while legislation is pending in seven other states (Arizona, Colorado, Florida, Hawaii, Nevada, Oregon, and Wyoming). In time, the requirement will extend to all jurisdictions of the United States.

In the important area of coping with obsolescence the accounting profession is leading the way in requiring continuing education as a condition for the renewal of license. This action recognizes that education is a life-long process and that formal education should address the need of learning to learn in addition to imparting skills which have immediate application.

Coping with the Demands
for Equality of Opportunity

Minorities are underrepresented in all professions, including accounting. Mitchell observed that in 1969 there were only 136 black CPAs among a population of over 100,000, of whom 108 were employed by CPA firms (only one black was in the top echelon of a CPA firm) [66].

The profession is taking strenuous action to improve its image in this quarter. CPA firms are donating advisory services to minority businesses; offering part-time employment, internships and other incentives; giving financial aid to educational programs for the minorities; sponsoring conferences and workshops; and taking policy steps which will effectuate equal opportunity [67].

In part, the payoff to these efforts is reflected in the statistical data in Exhibit 9, which shows very significant growth rates for minorities in accounting over the past decade.

The minorities are also helping themselves, and have assumed a new posture of aggressiveness. The American Woman's Society of Certified Public Accountants (AWSCPA) was formed in 1933, and the American Society of Women

EXHIBIT 60
Guidelines recommended in the Resolution on
Continuing Education for adoption by states.
SOURCE: Elmer G. Beamer, "Continuing Education—A Profes-
sional Requirement," *Journal of Accountancy,* January 1972,
p. 36.

I. **Basic requirement**
   A. In the 3-year period immediately preceding reregistration, the
      applicant must have completed 120 hours or 15 days of ac-
      ceptable continuing education (a 1-day program should be
      considered to equal 8 hours).
      1. Measurement is in full hours only (a 50-minute period
         equals 1 hour).
      2. Only class hours or the equivalent (and not hours devoted
         to preparation) are counted.
      3. Service as lecturer or discussion leader will be included to
         the extent that it contributes to his professional compe-
         tence (repetitious presentations should not be counted).
   B. The effective date of the requirement should be 3 years after
      its adoption. With respect to any individual, the regulation
      should become effective on the effective date of the require-
      ment or 3 years after his initial registration, whichever is later.
   C. The board of accountancy should have authority to make ex-
      ceptions for reasons of health, military service, foreign resi-
      dency, retirement, etc.

II. **Programs which qualify**
   A. The overriding consideration in determining whether a specific
      program qualifies is that it should be a "formal program of
      learning which contributes directly to the professional compe-
      tence of an individual after he has been licensed to practice
      public accounting."
   B. Formal programs requiring class attendance should qualify
      only if:
      1. An outline is prepared in advance and preserved.
      2. The program is at least 1 hour (50-minute periods) in
         length.

II. Programs which qualify

       3. The program is conducted by a qualified instructor.

       4. A record of registration or attendance is maintained.

C. The following are deemed to qualify provided the above are met:

    1. Professional development programs of the AICPA and the state societies.

    2. Technical sessions at meetings of AICPA, state societies and chapters.

    3. University or college courses.

       (a) Credit courses—each *semester hour* credit shall equal 15 hours toward the requirement. A *quarter hour* credit shall equal 10 hours.

       (b) Noncredit short courses.

    4. Formal organized in-firm educational programs.

    5. Programs in other organizations (accounting, industrial, professional, etc.).

D. Formal correspondence or other individual study programs which require registration and provide evidence of satisfactory completion will qualify with the amount of credit to be determined by the board of accountancy.

E. The state board of accountancy should look to the state society for assistance in interpreting the acceptability of and credit to be allowed for individual courses. The American Institute of CPAs offers its assistance, on request of state boards or state societies, in making these evaluations.

III. Controls and reporting

A. The candidate should provide a signed statement of the continuing education in which he has participated showing:

1. Sponsoring organization.

2. Location of course.

3. Title and/or description of content.

4. Dates attended.

5. Hours claimed.

Accountants in 1938.* In recent years, however, they have stepped up their efforts on behalf of opportunities for women in accounting, and particularly with respect to recruiting. Gayle Rayburn has completed a recent survey of the work experience of women in accounting and arrived at these findings [68]:

1. That most women remain in accounting careers because they find the work interesting and challenging. The nature of the work experience is a much greater inducement to women than salary, prestige or similar factors.

2. That 62.5% of women with full-time employment in accounting in 1970 earned over $12,000 and 8% earned over $25,000.

3. That 46% of women with full-time employment in accounting were married, as opposed to 40% who were single, 9% who were divorced or separated, and 5% who were widows. 36% were mothers.

4. That "even though prejudice against women still appears to exist, the opportunities today are much greater than ever before. Sex is no longer the main consideration; ability and the personality to inspire confidence and respect are most important. If a woman today has mastery of the profession, she may find opportunities not available to the man."

Turning to black accountants, a small group of them met in 1970 in New York City and formed the National Association of Black Accountants (NABA). Among its first activities was a survey intended to sample the quality of working life for black accountants in the employ of major CPA firms. Their survey notes that "blacks began entering public accounting in meaningful numbers in 1969 with the hope that the recruiters' pronouncements of equal opportunity would come to fruition." It noted that the work experience and satisfaction levels of the first wave of recruits would be critical in terms of positive feedback to the college campus. The survey found that "61% of the respondents report good to outstanding work experience." The report concludes with the positive note that "the public accounting profession has among its number, some of the most brilliant minds in the world. They successfully assist clients daily in their efforts to solve business problems. With this kind of talent in its midst there is no reason why the public accounting profession cannot use such energies to provide leadership in the quest for equal opportunity in the business community and indeed in the nation [69]."

Clearly progress is being made in the fight against inequality of opportunity in the accounting profession.

Coping with Organization Change

We pause to consider how the large public accounting firm is coping with the need for organizational change. James E. Sorenson notes that "the growth of

* See Appendix A.

EXHIBIT 61
A decentralized, matrix type of organization for
auditing in a major CPA firm.

SOURCE: *Modern Auditing: The Arthur Young Approach* (New York: Arthur Young & Co., 1973), p. 11.

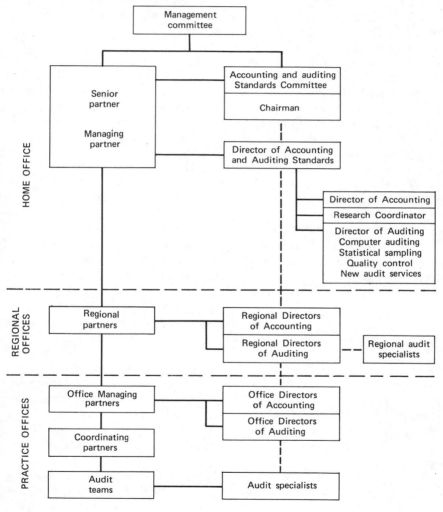

the public accounting profession has been characterized by phenomenal changes in organization structure . . . Large public accounting firms appear to be unique since no other currently known profession has been able to develop professionally through the widespread use of nationally or regionally organized firms [70]." Joseph J. Lengermann describes the traditional large CPA firm as being hierarchical in its organizational structure [71], and according to Emery and Trist [72], viable organizations of this type will modify to matrix-form organizations when they encounter turbulent * environments. CPA firms today indeed operate in a turbulent environment and organizational changes are crucial to the continued development of the profession.

A matrix type of organization differs from an hierarchical one primarily in terms of the flow of authority: the former is typified by decentralization. Teamwork is crucial to matrix organizations and persons may often have to report to a number of superiors. Some matrix organizations distinguish between programmatic and resource organization structures, so that individuals may belong to a resource unit which may be called upon to perform in one or more programmatic areas.

A recent publication indicates the emergence of a matrix organization by one major public accounting firm (Exhibit 61), which we believe to be indicative of the general trend among major CPA firms. The prominent features of the new organization structures in public accounting are the greater reliance on staff specialists, teamwork and the integration of services.

These changes at the level of the firm, when added to such major restructuring as seen in the newly formed Financial Accounting Foundation and the reorganization of the AICPA, indicate clearly that the profession is coping with the need for organizational change.

EPILOGUE

We have introduced you to one of the most vital institutions of our times. Our objective has been to increase your awareness of what the accounting profession is, what it does, and where it is headed. The profession has come a long way since its debut in the ancient civilizations of the world. Throughout its long history, the profession has shown a unique capacity to adapt to changing conditions. In the current period of turbulence it is demonstrating this capacity again.

The accounting function is more than a set of tools, and a principal facility of the accountant has been his ability to shed archaic tools and master new ones. Thus, like whitening bones in the desert, the artifacts of accounting are

---

* A turbulent field can be visualized as one in which not only the object (say, an automobile) but the field itself (the road) are in a dynamic state of motion.

strewn along the sands of time: braided string, clay tablets, papyrus scrolls, the abax, calculus, abacus, and counters. Progressively, journals, ledgers, and more recent artifacts are finding their way to the scrap heap in favor of such new tools as on-line and real-time systems.

The concern with history is yielding to a growing ability to understand and cope with the future. The long-established art of accounting is being augmented by an increasingly sophisticated *science* of accounting; a science which insists on inquiring into the meaning of things.

In recent years the profession has come to understand the broad socioeconomic consequence of its actions and has demonstrated a willingness to have others join in the process of formulating policies which will optimize the allocation of scarce resources and reward those who use them with the greatest efficiency.

The final measure of the profession, however, is the quality of its members, for the living profession is made up of people who care deeply about the world in which they live and who strive to make it a better place for everyone. It is a profession which offers unlimited opportunities to those who wish to effect change through positive action.

REFERENCES

1. ABRAHAM J. BRILOFF, *Unaccountable Accounting* (New York: Harper & Row, 1972).

2. DAVID HACKETT FISCHER, *Historians' Fallacies: Toward a Logic of Historical Thought* (New York: Harper Torchbooks, 1970). The treatment of fallacies of factual significance begins on p. 64.

3. Ibid., pp. 71–72.

4. Ibid., p. 74.

5. THOMAS B. MACAULAY, "History," Complete Writings, 20 vols. (Boston, 1900), 11:245, as cited in #2, p. 65.

6. RALPH B. PERRY, *Puritanism and Democracy* (New York, 1944), p. 53, as cited in #2, p. 75.

7. PAUL D. MONTAGNA, "The Public Accounting Profession," *American Behavioral Scientist*, March–April, 1971, p. 489.

8. D. LERNER, *The Passing of Traditional Society*, (Glencoe, Ill.: Free Press, 1958), p. 54. In a similar vein, the preeminent philosopher of the behavioral school, G. Homas, concludes that "if a serious effort is made to construct theories that will explain social phenomena, it turns out that their general propositions are not about the equilibrium of societies but about the behavior of men" in "Bringing Man Back In," *American Sociological Review*, vol. 29, p. 818.

9. See JOHN P. GRENSIDE, "Accountants' Reports on Profit Forecasts in the U.K.," *Journal of Accountancy*, May 1970, pp. 47–53.

10. See RICHARD J. ASHBROOK and D. R. CARMICHAEL, "Reporting on Forecasts: A Survey of Attitudes," *Journal of Accountancy*, August 1973, p. 38.

11. Ibid., p. 46. Also see JOHN C. CORLESS and CORINE T. NORGAARD, "User Responses to CPA Reports on Forecasts," *Technical Research Report 2* (New York: American Institute of Certified Public Accountants, 1973), and JOHN J. CLARK and PIETER ELGERS, "Forecasted Income Statements: An Investor Perspective," *Accounting Review*, October 1973, p. 668.

12. Referenced in *Journal of Accountancy*, March 1972, p. 9.

13. HENRY W. SWEENEY, "German Inflation Accounting," *Journal of Accountancy*, February 1928, pp. 104–116; "How Inflation Affects Balance Sheets," *Accounting Review*, December 1934, pp. 275–299; *Stabilized Accounting* (New York: Harper & Row, 1936); and "Stabilized Depreciation," *Accounting Review*, September 1931, pp. 165–178; and JOEL DEAN, "Measurement of Profits for Executive Decisions," *Accounting Review*, April 1951, pp. 185–196.

14. Published by the American Institute of Certified Public Accountants in 1969. JAMES A. HEINTZ in "Price-Level Restated Financial Statements and Investment Decision Making," *Accounting Review*, October 1973, pp. 679–689 has conducted a laboratory experiment which purports to show that the information value of price-level adjusted data is inconsequential to investment decisions.

15. For an articulate discussion of the need for current values in financial reporting, see HOWARD ROSS, *The Elusive Art of Accounting* (New York: Ronald Press, 1966).

16. ALVIN TOFFLER, *Future Shock* (New York: Random House, 1970), p. 490 attributes the term "post-industrial society" to Daniel Bell. On the same subject see JOHN KENNETH GALBRAITH, *The New Industrial State* (Boston: Houghton-Mifflin, 1958); ELI GINZBERG, et al., *The Pluralistic Economy* (New York: McGraw-Hill, 1966). The fact that more than 50% of the U.S. working population is white collar appears in TOFFLER, op.cit., pp. 14–15. Other countries conforming to this pattern include Japan, Sweden, Britain, Belgium, Canada, and the Netherlands.

17. TOFFLER, op.cit., p. 233.

18. The most extensive discussion of human resources accounting to this point appears in ERIC G. FLAMHOLTZ, *Human Resources Accounting* (Belmont, Ca.: Dickenson, 1974). Also, see JAMES C. HEKIMIAN and CURTIS H. JONES, "Put People on Your Balance Sheet," *Harvard Business Review*, January–February 1967, pp. 105–113.

19. Study Group on the Objectives of Financial Statements, *Objectives of Financial Statements* (New York: American Institute of Certified Public Accountants, October 1973).

20. Ibid., p. 14.

21. The quotations appear in order in #19, pp. 17, 20, 24, 26, 34, 46, 51, 55. A summary of the objectives of financial statements is provided in #19, pp. 61–66.

22. RALPH W. ESTES, *Accounting and Society* (Los Angeles: Melville, 1973).

23. Ibid., pp. 377–383 and 232–238, respectively.

24. See, for example, *Social Measurement* (New York: American Institute of Certified Public Accountants, 1972); A. CHARNES, C. COLANTONI, W. W. COOPER, and K. O. KORTANEK, "Economic Social and Enterprise Accounting and Mathematical Models," *Accounting Review*, January 1972, pp. 85–108; DAVID F. LINOWES, "The Accountant's Enlarged Professional Responsibilities," *Journal of Accountancy*, February 1973, pp. 47–51; and M. E. FRANCIS, "Accounting and Evaluation of Social Programs," *Accounting Review*, April 1973, pp. 245–257.

25. See "First Attempts at a Corporate 'Social Audit,' " *Business Week*, September 23, 1972, pp. 88–92; also RAYMOND A. BAUER and DAN H. FEEN, JR., *The Corporate Social Audit* (New York: Russell Sage Foundation, 1972).

26. RAYMOND A. BAUER, ed., *Social Indicators* (Cambridge, Mass.: MIT Press, 1966); ALBERT D. BIDERMAN, "Social Indicators and Goals," in Ibid., pp. 68–153; KENNETH G. LAND, "On the Definition of Social Indicators," *The American Sociologist*, November 1971, pp. 322–325; ELEANOR B. SHELDON and HOWARD E. FREEMAN, "Notes on Social Indicators: Premises and Potential," *Policy Sciences*, vol. 1 (1970), pp. 97–111; and U.S. Department of Health, Education and Welfare, *Toward a Social Report* (Washington, D.C.: U.S. Government Printing Office, 1969).

27. STANLEY C. ABRAHAM, "A System Dynamics Model of a Criminal Justice System," *AIS Working Paper 72–15* (Los Angeles: UCLA Accounting-Information Systems Research Program, April 1972).

28. A serious effort is being made to improve productivity measures in the federal government: see *Measuring and Enhancing Productivity in the Federal Sector* (Washington, D.C.: U.S. Government Printing Office, June 1972).

29. The appreciative act is as old as homo sapiens, yet formal appreciation is of more recent vintage. See GEOFFREY VICKER, *The Art of Judgment* (New York: Basic Books, 1965); and STANLEY C. ABRAHAM, "Appreciating the Environment of the Graduate School of Management, UCLA" (manuscript, UCLA Graduate School of Management, June 1972). The need for a systemic or holistic viewpoint is articulated forcefully by C. WEST CHURCHMAN, *The Systems Approach* (New York: Dell, 1968).

30. Also, see BERTRAM M. GROSS, "The State of the Nations: Social Systems Accounting," in RAYMOND A. BAUER, ed., op. cit. (26), pp. 154–271; NANCY and RICHARD RUGGLES, "A Proposal for a System of Social Accounts" (New York: National Bureau of Economic Research, 1971); DR SCOTT, *The Cultural Signifi-*

cance of Accounts (New York: Henry Holt, 1931); MICHAEL SPRINGER, "Social Indicators, Reports and Accounts: Toward the Management of Society," *Annals of the American Academy of Political and Social Science,* vol. 338, 1970; and RALPH V. LUCANO, "Relationship Between National and Income Accounting," *Federal Accountant,* March 1962, pp. 14–20.

31. ROBERT U. AYRES, *Technological Forecasting* (New York: McGraw-Hill, 1969), pp. 29–30.

32. JOHN L. CAREY, *The CPA Plans for the Future* (New York: American Institute of Certified Public Accountants, 1965).

33. MAURICE MOONITZ, ed., *Public Accounting 1980* (Palo Alto, Ca.: California Certified Public Accountants Foundation for Education and Research, 1970).

34. CHARLES T. HORNGREN, "The Accounting Discipline in 1999," *Accounting Review,* January 1971, pp. 1–11.

35. Ibid., p. 11.

36. We have reference here to institutional as well as self-image of individuals. For the role of self-image in change processes see KENNETH E. BOULDING, *The Image* (Ann Arbor, Mich.: Ann Arbor Paperbacks, 1961); also, MARTIN BUBER, *I and Thou* (New York: Charles Scribner's Sons, 1958); PAUL PFUETZE, *The Social Self* (New York: Brookman Associates, 1954), and GEORGE HERBERT MEAD, *On Social Psychology* (Chicago: University of Chicago Press, 1964). PHILIP M. PIAKER cautions that change hinges on the fundamental attitudes of accountants in "Acceptance of Change Among Accountants: An Examination of Attitudes Towards Current Controversies," *CPA Journal,* February 1973, pp. 132–138.

37. JOHN MCHALE in "A Survey of Futures Research in the United States," *The Futurist,* December 1970, p. 201, reveals this frequency in the use of different techniques in his sample:

Scenarios	45	Objective trees	2
Delphi	41	Operations research	2
Simulation gaming	29	Survey research	2
Trend extrapolation	19	Casual methods	1
Dynamic modelling	7	Decision matrices	1
Gross impact analysis	5	Growth curves	1
Correlation plotting	4	Interviewing	1
Expert position papers	3	Operational gaming	1
Relevance trees	3	PERT adaptations	1
Analogy	2	Role play gaming	1
Economic projection	2	Speculation (formal)	1
Morphology	2	Values analysis	1

And, from the same survey, the applications which these studies have addressed:

Technological forecasting	41	Long-range planning	2
Socioeconomic forecasting	21	Population growth	2

Economic projections	21	Problem-solving	2
Market analysis	15	Product development	2
Corporate planning studies	10	Public affairs forecasting	2
Organizational studies	7	Resources planning	2
Educational planning	7	Sociotechnical integration	2
Corporate journal publication	6	Biotechnical forecasting	1
Policy research	6	Family psychotherapy	1
Environmental control	5	General systems analysis	1
Research and development	5	Auto-industry projections	1
Urban planning	5	Technological change	1
Holistic futures	5	Leisure, future of	1
Business forecasting	4	Life extension	1
Individual/society	4	Life styles	1
Political forecasting	4	Medical care systems	1
Manpower utilization	3	Personnel research	1
Social problem-solving	3	Psychiatry futures	1
Society, alternative futures	3	Race relations/ethnicity	1
Urban design	3	Regional development	1
Aero system planning	2	Sex education	1
Conference organization	2	Social systems analysis	1
Educational forecasting	2	Social systems forecasting	1
Educational programs	2	State planning	1
Geopolitical forecasting	2	Threat projection	1
Health planning	2		

38. NORMAN DALKEY and OLAF HELMER, "An Experimental Application of the Delphi Method to the Use of Experts," *Management Science*, April 1963; ALAN R. FUSFELD, "The Delphi Technique: Survey and Comment," *Working Paper No. 520–71* (Cambridge, Mass.: Alfred P. Sloan School of Management, March 1971); OLAF HELMER, "The Use of the Delphi Technique in Problems of Educational Innovation," Report P–3499 (Santa Monica, Ca.: Rand Corporation, December 1966); and MURRAY TUROFF, "The Design of a Policy Delphi," *Technological Forecasting and Social Change*, vol. 2 (1970), pp. 149–171.

39. For example, HERMAN KAHN and ANTHONY WIENER, *The Year 2000: A Framework of Speculation on the Next Thirty-Three Years* (New York: Macmillan, 1967); HERMAN KAHN, *On Escalation: Metaphors and Scenarios* (New York: Praeger, 1965); and HERMAN KAHN with B. BRUCE–BRIGGS, "Alternative U.S. Futures— Scenarios and Branch Points," in *Things to Come: Thinking about the 70's and 80's*, by the same authors (New York: Macmillan, 1972).

40. Systems dynamics has been used by Forrester to analyze *Industrial Dynamics* (Cambridge, Mass.: MIT Press, 1961); *Urban Dynamics* (Cambridge, Mass.: MIT Press, 1969); and *World Dynamics* (Cambridge, Mass.: Wright–Allen Press, 1969). ASHBY refers to "richly joined systems" in *Design for a Brain*, 2nd ed. (London:

Chapman & Hall, 1960), and makes the observation on page 205, "in a set of sub-systems . . . richly joined, each variable is as much affected by variables in other subsystems as by those in its own. When this occurs, the division of the whole in subsystems ceases to have any natural basis."

41. ROBERT BOYD in "The Dynamic World Optimist," *Technology Review*, October–November 1972, pp. 50–60, repeated Forrester's *World Dynamic* study above, but substituted assumptions that new technological advances would take place in response to the critical needs in the future. Among other successful applications of systems dynamics in DONELLA MEADOWS, DENNIS MEADOWS, JERGEN RANDERS, and WILLIAM BEHRENS III in *The Limits to Growth* (New York: Universe Books, 1972), and STANLEY C. ABRAHAM, "A Systems Dynamics Model of a Criminal Justice System," *Working Paper 72–15* (Los Angeles: UCLA Accounting-Information Systems Research Program, April 1972).

42. Morphological analysis is the brainchild of FRITZ ZWICKY, *Morphology of Propulsive Power* (Pasadena, Ca.: Society for Morphological Research, 1962). For a morphology of social structures of the future see E. METTLER in W. J. J. GORDON, *Synectics: The Development of Creative Capacity* (New York: Harper & Row, 1961), and ALBERT G. WILSON, ed., *Exercises in Imagining the Future* (Los Angeles: UCLA Extension Courses, Fall 1970).

43. See W. J. J. GORDON, Ibid., and MARVIN DUNNETTE, JOHN CAMPBELL, and KAY JAASTAD, "The Effect of Group Participation on Brainstorming Effectiveness for the Two Industrial Samples," *Journal of Applied Psychology*, vol. 47 (1963), pp. 30–37. Dialectical analysis is a related technique consisting of situation analysis in which two fully developed points of view—the plan and counterplan—are generated and juxtaposed. See RICHARD O. MASON, "A Dialectical Approach to Strategic Planning," *Management Science*, vol. 15; no. 8, April, 1969.

44. A useful guide through the legal environment of accounting is provided by DENZIL Y. CAUSEY, JR., *Duties and Liabilities of the CPA* (Austin, Tx.: Bureau of Business Research, The University of Texas at Austin, 1973). Also, R. M. V. DICKERSON, *Accountants and the Law of Negligence* (Toronto, Canada: The Canadian Institute of Chartered Accountants, 1966); and KENNETH F. BYRD, "Accountancy and the Onslaught of Case Law in North America," *Accountant*, July 8, 1967, pp. 34–41.

45. The principal figure in the case was Philip Musica, a bootlegger, who acquired financial control of McKesson & Robbins under the alias of Frank Donald Coster. See ROBERT SHAPLEN, "Annals of Crime—The Metamorphosis of Philip Musica," *New Yorker*, October 22, 1955 and October 29, 1955; also the accounts in the *New York Times* on December 7 and 9, 1938.

46. The settlement represented the return of auditing fees paid to Price Waterhouse & Co. between 1933 and 1938.

47. In *Statement of Auditing Procedure No. 1: Extensions of Auditing Procedure* (New York: American Institute of Certified Public Accountants, October 1939).

48. 455 F. 2d 847 (4th Cir. 1972).

49. 256 App. Div. 226, 9 N.Y.S. 2d 554 (1939); also, *Smith v. London Assurance Corp.*, 109 App. Div. 882, 96 N.Y.S. 820 (1905).

50. 27 App. Div. 2d 830, 277 N.Y.S. 2d 996 (1967), *aff'd*, 21 N.Y. 2d 995, 290 N.Y.S. 2d 919, 238 N.E. 2d 322 (N.Y. Ct. App. 1968).

51. 255 N.Y. 179, 174 N.E. 441 (1931).

52. 283 F. Supp. 643 (S.D.N.Y. 1968).

53. 401 F. 2d 833 (2d Cir. 1968).

54. 425 F. 2d 796 (2d Cir. 1969), *cert. denied*, 397 U.S. 1006 (1970).

55. 328 F 2d 854, 863 (2d Cir. 1964). The quotation is from CAUSEY, op. cit. (44), p. 113–114.

56. See *CCH Fed. Sec. L. Rep.* 193, 917 (C.D. Cal 1973).

57. For an excellent treatment of the problems which are posed by the security of computer systems, see LANCE J. HOFFMAN, ed., *Security and Privacy in Computer Systems* (Los Angeles: Melville, 1973).

58. There have been numerous dire predictions of the accountant's failure to close the technological gap, including GEOFFREY B. HORWITZ, "EDP Auditing—The Coming of Age," *Journal of Accountancy,* August 1970, pp. 48–56; RICHARD C. REA, "Accountants—A Vanishing Breed," *Ohio CPA,* Spring 1969, pp. 73–79; THOMAS V. MCRAE, "The Decline and Fall of the Accounting Profession," *Accounting Forum,* December 1969, pp. 21–23; and C. V. CROSSMAN, "The Decline and Fall of the Accounting Profession," *Cost and Management,* July–August 1968, pp. 33–34.

59. An excellent summary of what one major CPA firm is doing in bringing modern technology to bear on the audit function is *Modern Auditing: The Arthur Young Approach* (New York: Arthur Young, 1973), and *Computer Auditing in the Seventies* (New York: Arthur Young, 1970). Auditing "around," "through," and "with" the computer is discussed in GORDON B. DAVIS, *Auditing & EDP* (New York: American Institute of Certified Public Accountants, 1968).

60. ALVIN TOFFLER, *Future Shock* (New York: Random House, 1970), pp. 9–18; also, JOHN W. GARDNER, *Self-Renewal* (New York: Harper & Row, 1963); see page 13 where the author advocates that "the ultimate goal of the educational system is to shift to the individual the burden of pursuing his own education."

61. GEORGE S. ODIORNE, *Training by Objectives* (New York: Macmillan, 1970), p. 13.

62. See MILTON F. USRY and GEORGE W. DRULL, JR., "Dimensions of Professional Development," *Journal of Accountancy,* September 1973, pp. 108–110.

63. See JOSEPH O'ROURKE, "The Role of Colleges and Universities in Professional Development," *Journal of Accountancy*, March 1973, pp. 91–93.

64. *Report of the Committee on Education and Experience Requirements for CPAs* (New York: American Institute of Certified Public Accountants, 1969).

65. In ELMER G. BEAMER, "Continuing Education—A Professional Requirement," *Journal of Accountancy*, January 1972), pp. 33–39.

66. BERT N. MITCHELL, "The Black Minority in the CPA Profession," *Journal of Accountancy*, October 1969, pp. 41–48.

67. As reported in *The CPA*, June 1969, p. 15, a resolution of the Council of the AICPA reads:

    1. That a special campaign be undertaken to encourage young men and women of high potential from disadvantaged groups to attend college and major in accounting.
    2. That special efforts be made to provide educational opportunities for young men and women from disadvantaged groups so that they may enter the accounting profession without educational disadvantage.
    3. That such men and women be hired by individuals and firms in order to integrate the accounting profession in fact as well as in ideal.

68. L. GAYLE RAYBURN, "Recruitment of Women Accountants," *Journal of Accountancy*, November 1971, pp. 51–57.

69. WILLIAM AIKEN, *The Black Experience in Large Public Accounting Firms* (New York: National Association of Black Accountants, Fall 1971), pp. 7, 8, 10; also appears in *Journal of Accountancy*, August 1972, pp. 60–63.

70. JAMES E. SORENSON, "Professional and Bureaucratic Organization in the Public Accounting Field," *Accounting Review*, July 1967, p. 553.

71. JOSEPH J. LENGERMANN, "Supposed and Actual Differences in Professional Autonomy Among CPAs as Related to Type of Work Organization and Size of Firm," *Accounting Review*, October 1971, pp. 665–675.

72. F. E. EMERY and E. L. TRIST, "The Causal Texture of Organizational Environments," *Human Relations*, vol. 18 (1965), pp. 21–32; and in F. E. EMERY, ed., *Systems Thinking* (London: Penguin Books, 1969), pp. 241–257. The authors refer to four environmental fields or conditions, i.e., (*a*) placid–randomized, (*b*) placid–clustered, (*c*) disturbed–reactive, and (*d*) turbulent.

APPENDIX

A

ACCOUNTING
ASSOCIATIONS

1. AMERICAN ACCOUNTING ASSOCIATION (AAA)
   653 South Orange Avenue
   Sarasota, Florida 33577
   Founded: 1916
   Purpose: Promotes education and research in accounting.
   The AAA contracts research and provides Ph.D.
   fellowships in accounting.
   Publications: *The Accounting Review*, research monographs
   and special studies
   Membership: 15,000

2. AMERICAN INSTITUTE OF CERTIFIED PUBLIC
   ACCOUNTANTS (AICPA)
   666 Fifth Avenue
   New York, New York 10019
   Founded: (American Association of Public Accountants)
   1887
   Purpose: Promotes professional, technical, and ethical
   standards. Maintains liaison between academic,
   government, business, and the profession
   through divisions such as Management of an Accounting Practice; Management Services; Federal
   Taxation; Professional Ethics; Trial Board; Professional Development Board; Practice Review;
   Relations with Federal Government; Board of

	Examiners; Audit Procedure; Relations with Universities; Relations with State Societies. Maintains a library of 53,000 volumes.
Publications:	*Journal of Accountancy, Management Adviser, The CPA, Tax Adviser,* research studies, books, etc.
Qualifications:	Applicants must have a valid, unrevoked CPA certificate issued by the regulatory body of any state or other U.S. jurisdiction, and must have passed an examination in accounting and related subjects satisfactory to the Board of Directors of the AICPA.
Membership:	88,168

3. AMERICAN SOCIETY OF WOMEN ACCOUNTANTS
   (Affiliate of the AWSCPA)
   327 South LaSalle Street
   Chicago, Illinois 60604

Founded:	1938
Purpose:	Professional society for women accountants.
Publications:	*The Woman CPA*
Membership:	4400

4. AMERICAN WOMAN'S SOCIETY OF CERTIFIED
   PUBLIC ACCOUNTANTS
   327 South LaSalle Street
   Chicago, Illinois 60604

Founded:	1933
Purpose:	Improves women's professional competence and their professional status within the business community. Maintains relevant statistics pertaining to women CPAs.
Publications:	*The Woman CPA, AWSCPA News*
Membership:	1237

5. ASSOCIATION OF WATER TRANSPORTATION
   ACCOUNTING
   P.O. Box 53
   Bowling Green Station
   New York, New York 10004

Founded:	1912
Purpose:	Promotes general systemization and greater uniformity in water transportation accounting sys-

tems and government reports. Committees include Forms and Procedures; ICC; Maritime Administration; Renegotiations; Taxation and Legislation; Uniform System of Accounts; Federal Maritime Commission.

Publications:	Bulletin and the annual report
Membership:	241
Qualifications:	Accountants or financial officers of companies which engage in transportation by water. Associate members include CPAs, bank officers, etc.

6. FEDERAL GOVERNMENT ACCOUNTANTS ASSOCIATION
727 South 23rd Street
Suite 120
Arlington, Virginia 22202

Founded:	1950
Purpose:	Professional society of governmental financial managers.
Publications:	*Federal Accountant, Federal Financial Management Topics, FGAA Year Book*
Membership:	7,600
Qualifications:	Full membership requires six or more years of government experience involving the professional performance of financial management activities in an administrative, supervisory, and/or operational capacity. Associate and affiliate memberships require less stringent qualifications.

7. FEDERATION OF TAX ADMINISTRATORS
1313 East 60th Street
Chicago, Illinois 60637

Founded:	1937
Purpose:	Advances standards and improves methods of tax administration.
Publications:	*Tax Administrator News*, research reports and annual proceedings of the National Association of Tax Administrators, National Tobacco Tax Association, and North American Gasoline Tax Conference.
Membership:	No public members

8. FINANCIAL EXECUTIVES INSTITUTE
    633 Third Avenue
    New York, New York 10017
    Founded: 1931
    Purpose: Professional society for financial and managerial
                      executives.
    Publications: *Financial Executive, FEI Bulletin*, research stud-
                      ies, monographs, books, etc.
    Membership: 8000
    Qualifications: Applicants are sponsored by two Institute
                      members and must meet high standards of per-
                      sonal character. Must be employed in a position
                      which demands the formulation of policies and
                      the administration of the financial function in an
                      enterprise of a size and reputation connotating
                      prestige among business organizations.

9. HOSPITAL FINANCIAL MANAGEMENT
    ASSOCIATION
    840 North Lake Shore Drive
    Chicago, Illinois 60611
    Founded: 1946
    Purpose: Conducts correspondence courses, holds annual
                      institute at the University of Colorado, Boulder,
                      and gives two annual examinations (successful
                      candidates are awarded the rating of *Fellow* or
                      CMPA. Promotes uniformity of accounting pro-
                      cedures and statistical data. Maintains a lending
                      and reference library and a no-fee placement ser-
                      vice.
    Publications: *Hospital Financial Management*, textbooks,
                      compilations, etc. Publications catalog is avail-
                      able on request.

10. INSTITUTE OF INTERNAL AUDITORS, INC.
    5500 Diplomat Circle
    Orlando, Florida 32810
    Founded: 1941
    Purpose: Holds educational seminars, maintains a library
                      of 1000 volumes, conducts research projects and
                      certification program, publishes a variety of items
                      to educate members.

Publications: *Internal Auditor, Auditing News, Members' News Bulletin,* membership directory, a bibliography of internal auditing, research reports, textbooks, workbooks, instructors guides and case histories.

Membership: 9200

Qualifications: Individuals must have direct jurisdiction over internal auditing activities or be actively engaged as internal auditors. For individuals who do not meet the qualifications as a member there are less stringent qualifications for educational, associate, student, or retired classifications.

11. INSTITUTE OF NEWSPAPER CONTROLLERS AND
FINANCE OFFICERS (INCFO)
P.O. Box 68
Fairhaven, New Jersey 07701

Founded: 1947

Purpose: Conducts research on accounting methods and procedures of newspapers. Publishes manuals on newspaper accounting methods and procedures. INCFO is the international press association for financial, accounting, and business management.

Publications: *Newspaper Controller*

Membership: 650

Qualifications: Applicants for active membership must perform or supervise the commonly accepted duties of controllers or finance officers of business entities which are engaged in the publication of newspapers.

12. INTERNATIONAL TAX INSTITUTE, INC.
70 Pine Street
New York, New York 10005

Founded: 1961

Purpose: Holds numerous Public Technical Meetings each year dealing with problems in its field; files statements and appears before Congressional tax committees; supplies its members with information relating to taxation of international operations.

Publications: Reports and bulletins to members, "DISC Tax Guide for Manufacturers," (in process) "Export Tax Guide for Manufacturers," and seven volumes of papers delivered at the Public Technical Meetings.

Membership: 460

Qualifications: Lawyers, public accountants, and executives having knowledge and experience in the field of international taxation.

13.   MUNICIPAL FINANCE OFFICERS ASSOCIATION OF THE U.S. AND CANADA (MFOA)
1313 East 60th Street
Chicago, Illinois 60637

Founded: 1906

Purpose: Provides technical inquiry service and sponsors the National Committee on Governmental Accounting.

Publications: MFOA *News Letter, Governmental Finance,* membership directory, special bulletins and reports on technical problems, and specialized books in the field of public finance.

Membership: 5212

14.   NATIONAL ASSOCIATION OF ACCOUNTANTS
919 Third Avenue
New York, New York 10022

Founded: 1919

Purpose: Conducts research into accounting methods and procedures and the management purposes served. Operates continuing education programs. Maintains a library and offers technical services. Sponsors the Certificate in Management Accounting by examination.

Publications: NAA *Management Accounting,* research reports, accounting practice reports, special publications

Membership: 70,000

Qualifications: Open to those with an interest in management accounting.

15. NATIONAL ASSOCIATION OF BLACK
    ACCOUNTANTS
    P.O. Box 726
    FDR Post Office Station
    New York, New York 10022
    Founded: 1970
    Purpose: Promotes the interest of black accountants in the
                       field of public accounting.
    Publications: Research studies

16. NATIONAL ASSOCIATION OF COUNTY
    TREASURERS AND FINANCE OFFICERS
    % Helen Singleton, County Treasurer
    Hidalgo County
    Edinburg, Texas 78539
    Purpose: Promotes improved, efficient accounting and fi-
                       nancial procedures in the administration of
                       county business.
    Membership: 600

17. NATIONAL ASSOCIATION OF STATE AUDITORS,
    COMPTROLLERS, AND TREASURERS
    % Raymond Hawksley
    State Capital, Room 102
    Providence, Rhode Island 02903
    Founded: 1916
    Purpose: Studies government operations, particularly fi-
                       nancial, tax, and administration.
    Publications: Annual proceedings, directory
    Membership: 160

18. NATIONAL ASSOCIATION OF STATE BOARDS
    OF ACCOUNTANCY
    666 Fifth Avenue
    New York, New York 10019
    Founded: 1908
    Purpose: Promotes the adoption and enforcement of uni-
                       form standards of professional conduct, educa-
                       tional qualifications, and other requirements for
                       licensing public accountants.
    Publications: Monthly newsletter and periodic reports

Qualifications: Service on a state board of accountancy or the AICPA Board of Examiners.

19. NATIONAL ASSOCIATION OF TAX ADMINISTRATORS
1313 East 60th Street
Chicago, Illinois 60637
Purpose: Associated organization of the Federation of Tax Administrators.
Publications: *Revenue Administration*
Qualifications: State and local tax agencies only.

20. NATIONAL COMMITTEE ON GOVERNMENTAL ACCOUNTING
1313 East 60th Street
Room 450
Chicago, Illinois 60637
Founded: 1934
Purpose: Promotes uniformity in accounting and reporting.
Publications: *Governmental Accounting, Auditing, and Financial Reporting*

21. NATIONAL SOCIETY OF ACCOUNTANTS FOR COOPERATIVES
Box 4765 Duke Station
Durham, North Carolina
Founded: 1935
Purpose: United persons performing services for cooperatives and nonprofit associations.
Publications: *Cooperative Accountant*
Membership: 1500

22. NATIONAL SOCIETY OF CONTROLLERS AND FINANCIAL OFFICERS OF SAVINGS INSTITUTIONS
111 East Wacker Drive
Chicago, Illinois 60601
Founded: 1949
Purpose: Provides technical information exchange.
Publications: Monthly newsletter covering topical subjects: technical publications covering broad spectrum

of operational subjects. Circulation to members only.

23. NATIONAL SOCIETY OF PUBLIC ACCOUNTANTS
(NSPA)
1717 Pennsylvania Avenue, NW
Suite 1200
Washington, D.C. 20006
Founded: 1940
Purpose: Operates correspondence courses, advances the positions of public accountants through its committees: Education, Ethics and Grievances, Insurance, National Affairs, Public Relations, State Affairs.
Publications: *National Public Accountant, NSPA Washington Reporter*
Membership: 14,000

24. NATIONAL TAX ASSOCIATION–TAX INSTITUTE
OF AMERICA (NTA–TIA)
21 East State Street
Columbus, Ohio 43215
Founded: 1907
Purpose: Promotes scientific nonpolitical study of taxation, better understanding of the common interests of national, state, and local governments in tax matters, and public finance.
Publications: *National Tax Journal, NTA–TIA Bookshelf,* proceedings of the annual conference
Membership: 2500

25. SOCIETY OF INSURANCE ACCOUNTANTS
14 Ardsley Road
Glen Ridge, New Jersey 07028
Founded: 1960
Purpose: Examines matters of interest to insurance accountants through its committees: Accountants, Auditing, Statistical, Educational, Tax, and Legislative.
Publications: Committee reports of meetings, proceedings of annual conference, triennial newsletter. Circulation to membership only.

Membership: 500
Qualifications: Officers and employees of insurance companies and other organizations affiliated with the insurance field. Associate members include employees of CPA firms, actuarial and legal tax consultants.

26. TAX EXECUTIVES INSTITUTE (TEI)
     425 Thirteenth Street, NW
     Washington, D.C. 20004
     Founded: 1944
     Purpose: Professional society of executive administrators and directors of tax affairs for corporations and other businesses.
     Publications: *TEI News, Tax Executive*
     Membership: 2800
     Qualifications: Membership is restricted to tax executives in business.

B

ACCOUNTING
PERIODICALS

1. *Accounting Forum*

Baruch College School of Business
and Public Administration
The City University of New York
17 Lexington Avenue
New York, New York 10010
Circulation: 1500
Semiannually

2. *Accounting Review*

American Accounting Association
653 South Orange Avenue
Sarasota, Florida 33577
Circulation: 20,000
Quarterly

3. *Arizona Society of Certified
   Public Accountants
   Quarterly*

Arizona Society of Certified Public
   Accountants
3130 North Third Avenue
Phoenix, Arizona 85013
Circulation: 720
Quarterly

4. *Asset—Missouri Society of
   Certified Public
   Accountants*

Missouri Society of Certified Public
   Accountants
1925 Railway Exchange Building
St. Louis, Missouri 63101
Three times a year

5. *California Accountant*

Society of California Accountants
3887 State Street
Santa Barbara, California 93105
Monthly

6. *California CPA Quarterly*

California Society of Certified
    Public Accountants
1000 Welch Road
Palo Alto, California 94304
Circulation: 8900
Quarterly

7. *Certificate*

District of Columbia Institute of
    Certified Public Accountants
710 Pennsylvania Avenue
Washington, D.C. 20004
Monthly

8. *CPA Journal*
    (Formerly *New York*
    CPA)

New York State Society of Certified
    Public Accountants
355 Lexington Avenue
New York, New York 10017
Circulation: 25,000
Monthly

9. *Colorado CPA Report*

Colorado Society of Certified Public
    Accountants
1200 Lincoln Street
#530
Denver, Colorado 80203
Circulation: 2000
Quarterly

10. *Connecticut CPA*

Connecticut Society of Certified
    Public Accountants
179 Allyn Street, Suite 501
Hartford, Connecticut 06103
Circulation: 1800
Quarterly

11. *Cooperative Accountant*

National Society of Accountants for Cooperatives
Box 4765 Duke Station
Durham, North Carolina 27706
Circulation: 1400
Quarterly

12. *Current Asset*

Delaware Society of Certified Public Accountants
1815 Newport Gap Pike
Wilmington, Delaware 19808
Monthly

13. *Empirical Research in Accounting: Selected Studies*

Institute of Professional Accounting
Graduate School of Business
University of Chicago
Chicago, Illinois 60637
Annually

14. *Federal Accountant*

Federal Government Accountants Association
Editorial Office: 1730 M. Street, NW
Washington, D.C. 20036
Circulation: 7000
Quarterly

15. *Financial Executive*

Financial Executives Institute
50 West 44th Street
New York, New York 10036
Circulation: 14,750
Monthly

16. *Florida Certified Public Accountant*

Florida Institute of Certified Public Accountants
P.O. Box 14387
Gainesville, Florida 32601
Circulation: 4000
Semiannually

17. *Footnote*

Minnesota Society of Certified
  Public Accountants
1102 Wesley Temple Building
Minneapolis, Minnesota 55403
Monthly

18. *Georgia CPA*

Georgia Society of Certified Public
  Accountants
1524 William Oliver Building
Atlanta, Georgia 30303
Quarterly

19. *Governmental Finance*

Municipal Finance Officers
  Association of the U.S. and
  Canada
1313 East 60th Street
Chicago, Illinois 60637
Quarterly

20. *Hospital Financial
    Management*

Hospital Financial Management
  Association
840 North Lake Shore Drive, Suite
  605
Chicago, Illinois 60611
Circulation: 10,000
Monthly (except July and August)

21. *Idaho Society of Certified
    Public Accountants
    Bulletin*

Idaho Society of Certified Public
  Accountants
P.O. Box 149
Caldwell, Idaho
Bimonthly

22. *Illinois CPA*

Illinois Society of Certified Public
  Accountants
208 South LaSalle Street
Chicago, Illinois 60604
Circulation: 5600
Quarterly

23. *Internal Auditor*

Institute of Internal Auditors
170 Broadway
New York, New York 10038
Circulation: 9200
Bimonthly

24. *International Journal of*
     Accounting Education
     and Research

Center for Internal Education and
    Research in Accounting
320 Commerce West, Box 109
University of Illinois
Urbana, Illinois 61801
Circulation: 1200
Semiannually

25. *ISCPA Bulletin*

Iowa Society of Certified Public
    Accountants
627 Insurance Exchange Building
Des Moines, Iowa 50309
Bimonthly

26. *Journal of Accountancy*

American Institute of Certified
    Public Accountants
666 Fifth Avenue
New York, New York 10019
Circulation: 132,000
Monthly

27. *Journal of Accounting*
     Research

University of Chicago Graduate
    School of Business
Chicago, Illinois 60637
Circulation: 2500
Semiannually

28. *Journal of Taxation*

Tax Research Group, Inc.
512 North Florida Avenue
Tampa, Florida 33602
Editorial Office: 125 East 56th
    Street
New York, New York 10022
Circulation: 15,600
Monthly

29. *Kentucky Accountant*

Kentucky Society of Certified
   Public Accountants
310 West Liberty
Louisville, Kentucky 40202
Circulation: to membership
Monthly

30. *Louisiana Certified Public
     Accountant*

Society of Louisiana Certified
   Public Accountants
408 Perdido Building
822 Perdido Street
New Orleans, Louisiana 60112
Circulation: 1600
Quarterly

31. *Management Accounting*

National Association of
   Accountants
919 Third Avenue
New York, New York 10022
Circulation: 68,000
Monthly

32. *Management Adviser*

American Institute of Certified
   Public Accountants
666 Fifth Avenue
New York, New York 10019
Circulation: 17,000
Bimonthly

33. *Maryland CPA Quarterly*

Maryland Association of Certified
   Public Accountants
1012 Keyser Building
Baltimore, Maryland 21202
Quarterly

34. *Massachusetts CPA Review*

Massachusetts Society of Certified
   Public Accountants
One Center Plaza
Boston, Massachusetts 02108
Circulation: 3100
Bimonthly

35. *Michigan CPA*

Michigan Association of Certified
   Public Accountants
1311 East Jefferson Avenue
Detroit, Michigan 48207
Circulation: 3300
Bimonthly

36. *Mississippi Certified Public
Accountant*

Mississippi Society of Certified
   Public Accountants
515 First Federal Building
Jackson, Mississippi
Annually

37. *Modern Accountant*

Independent Accountants
   Association of Michigan
304 Hollister Building
Lansing, Michigan 48933
Monthly

38. *Montana CPA*

Montana Society of Certified Public
   Accountants
University of Montana
School of Business Administration
Missoula, Montana 59801
Bimonthly

39. *National Public
Accountant*

National Society of Public
   Accountants
1717 Pennsylvania Avenue, NW
Washington, D.C. 20006
Circulation: 15,500
Monthly

40. *National Tax Journal*

National Tax Association
21 East State Street
Columbus, Ohio 43215
Quarterly

41. *Nebraska CPA*

Nebraska Society of Certified Public
   Accountants
811 Mulder Drive
Lincoln, Nebraska 68510
Semiannually

42. *New Jersey CPA*

New Jersey Society of Certified
    Public Accountants
550 Broad Street
Newark, New Jersey 07102
Circulation: 3000
Quarterly

43. *New Mexico CPA Reporter*

New Mexico Society of Certified
    Public Accountants
Korber Building
Albuquerque, New Mexico
Quarterly

44. *Newspaper Controller*

Institute of Newspaper Controllers
    and Finance Officers
P.O. Box 68
Fairhaven, New Jersey 07701
Monthly

45. *Ohio CPA*

Ohio Society of Certified Public
    Accountants
79 East State Street
Columbus, Ohio 43215
Circulation: 3900
Quarterly

46. *Oklahoma CPA*

Oklahoma Society of Certified
    Public Accountants
265 West Court, Lincoln Office
    Plaza
4545 Lincoln Boulevard
Oklahoma City, Oklahoma 73105
Circulation: 1500
Quarterly

47. *Oregon Certified Public
    Accountant*

Oregon Society of Certified Public
    Accountants
720 Oregon Bank Building
Portland, Oregon 97204
Monthly

48. *Pennsylvania CPA*
    Spokesman

Pennsylvania Institute of Certified
    Public Accountants
1100 Lewis Tower Building
Philadelphia, Pennsylvania 19102
Circulation: 6100
Six times a year

49. *Practical Accountant*

Institute for Continuing
    Professional Development, Inc.
40 West 57th Street
New York, New York 10019
Circulation: 20,000
Bimonthly

50. *Tax Adviser*

American Institute of Certified
    Public Accountants
666 Fifth Avenue
New York, New York 10019
Monthly

51. *Tax Executive*

Tax Executives Institute
1111 E Street, NW
Washington, D.C.
Quarterly

52. *Tax Policy*

Tax Institute of America
457 Nassau Street
Princeton, New Jersey 08540
Circulation: 1150
Monthly

53. *Tax Topics*

National Association of Tax
    Accountants
P.O. Box 38
Colorado Springs, Colorado 80301
Monthly

54. *Taxation for Accountants*

Taxation Research Groups, Ltd.
320 North Sixth Street
Prospect Park, New Jersey 07508
Monthly

55. *Taxes—The Tax Magazine*

Commerce Clearing House, Inc.
4025 West Peterson Avenue
Chicago, Illinois 60646
Circulation: 14,500
Monthly

56. *Tennessee CPA*

Tennessee Society of Certified
    Public Accountants
Room 317 Frost Building
161 Eighth Avenue N.
Nashville, Tennessee 37203
Monthly

57. *Texas Certified Public
    Accountant*

Texas Society of Certified Public
    Accountants
200 Corrigan Tower
Dallas, Texas 75201
Circulation: 7100
Quarterly

58. *Virginia Accountant*

Virginia Society of Certified Public
    Accountants
809 Mutual Building
Richmond, Virginia 23219
Circulation: 2200
Quarterly

59. *Washington CPA*

Washington Society of Certified
    Public Accountants
1114 Northern Life Tower Building
Seattle, Washington 98101
Bimonthly

60. *West Virginia CPA*

West Virginia Society of Certified
    Public Accountants
P.O. Box 1236
Huntington, West Virginia 25714
Quarterly

61. *Wisconsin CPA*

Wisconsin Society of Certified
  Public Accountants
176 West Wisconsin Avenue
Milwaukee, Wisconsin 53202
Circulation: 1650
Quarterly

62. *Woman CPA*

American Woman's Society of
  Certified Public Accountants and
  the American Society of Women
  Accountants
327 South LaSalle Street
Chicago, Illinois 60604
Bimonthly

C

CONCEPTS OF PROFESSIONAL ETHICS AND RULES OF CONDUCT

I. CONCEPTS OF PROFESSIONAL ETHICS *

A distinguishing mark of a professional is his acceptance of responsibility to the public. All true professions have therefore deemed it essential to promulgate codes of ethics and to establish means for ensuring their observance.

The reliance of the public, the government and the business community on sound financial reporting and advice on business affairs, and the importance of these matters to the economic and social aspects of life impose particular obligations on certified public accountants.

Ordinarily those who depend upon a certified public accountant find it difficult to assess the quality of his services; they have a right to expect, however, that he is a person of competence and integrity. A man or woman who enters the profession of accountancy is assumed to accept an obligation to uphold its principles, to work for the increase of knowledge in the art and for the improvement of methods, and to abide by the profession's ethical and technical standards.

The ethical Code of the American Institute emphasizes the profession's responsibility to the public, a responsibility that has grown as the number of investors has grown, as the relationship between corporate managers and stockholders has become more impersonal and as government increasingly relies on accounting information.

* SOURCE: *Codes of Professional Ethics* (New York: American Institute of Certified Public Accountants, March 1, 1973). "Concepts of Professional Ethics" appear on pp. 6–16 and "Rules of Conduct" on pp. 18–25.

181

The Code also stresses the CPA's responsibility to clients and colleagues, since his behavior in these relationships cannot fail to affect the responsibilities of the profession as a whole to the public.

The Institute's Rules of Conduct set forth minimum levels of acceptable conduct and are mandatory and enforceable. However, it is in the best interests of the profession that CPAs strive for conduct beyond that indicated merely by prohibitions. Ethical conduct, in the true sense, is more than merely abiding by the letter of explicit prohibitions. Rather it requires unswerving commitment to honorable behavior, even at the sacrifice of personal advantage.

The conduct toward which CPAs should strive is embodied in five broad concepts stated as affirmative ethical principles:

Independence, Integrity, and Objectivity. A certified public accountant should maintain his integrity and objectivity and, when engaged in the practice of public accounting, be independent of those he serves.

Competence and Technical Standards. A certified public accountant should observe the profession's technical standards and strive continually to improve his competence and the quality of his services.

Responsibilities to Clients. A certified public accountant should be fair and candid with his clients and serve them to the best of his ability, with professional concern for their best interests, consistent with his responsibilities to the public.

Responsibilities to Colleagues. A certified public accountant should conduct himself in a manner which will promote cooperation and good relations among members of the profession.

Other Responsibilities and Practices. A certified public accountant should conduct himself in a manner which will enhance the stature of the profession and its ability to serve the public.

The foregoing ethical principles are intended as broad guide lines as distinguished from enforceable Rules of Conduct. Even though they do not provide a basis for disciplinary action, they constitute the philosophical foundation upon which the Rules of Conduct are based.

The following discussion is intended to elaborate on each of the ethical principles and provide rationale for their support.

Independence, Integrity, and Objectivity. *A certified public accountant should maintain his integrity and objectivity and, when engaged in the practice of public accounting, be independent of those he serves.*

The public expects a number of character traits in a certified public accountant but primarily integrity and objectivity and, in the practice of public accounting, independence.

Independence has always been a concept fundamental to the accounting profession, the cornerstone of its philosophical structure. For no matter how competent any CPA may be, his opinion on financial statements will be of little value to those who rely on him—whether they be clients or any of his unseen audience of credit grantors, investors, governmental agencies and the like—unless he maintains his independence.

Independence has traditionally been defined by the profession as the ability to act with integrity and objectivity.

Integrity is an element of character which is fundamental to reliance on the CPA. This quality may be difficult to judge, however, since a particular fault of omission or commission may be the result either of honest error or a lack of integrity.

Objectivity refers to a CPA's ability to maintain an impartial attitude on all matters which come under his review. Since this attitude involves an individual's mental processes, the evaluation of objectivity must be based largely on actions and relationships viewed in the context of ascertainable circumstances.

While recognizing that the qualities of integrity and objectivity are not precisely measurable, the profession nevertheless constantly holds them up to members as an imperative. This is done essentially by education and by the Rules of Conduct which the profession adopts and enforces.

CPAs cannot practice their calling and participate in the world's affairs without being exposed to situations that involve the possibility of pressures upon their integrity and objectivity. To define and proscribe all such situations would be impracticable. To ignore the problem for that reason, however, and to set no limits at all would be irresponsible.

It follows that the concept of independence should not be interpreted so loosely as to permit relationships likely to impair the CPA's integrity or the impartiality of his judgment, nor so strictly as to inhibit the rendering of useful services when the likelihood of such impairment is relatively remote.

While it may be difficult for a CPA always to appear completely independent even in normal relationships with clients, pressures upon his integrity or objectivity are offset by powerful countervailing forces and restraints. These include the possibility of legal liability, professional discipline ranging up to revocation of the right to practice as a CPA, loss of reputation and, by no means least, the inculcated resitance of a disciplined professional to any infringement upon his basic integrity and objectivity. Accordingly, in deciding which types of relationships should be specifically prohibited, both the magnitude of the threat posed by a relationship and the force of countervailing pressures have to be weighed.

In establishing rules relating to independence, the profession uses the criterion of whether reasonable men, having knowledge of all the facts and taking into consideration normal strength of character and normal behavior under the circumstances, would conclude that a specified relationship between a CPA and a client poses an unacceptable threat to the CPA's integrity or objectivity.

When a CPA expresses an opinion on financial statements, not only the fact but also the appearance of integrity and objectivity is of particular importance. For this reason, the profession has adopted rules to prohibit the expression of such an opinion when relationships exist which might pose such a threat to integrity and objectivity as to exceed the strength of countervailing forces and restraints. These relationships fall into two general categories: (1) certain financial relationships with clients and (2) relationships in which a CPA is virtually part of management or an employee under management's control.

Although the appearance of independence is not required in the case of management advisory services and tax practice, a CPA is encouraged to avoid the proscribed relationships with clients regardless of the type of services being rendered. In any event, the CPA, in all types of engagements, should refuse to subordinate his professional judgment to others and should express his conclusions honestly and objectively.

The financial relationships proscribed when an opinion is expressed on financial statements make no reference to fees paid to a CPA by a client. Remuneration to providers of services is necessary for the continued provision of those services. Indeed, a principal reason for the development and persistence in the professions of the client–practitioner relationship and of remuneration by fee (as contrasted with an employer–employee relationship and remuneration by salary) is that these arrangements are seen as a safeguard of independence.

The above reference to an employer–employee relationship is pertinent to a question sometimes raised as to whether a CPA's objectivity in expressing an opinion on financial statements will be impaired by his being involved with his client in the decision-making process.

CPAs continually provide advice to their clients, and they expect that this advice will usually be followed. Decisions based on such advice may have a significant effect on a client's financial condition or operating results. This is the case not only in tax engagements and management advisory services but in the audit function as well.

If a CPA disagrees with a client on a significant matter during the course of an audit, the client has three choices—he can modify the financial statements (which is usually the case), he can accept a qualified report or he can discharge the CPA. While the ultimate decision and the resulting financial statements clearly are those of the client, the CPA has obviously been a significant factor in the decision-making process. Indeed, no responsible user of financial statements would want it otherwise.

It must be noted that when a CPA expresses an opinion on financial statements, the judgments involved pertain to whether the results of operating decisions of the client are fairly presented in the statements and not on the underlying wisdom of such decisions. It is highly unlikely, therefore, that being a factor in the client's decision-making process would impair the CPA's objectivity in judging the fairness of presentation.

The more important question is whether a CPA would deliberately compromise his integrity by expressing an unqualified opinion on financial statements which were prepared in such a way as to cover up a poor business decision by the client and on which the CPA had rendered advice. The basic character traits of the CPA as well as the risks arising from such a compromise of integrity, including liability to third parties, disciplinary action and loss of right to practice, should preclude such action.

Providing advice or recommendations which may or may not involve skills logically related to a client's information and control system, and which may affect the client's decision-making, does not in itself indicate lack of independence. However, the CPA must be alert to the possibility that undue identification with the management of the client or involvement with a client's affairs to such a degree as to place him virtually in the position of being an employee, may impair the apparance of independence.

To sum up, CPAs cannot avoid external pressures on their integrity and objectivity in the course of their professional work, but they are expected to resist these pressures. They must, in fact, retain their integrity and objectivity in all phases of their practice and, when expressing opinions on financial statements, avoid involvement in situations that would impair the credibility of their independence in the minds of reasonable men familiar with the facts.

Competence and Technical Standards.   *A certified public accountant should observe the profession's technical standards and strive continually to improve his competence and the quality of his services.*

Since accounting information is of great importance to all segments of the public, all CPAs, whether in public practice, government service, private employment or academic pursuits, should perform their work at a high level of professionalism.

A CPA should maintain and seek always to improve his competence in all areas of accountancy in which he engages. Satisfaction of the requirements for the CPA certificate is evidence of basic competence at the time the certificate is granted, but it does not justify an assumption that this competence is maintained without continuing effort. Further, it does not necessarily justify undertaking complex engagements without additional study and experience.

A CPA should not render professional services without being aware of, and complying with, the applicable technical standards. Moreover, since published technical standards can never cover the whole field of accountancy, he must keep broadly informed.

Observance of the rule on competence calls for a subjective determination by a CPA with respect to each engagement. Some engagements will require a higher level of knowledge, skill and judgment than others. Competence to deal with an unfamiliar problem may be acquired by research, study or consultation with a practitioner who has the necessary competence. If a CPA is unable to gain sufficient competence through these means, he should suggest, in fairness to his client and the public, the engagement of someone competent to perform the needed service, either independently or as an associate.

The standards referred to in the rules are elaborated and refined to meet changing conditions, and it is each CPA's responsibility to keep himself up to date in this respect.

Responsibilities to Clients.
A certified public accountant should be fair and candid with his clients and serve them to the best of his ability, with professional concern for their best interests, consistent with his responsibilities to the public.

As a professional person, the CPA should serve his clients with competence and with professional concern for their best interests. He must not permit his regard for a client's interest, however, to override his obligation to the public to maintain his independence, integrity and objectivity. The discharge of this dual responsibility to both clients and the public requires a high degree of ethical perception and conduct.

It is fundamental that the CPA hold in strict confidence all information concerning a client's affairs which he acquires in the course of his engagement. This does not mean, however, that he should acquiesce in a client's unwillingness to make disclosures in financial reports which are necessary to fair presentation.

Exploitation of relations with a client for personal advantage is improper. For example, acceptance of a commission from any vendor for recommending his product or service to a client is prohibited.

A CPA should be frank and straightforward with clients. While tact and diplomacy are desirable, a client should never be left in doubt about the CPA's position on any issue of signicance. No truly professional man will subordinate his own judgment or conceal or modify his honest opinion merely to please. This admonition applies to all services including those related to management and tax problems.

When accepting an engagement, a CPA should bear in mind that he may find it necessary to resign if conflict arises on an important question of principle. In cases of irreconcilable difference, he will have to judge whether the importance of the matter requires such an action. In weighing this question, he can feel assured that the practitioner who is independent, fair, and candid is the better respected for these qualities and will not lack opportunities for constructive service.

Responsibilities to Colleagues.   *A certified public accountant should conduct himself in a manner which will promote cooperation and good relations among members of the profession.*

The support of a profession by its members and their cooperation with one another are essential elements of professional character. The public confidence and respect which a CPA enjoys is largely the result of the cumulative accomplishments of all CPAs, past and present. It is, therefore, in the CPA's own interest, as well as that of the general public, to support the collective efforts of colleagues through professional societies and organizations and to deal with fellow practitioners in a manner which will not detract from their reputation and well-being.

Although the reluctance of a professional to give testimony that may be damaging to a colleague is understandable, the obligation of professional courtesy and fraternal consideration can never excuse lack of complete candor if the CPA is testifying as an expert witness in a judicial proceeding or properly constituted inquiry.

A CPA has the obligation to assist his fellows in complying with the Code of Professional Ethics and should also assist appropriate disciplinary authorities in enforcing the Code. To condone serious fault can be as bad as to commit it. It may be even worse, in fact, since some errors may result from ignorance rather than intent and, if let pass without action, will probably be repeated. In situations of this kind, the welfare of the public should be the guide to a member's action.

While the Code proscribes certain specific actions in the area of relationships with colleagues, it should be understood that these proscriptions do not define the limits of desirable intraprofessional conduct. Rather, such conduct encompasses the professional consideration and courtesies which each CPA would like to have fellow practitioners extend to him.

It is natural that a CPA will seek to develop his practice. However, in doing so he should not seek to displace another accountant in a client relationship, or act in any way that reflects negatively on fellow practitioners.

A CPA may, of course, provide services to those who request it, even though they may be served by another practitioner in another area of service, or he may succeed another practitioner at a client's request. In such circumstances it is desirable before accepting an engagement that the CPA who has been approached should advise the accountant already serving the client. Such action is indicated not only by considerations of professional courtesy but by good business judgment.

A client may sometimes request services requiring highly specialized knowledge. If the CPA lacks the expertise necessary to render such services, he should call upon a fellow practitioner for assistance or refer the entire engagement to another. Such assistance or referral brings to bear on the client's needs both the referring practitioner's knowledge of the client's affairs and the technical expertise of the specialist brought into the engagement. The rules encourage referrals by helping to protect the client relationships of the referring practitioner.

Other Responsibilities and Practices. *A certified public accountant should conduct himself in a manner which will enhance the stature of the profession and its ability to serve the public.*

In light of the importance of their function, CPAs and their firms should have a keen consciousness of the public interest and the needs of society. Thus, they should support efforts to achieve equality of opportunity for all, regardless of race, religious background or sex, and should contribute to this goal by their own service relationships and employment practices.

The CPA is a beneficiary of the organization and character of his profession. Since he is seen as a representative of the profession by those who come in contact with him, he should behave honorably both in his personal and professional life and avoid any conduct that might erode public respect and confidence.

Solicitation to obtain clients is prohibited under the Rules of Conduct because it tends to lessen the professional independence toward clients which is essential to the best interests of the public. It may also induce an unhealthy rivalry within the profession and thus lessen the cooperation among members which is essential to advancing the state of the art of accounting and providing maximum service to the public.

Advertising, which is a form of solicitation, is also prohibited becaue it could encourage representations which might mislead the public and thereby reduce or destroy the profession's usefulness to society. However, a CPA should seek to establish a reputation for competence and character, and there are many acceptable means by which this can be done. For example, he may make himself known by public service, by civic and political activities, and by joining associations and clubs. It is desirable for him to share his knowledge with interested groups by accepting requests to make speeches and write articles. Whatever publicity occurs as a natural by-product of such activities is entirely proper. It would be wrong, however, for the CPA to initiate or embellish publicity.

Promotional practices, such as solicitation and advertising, tend to indicate a dominant interest in profit. In his work, the CPA should be motivated more by desire for excellence in performance than for material reward. This does not mean that he need be indifferent about compensation. Indeed, a professional man who cannot maintain a respectable standard of living is unlikely to inspire confidence or to enjoy sufficient peace of mind to do his best work.

In determining fees, a CPA may assess the degree of responsibility assumed by undertaking an engagement as well as the time, manpower and skills required to perform the service in conformity with the standards of the profession. He may also take into account the value of the service to the client, the customary charges of professional colleagues and other considerations. No single factor is necessarily controlling.

Clients have a right to know in advance what rates will be charged and approximately how much an engagement will cost. However, when professional judgments are involved, it is usually not possible to set a fair charge until an engagement has been completed. For this reason CPAs should state their fees for proposed engagements in the form of estimates which may be subject to change as the work progresses.

Other practices prohibited by the Rules of Conduct include using any firm designation or description which might be misleading, or practicing as a professional corporation or association which fails to comply with provisions established by Council to protect the public interest.

A member, while practicing public accounting, may not engage in a business or occupation which is incompatible therewith. While certain occupations are clearly incompatible with the practice of public accounting, the profession has never attempted to list them for in most cases the individual circumstances indicate whether there is a problem. For example, there would be a problem of incompatibility if a practicing CPA were to sell insurance or securities because these occupations involve solicitation and promotional activities which might be used to promote a public accounting practice. Moreover, they might, under some circumstances, jeopardize the CPA's independence.

Paying a commission is prohibited in order to eliminate the temptation to compensate anyone for referring a client. Receipt of a commission is proscribed since practitioners should look to the client, and not to others, for compensation for services rendered. The practice of paying a fee to a referring CPA irrespective of any service performed or responsibility assumed by him is proscribed because there is no justification for a CPA to share in a fee for accounting services where his sole contribution was to make a referral.

Over the years the vast majority of CPAs have endeavored to earn and maintain a reputation for competence, integrity and objectivity. The success of these efforts has been largely responsible for the wide public acceptance of accounting as an honorable profession. This acceptance is a valuable asset which should never be taken for granted. Every CPA should constantly strive to see that it continues to be deserved.

II. RULES OF CONDUCT

These Rules of Conduct were adopted by the membership and became effective March 1, 1973. In the footnotes below, the references to specific rules or numbered Opinions indicate that revised sections are derived therefrom; where modifications have been made to the former rule or Opinion, it is noted. The reference to "prior rulings" indicates a position previously taken by the ethics division in response to a specific complaint or inquiry, but not previously published. The reference to "new" indicates a substantive addition adopted by the membership.

Definitions

The following definitions of terminology are applicable wherever such terminology is used in the rules and interpretations.

Client. The person(s) or entity which retains a member or his firm, engaged in the practice of public accounting, for the performance of professional services.

Council. The Council of the American Institute of Certified Public Accountants.

Enterprise. Any person(s) or entity, whether organized for profit or not, for which a CPA provides services.

Firm. A proprietorship, partnership or professional corporation or association engaged in the practice of public accounting, including individual partners or shareholders thereof.

Financial Statements. Statements and footnotes related thereto that purport to show financial position which relates to a point in time or changes in financial position which relate to a period of time, and statements which use a cash or other incomplete basis of accounting. Balance sheets, statements of income, statements of retained earnings, statements of changes in financial position and statements of changes in owners' equity are financial statements.

Incidental financial data included in management advisory services reports to support recommendations to a client, and tax returns and supporting schedules do not, for this purpose, constitute financial statements; and the statement, affidavit or signature of preparers required on tax returns neither constitutes an opinion on financial statements nor requires a disclaimer of such opinion.

Institute. The American Institute of Certified Public Accountants.

Interpretations of Rules of Conduct. Pronouncements issued by the Division of Professional Ethics to provide guidelines as to the scope and application of the Rules of Conduct.

Member. A member, associate member or international associate of the American Institute of Certified Public Accountants.

Practice of Public Accounting. Holding out to be a CPA or public accountant and at the same time performing for a client one or more types of services rendered by public accountants. The term shall not be limited by a more restrictive definition which might be found in the accountancy law under which a member practices.

Professional Services. One or more types of services performed in the practice of public accounting.

Applicability of Rules

The Institute's Code of Professional Ethics derives its authority from the by-laws of the Institute which provide that the Trial Board may, after a hearing, admonish, suspend or expel a member who is found guilty of infringing any of the by-laws or any provisions of the Rules of Conduct.*

The Rules of Conduct which follow apply to all services performed in the practice of public accounting including tax † and management advisory services ‡ except (*a*) where the wording of the rule indicates otherwise and (*b*) that a member who is practicing outside the United States will not be subject to discipline for departing from any of the rules stated herein so long as his conduct is in accord with the rules of the organized accounting profession in the country in which he is practicing.§ However, where a member's name is associated with financial statements in such a manner as to imply that he is acting as an independent public accountant and under circumstances that would entitle the reader to assume that United States practices were followed, he must comply with the requirements of Rules 202 and 203."

A member may be held responsible for compliance with the Rules of Conduct by all persons associated with him in the practice of public accounting who are either under his supervision or are his partners or shareholders in the practice.¶

A member engaged in the practice of public accounting must observe all the Rules of Conduct. A member not engaged in the practice of public accounting must observe only Rules 102 and 501 since all other Rules of Conduct relate

---

* By-law Section 7.4.
† Opinion No. 13.
‡ Opinion No. 14.
§ Prior ruling.
" Rules 2.01, 2.02, 2.03 and prior rulings.
¶ New.

solely to the practice of public accounting.*

A member shall not permit others to carry out on his behalf, either with or without compensation, acts which, if carried out by the member, would place him in violation of the Rules of Conduct.†

Independence, Integrity, and Objectivity

Rule 101–Independence. A member or a firm of which he is a partner or shareholder shall not express an opinion on financial statements of an enterprise unless he and his firm are independent with respect to such enterprise.‡ Independence will be considered to be impaired if, for example:

A. During the period of his professional engagement, or at the time of expressing his opinion, he or his firm

1. Had or was committed to acquire any direct or material indirect financial interest in the enterprise; § or

2. Had any joint closely held business investment with the enterprise or any officer, director or principal stockholder thereof which was material in relation to his or his firm's net worth; ″ or

3. Had any loan to or from the enterprise or any officer, director or principal stockholder thereof.¶ This latter proscription does not apply to the following loans from a financial institution when made under normal lending procedures, terms and requirements:

   (a) Loans obtained by a member or his firm which are not material in relation to the net worth of such borrower.

   (b) Home mortgages.

   (c) Other secured loans, except loans guaranteed by a member's firm which are otherwise unsecured.**

B. During the period covered by the financial statements, during the period of the professional engagement or at the time of expressing an opinion, he or his firm

1. Was connected with the enterprise as a promoter, underwriter or voting trustee, a director or officer or in any capacity equivalent to that of a member of management or of an employee; †† or

---

* New.
† Opinion No. 2.
‡ Rule 1.01 (*shareholder* added to recognize corporate practice).
§ Rule 1.01.
″ Prior rulings.
¶ Prior rulings.
** Opinion No. 19.
†† Rule 1.01 (present Rule 1.01 uses the phrase *key employee*).

2. Was a trustee of any trust or executor or administrator of any estate if such trust or estate had a direct or material indirect financial interest in the enterprise; or was a trustee for any pension or profit-sharing trust of the enterprise.*

The above examples are not intended to be all-inclusive.

Rule 102–Integrity and Objectivity.   A member shall not knowingly misrepresent facts, and when engaged in the practice of public accounting, including the rendering of tax and management advisory services, shall not subordinate his judgment to others.† In tax practice, a member may resolve doubt in favor of his client as long as there is reasonable support for his position.‡

Competence and Technical Standards

Rule 201–Competence.   A member shall not undertake any engagement which he or his firm cannot reasonably expect to complete with professional competence.§

Rule 202–Auditing Standards.   A member shall not permit his name to be associated with financial statements in such a manner as to imply that he is acting as an independent public accountant unless he has complied with the applicable generally accepted auditing standards ″ promulgated by the Institute. Statements on Auditing Procedure issued by the Institute's committee on auditing procedure are, for purposes of this rule, considered to be interpretations of the generally accepted auditing standards, and departures from such statements must be justified by those who do not follow them.¶

Rule 203–Accounting Principles.   A member shall not express an opinion that financial statements are presented in conformity with generally accepted accounting principles if such statements contain any departure from an accounting principle promulgated by the body designated by Council to establish such principles which has a material effect on the statements taken as a whole, unless the member can demonstrate that due to unusual circumstances the financial statements would otherwise have been misleading. In such cases

---

* Prior rulings. In order that a member may arrange an orderly transition of his relationship with clients, sections B2 of Rule 101 relating to trusteeships and executorships will not become effective until two years following the adoption of these Rules of Conduct.

† New.

‡ Opinion No. 13.

§ New.

″ Ten generally accepted auditing standards are listed in Appendix A, page 26.

¶ New (replaces Rules 2.01–2.03).

his report must describe the departure, the approximate effects thereof, if practicable, and the reasons why compliance with the principle would result in a misleading statement.*

Rule 204–Forecasts.   A member shall not permit his name to be used in conjunction with any forecast of future transactions in a manner which may lead to the belief that the member vouches for the achievability of the forecast.†

Responsibilities to Clients

Rule 301–Confidential Client Information.   A member shall not disclose any confidential information obtained in the course of a professional engagement except with the consent of the client.‡

This rule shall not be construed (*a*) to relieve a member of his obligation under Rules 202 and 203, (*b*) to affect in any way his compliance with a validity issued subpoena or summons enforceable by order of a court, (*c*) to prohibit review of a member's professional practices as a part of voluntary quality review under Institute authorization or (*d*) to preclude a member from responding to any inquiry made by the ethics division or Trial Board of the Institute, by a duly constituted investigative or disciplinary body of a state CPA society, or under state statutes.§

Members of the ethics division and Trial Board of the Institute and professional practice reviewers under Institute authorization shall not disclose any confidential client information which comes to their attention from members in disciplinary proceedings or otherwise in carrying out their official responsibilities. However, this prohibition shall not restrict the exchange of information with an aforementioned duly constituted investigative or disciplinary body."

Rule 302–Contingent Fees.¶   Professional services shall not be offered or rendered under an arrangement whereby no fee will be charged unless a specified finding or result is attained, or where the fee is otherwise contingent upon the findings or results of such services. However, a member's fees may vary depending, for example, on the complexity of the service rendered.**

Fees are not regarded as being contingent if fixed by courts or other public

---

* New (replaces Rules 2.01–2.03).
† Restatement of Rule 2.04.
‡ Restatement of Rule 1.03.
§ Prior rulings.
" New.
¶ Restatement of Rule 1.04.
** New.

authorities or, in tax matters, if determined based on the results of judicial proceedings or the findings of governmental agencies.*

Responsibilities to Colleagues

Rule 401-Encroachment.† A member shall not endeavor to provide a person or entity with a professional service which is currently provided by another public accountant except:

1. He may respond to a request for a proposal to render services and may furnish service to those who request it.‡ However, if an audit client of another independent public accountant requests a member to provide professional advice on accounting or auditing matters in connection with an expression of opinion on financial statements, the member must first consult with the other accountant to ascertain that the member is aware of all the available relevant facts.§

2. Where a member is required to express an opinion on combined or consolidated financial statements which include a subsidiary, branch or other component audited by another independent public accountant, he may insist on auditing any such component which in his judgment is necessary to warrant the expression of his opinion."

A member who receives an engagement for services by referral from another public accountant shall not accept the client's request to extend his service beyond the specific engagement without first notifying the referring accountant, nor shall he seek to obtain any additional engagement from the client.¶

Rule 402–Offers of Employment. A member in public practice shall not make a direct or indirect offer of employment to an employee of another public accountant on his own behalf or that of his client without first informing such accountant. This rule shall not apply if the employee of his own initiative or in response to a public advertisement applies for employment.**

Other Responsibilities and Practices

Rule 501–Acts Discreditable. A member shall not commit an act discreditable to the profession.††

* Rule 1.04.
† Restatement of Rule 5.01.
‡ Rule 5.01.
§ New.
" Opinion No. 20.
¶ Rule 5.02 restated to include prior rulings.
** Rule 5.03, *or that of his client* added.
†† Rule 1.02.

Rule 502–Solicitation and Advertising. A member shall not seek to obtain clients by solicitation.* Advertising is a form of solicitation and is prohibited.†

Rule 503–Commissions. A member shall not pay a commission to obtain a client, nor shall he accept a commission for a referral to a client of products or services of others.‡ This rule shall not prohibit payments for the purchase of an accounting practice § or retirement payments to individuals formerly engaged in the practice of public accounting or payments to their heirs or estates."

Rule 504–Incompatible Occupations. A member who is engaged in the practice of public accounting shall not concurrently engage in any business or occupation which impairs his objectivity in rendering professional services or serves as a feeder to his practice.¶

Rule 505–Form of Practice and Name. A member may practice public accounting, whether as an owner or employee, only in the form of a proprietorship, a partnership, or a professional corporation whose characteristics conform to resolutions of Council.** (See Appendix B, page 28.)

A member shall not practice under a firm name which includes any fictitious name, indicates specialization or is misleading as to the type of organization (proprietorship, partnership, or corporation).†† However, names of one or more past partners or shareholders may be included in the firm name of a success or partnership or corporation.‡‡ Also, a partner surviving the death or withdrawal of all other partners may continue to practice under the partnership name for up to two years after becoming a sole practitioner.§§

A firm may not designate itself as Members of the American Institute of Certified Public Accountants unless all of its partners or shareholders are members of the Institute.""

* Rule 3.02.
† Rule 3.01.
‡ Restatement of Rule 3.04.
§ Prior rulings.
" Opinion No. 6.
¶ Restatement of Rule 4.04.
** Rule 4.06.
†† Prior rulings.
‡‡ Rule 4.02.
§§ Prior rulings.
"" Rule 4.01.

D

STATE SOCIETIES
OF CERTIFIED PUBLIC
ACCOUNTANTS *

Alabama Society of CPAs
J. G. Robertson, *Executive Secretary*
P.O. Box 4187, Montgomery, Ala. 36104

Alaska Society of CPAs
Jean B. Schmitt, *Secretary*
1545 Crosson, Fairbanks, Ak. 99701

Arizona Society of CPAs
Richard H. Bailey, *Executive Director*
2721 North Central Ave., Suite 1028 South, Phoenix, Ariz. 85004

Arkansas Society of CPAs
Miss Marque Schwarz, *Executive Director*
1210 Worthen Plaza, Little Rock, Ark. 72201

California Society of CPAs
Louis G. Baldacci, *Executive Director*
1000 Welch Road, Palo Alto, Ca. 94304

Colorado Society of CPAs
Gordon H. Scheer, *Executive Director*
1200 Lincoln St., Suite 530, Denver, Colo. 80203

Connecticut Society of CPAs
Jack Brooks, *Executive Director*
179 Allyn St., Hartford, Conn. 06103

---

* SOURCE: *Committee Handbook 1972–73* (New York: American Institute of Certified Public Accountants, 1972), pp. 165–169.

Delaware Society of CPAs
Walter S. Wallace, CPA, *Secretary*

Frank A. Gunnip & Co., 2625
Concord Pike, Wilmington, Del.
19803

District of Columbia Institute of
CPAs
Harvey R. Lampshire, *Executive
Director*

1200 18th St., NW, Suite 915,
Washington, D.C. 20036

Florida Institute of CPAs
Clifford C. Beasley, *Executive
Director*

P.O. Box 13455, University Station,
Gainesville, Fla. 32601

Georgia Society of CPAs
James Martin, Jr. *Executive Director*

1504 William Oliver Bldg., Atlanta,
Ga. 30303

Hawaii Society of CPAs
Mrs. Peg Dunham, *Executive
Director*

P.O. Box 1754, Honolulu, Hawaii
96806

Idaho Society of CPAs
Mrs. Jeannette B. Drury,
Administrative Secretary

P.O. Box 2896, Boise, Idaho 83701

Illinois Society of CPAs
Miss Jeannette M. Cochrane,
Executive Director

One IBM Plaza, Suite 1415,
Chicago, Ill. 60611

Indiana Association of CPAs
Jack E. Noble, *Executive Director*

439 Glendale Bldg., 6100 North
Keystone Ave., Indianapolis, Ind.
46220

Iowa Society of CPAs
William Martin, *Executive Secretary*

722 Insurance Exchange Bldg.,
Des Moines, Iowa 50309

Kansas Society of CPAs
John Killian, *Executive Director*

517 Capitol Federal Savings Bldg.,
Topeka, Kans. 66603

Kentucky Society of CPAs
Bernard W. Gratzer, *Executive
Secretary*

310 West Liberty St. Room 415,
Louisville, Ky. 40202

Society of Louisiana CPAs
Mrs. Mary Atkinson, *Executive
Secretary*

822 Perdido St., Suite 408, New
Orleans, La. 70112

Maine Society of Public Accountants
Owen C. Hall, CPA, *Secretary*

University of Maine
Portland–Gorham, 96 Falmouth St.,
Portland, Maine 04103

Maryland Association of CPAs
Thomas L. Woods, *Administrative Vice President*

1012 Keyser Bldg., Baltimore, Md. 21202

Massachusetts Society of CPAs
Miss Agnes L. Bixby, *Executive Secretary*

One Center Plaza, Boston, Mass. 02108

Michigan Association of CPAs
Robert A. Bogan, Jr., *Executive Director*

1311 East Jefferson, Detroit, Mich. 48207

Minnesota Society of CPAs
Clair G. Budke, *Executive Director*

1102 Wesley Temple Bldg.,
Minneapolis, Minn. 55403

Mississippi Society of CPAs
Robert L. Nickey, *Executive Director*

301 Bankers Trust Plaza, P.O. Box 808, Jackson, Miss. 39205

Missouri Society of CPAs
Donald E. Breimeier, *Executive Director*

1925 Railway Exchange Bldg., St. Louis, Mo. 63101

Montana Society of CPAs
Mrs. Pamela B. Anderson, *Executive Secretary*

P.O. Box 521, Helena, Mont. 59601

Nebraska Society of CPAs
Arnold Magnuson, *Executive Secretary*

504 Stuart Bldg., Lincoln, Nebr. 68508

Nevada Society of CPAs
Mrs. Marguerite Callahan, *Executive Secretary*

290 South Arlington Ave., Reno, Nev. 89501

New Hampshire Society of CPAs
Richard H. Clough, *Executive Director*

Hamilton S. Putnam & Associates, 4 Park St., Concord, New Hampshire 03301

New Jersey Society of CPAs
Herbert J. Rohrbach, Jr., *Executive Director*

550 Broad St., 11th Floor, Newark, N.J. 07102

New Mexico Society of CPAs
Mrs. Wanda File, *Executive Secretary*

120 Madeira, N.E., Suite 102, Albuquerque, N.M. 87108

New York State Society of CPAs
Robert L. Gray, CPA, *Executive Director*

355 Lexington Ave., New York, N.Y. 10017

North Carolina Association of CPAs
Thomas C. Wagstaff, *Executive Secretary*

P.O. Box 2185, Chapel Hill, N.C. 27514

North Dakota Society of CPAs
R. D. Koppenhaver, CPA, *Secretary–Treasurer*

Box 8104, University Station, Grand Forks, N.D. 58201

Ohio Society of CPAs
Victor A. Feldmiller, *Executive Director*

6161 Busch Blvd., P.O. Box 617, Worthington, Ohio 43085

Oklahoma Society of CPAs
Mrs. Retha Duggan, *Executive Director*

265 West Court, Lincoln Office Plaza, 4545 Lincoln Blvd., Oklahoma City, Okla. 73105

Oregon Society of CPAs
Robert W. Hensel, *Executive Director*

720 Oregon Bank Bldg., Portland, Ore. 97204

Pennsylvania Institute of CPAs
F. Willard Heintzelman, CPA, *Executive Director*

1100 Lewis Tower Bldg., Philadelphia, Pa. 19102

Instituto de Contadores Publicos Autorizados de Puerto Rico
Miss Maritza Lopez, *Executive Secretary*

P.O. Box 9851, Santurce, P.R. 00908

Rhode Island Society of CPAs
Stanley B. Thomas, *Executive Secretary*

170 Westminister Street, Room 1112, Providence, R.I. 02903

South Carolina Association of CPAs
J. Edgar Eubanks, *Executive Director*

P.O. Box 11187, 202 Columbia Bldg., Columbia, S.C. 29211

South Dakota Society of CPAs
Holly A. Pederson, CPA,
Secretary–Treasurer

University of South Dakota,
Vermillion, S.D. 57069

Tennessee Society of CPAs
Nels T. Moody, *Executive Director*

3904 Hillsboro Road, Nashville,
Tenn. 37215

Texas Society of CPAs
William H. Quimby, *Executive
Director*

200 Corrigan Tower, Dallas, Texas
75201

Utah Association of CPAs
Joseph F. Cowley, Jr., CPA,
Executive Secretary

Suite 1180, Kennecott Bldg., Salt
Lake City, Utah 84111

Vermont Society of CPAs
Richard H. Clough, *Executive
Director*

Hamilton S. Putnam & Associates, 4
Park St., Concord, New Hampshire,
03301

Virgin Islands Society of CPAs
Ezra A. Gomez, CPA,
Secretary–Treasurer

P.O. Box 511, St. Thomas, V.I.
00801

Virginia Society of CPAs
Mrs. Patricia P. Koontz, *Executive
Director*

809 Mutual Bldg., Richmond, Va.
23219

Washington Society of CPAs
Russell A. Davis, *Executive Director*

347 Logan Bldg., Seattle, Wash.
98101

West Virginia Society of CPAs
Mrs. Mary Neal, *Executive Secretary*

P.O. Box 1142, Charleston, W. Va.
25324

Wisconsin Society of CPAs
Joseph Sperstad, *Executive Director*

176 West Wisconsin Ave., Room
1001, Milwaukee, Wisc. 53203

Wyoming Society of CPAs
LeRoy L. Lee, CPA, *Executive
Director*

University Station, Box 3643
Laramie, Wyo. 82070

INDEX